About the author

Magenta Pixie is a channel for the higher dimensional, divine intelligence known as 'The White Winged Collective Consciousness of Nine'. The transmissions she receives from 'The Nine' have reached thousands of people worldwide via the extensive video collection on her YouTube channel. She has worked with people from all over the world as an intuitive consultant and ascension/consciousness coach. Magenta lives in the New Forest, UK.

Visit Magenta Pixie online at www.magentapixie.com

Also by Magenta Pixie:

Books:

Masters of the Matrix:
Becoming the Architect of Your Reality and
Activating the Original Human Template

Divine Architecture and the Starseed Template:
Matrix Memory Triggers for Ascension

MP3 Guided Meditation Collections:

Gateways Within

Euphoric Voyage

Sacred Quest

Elemental Dream

Cover design and diagrams by Daniel Saunders

Author photograph by Oliver McGuire of Visual Logistics
www.visuallogistics.co.uk

Print Edition 1, 2018

ISBN-13: 978-1720300243
ISBN-10: 1720300240

White Spirit Publishing
www.magentapixie.com
enquiries: catzmagick@mail.com

In no way may this text be construed as
encouraging or condoning any harmful or illegal act.
In no way may this text be construed as
able to diagnose, treat, cure or prevent
any disease, injury, symptom or condition.

Named individuals used throughout this text as examples
to explain concepts and situations are fictitious. Any similarity
to any persons, living or deceased, is purely coincidental.

The Infinite Helix and the Emerald Flame

Sacred Mysteries of Stargate Ascension

Magenta Pixie

For Daddy

Contents

Acknowledgements

To those who planted the seeds with me so the flowers in the garden may grow...
Brian McGuire, Liam McGuire, Chris Turner

To the one who takes the journey with me and together we make up the flame...
Daniel Saunders

To those who built the structure with me so the pillars may hold up the temple...
William Shaw, Gordon Blake

To those who support me in tending the garden. Together we shall find the dragon's egg amongst the Krystal powered herbs and the seashells kissed by mermaids...
Andrew Cutler, Sharon Lewendon

To the priestesses who stand by my personal 'Sophia stargate', who hold my hands within the circle of the silver flame...
Teresa McGuire, Keira McGuire, Abigail Blake, Rosie Miller, Bonnie Blake, Dee Taylor-Mason, Heike Jenkins, Dionne Travers, Dawn Holliday

To those to whom I pass the code of Sophia and the sword of truth...
Alexander Blake, Oliver McGuire, Christian McGuire

To my manifestations of the alchemical merge...
Krista, the hidden daughter of the flame and to my blessed and beloved Elizabeth

To the diamonds and the roses in my beautiful garden...
Gracie Mae, Imogen Rose, Riley Alexander, Rody David, Elora Marie

To the hidden 'fairy princess' who rides on the back of ladybirds and flies with robins. May you shine your divine feminine light forever, you are a true child of the Emerald City. Your sparkling ruby shoes will take you 'home', over the rainbow, and we will see you there...
Molly Robyn

and to all the starseeds of Earth as they ride the dragon...
This book is for you.

Foreword

Within this book are several 'transmission codes' or 'keycodes' from the White Winged Collective Consciousness of Nine.

Embedded within the writings are 'DNA activation codes' (multiple codices) that will assist in memory, awakening and knowing. This memory awakening can take many forms including activations through dreamtime, the daydream and meditations. This may present as visions, feelings, images, impulses, intrinsic knowings, deep intuition, synchronicity and communication with the voice of the inner mind or clairaudient perception.

For those who already work within this activated 'higher' state then please continue with your own practised form of preparation as you continue to read.

For beginners within this level of work, please make sure you are comfortable and hydrated.

Take your time and read only as much as you feel is right for you, perhaps a few pages at a time. This is expansive work as your memories are awakened and your DNA begins to reform and reshape in response to your energetic vibration as you read. Rest, relax and meditate before moving on to the next part of the book if need be.

The sacred flow of synchronicity will create a connection or 'web' with this material whereby only those who are able and ready to receive these activations through this information will do so, but we present the tools you need to be able to assimilate the information in this book, should you find yourself in a place outside your usual frequency.

Throughout this transmission, the title of this text is referred to as *The Infinite Helix*. Towards the end of the transmission, it becomes evident why the title was eventually presented as *The Infinite Helix and the Emerald Flame*. This transmission is presented organically, as my journey with the Nine occurred in real time as transcribed.

Happy reading and happy activations!

With an abundance of love and light,

Your scribe, Magenta Pixie x

Introduction:

TRANSMISSION - Dark Deeds, Pole Shift

A transmission from the White Winged Collective Consciousness of Nine was downloaded to me on February 24th 2018. I entitled this "Dark Deeds, Pole Shift, Indigo Revolution and the Law of One" and shared it via YouTube.[1]

This transmission was a response from the Nine to a question regarding the silencing of 'truthers' across social media platforms which began to make itself quite evident in February 2018, although many were predicting this long before that time.

I originally intended this text to be an analysis of that particular transmission, as an article. Yet the responses from the Nine to my questions branched off into so many different areas that this piece of writing ended up being a book, essentially following on from the material presented in my previous two books (*Masters of the Matrix* and *Divine Architecture and the Starseed Template*).[2]

The analysis of the above mentioned transmission was not completed and instead I present this work, following on from the teachings of 'Matrix Awareness' and 'Matrix Mastery' in *Masters of the Matrix* and 'Matrix Architecture' in *Divine Architecture and the Starseed Template*. I present now 'Matrix Transportation' within this transmission, *The Infinite Helix*.

Whilst I do ask some questions of the Nine relating to the question regarding the silencing of the starseeds on a global level, much more information regarding Matrix Transportation, ascension and DNA activation has come through within this esoteric 'conversation' with the sixth/seventh dimensional monadic light structure that is the White Winged Collective Consciousness of Nine.

The original transmission is given here in text form (overleaf). The video can be found via the video archive at magentapixie.com

---

1   YouTube, video-sharing website. www.youtube.com
2   *Masters of the Matrix: Becoming the Architect of Your Reality and Activating the Original Human Template* (2016) and *Divine Architecture and the Starseed Template: Matrix Memory Triggers for Ascension* (2017), books by Magenta Pixie.

Dark Deeds, Pole Shift, Indigo Revolution and the Law of One

Dear Pixie,

You asked us...

"The truthers are being silenced at the moment across social media. What will be the outcome of this? Are we all at risk of losing our platforms and no longer being able to spread the message and deliver truth to humanity? What can we do?"

We would respond by saying that there is an attempt to silence those starseeds with the loudest voices and the widest reach who stand in opposition to their agenda. The truthers that you speak of are not actually 'being silenced'. The attempt is being made but it will not be successful. The energetics within the field, that which we would call 'positive polarised frequency', is predominant within your dimension. Therefore, only that which matches the frequency of your dimension has longevity. The dissolution of the process of the veils has created a situation whereby actions, thoughts, words and deeds that align with the negatively polarised frequency are dissolving.

We are aware that this process is not tangible to a great many individuals upon your planet. The dissolving, destructuring and dismantling of the core negative structures within the fourth dimension has been occurring for some time and the match to this is now filtering into the third dimension.

There are those who can see this dissolution we speak of but one has to look 'behind the scenes' if you will.

What we are saying here, as we have said before, is that there is a flip back into positive polarised frequency from that which was created with negatively polarised intention.

We cannot say that all negatively polarised intention will flip but those that do flip into positive polarisation are the majority of negatively polarised intentions.

The few remaining negatively polarised intentions that remain and actually manifest within physicality are held in place by a magickal structure. This magickal structure has to use far more concentration and power than has been the case in the past upon your planet due to the predominant positively polarised frequencies.

This action takes much focus. This action is not sustainable for long periods and it has a 'side effect' shall we say? That of burning itself out.

Therefore the service-to-self factions, those that you call 'cabal', 'Illuminati', 'global elite' or 'deep state' have to be very choosy as to which machination they lend their focus to. Many machinations are seeded but only a small minority can manifest to fruition and those that do have the burn out side effect we speak of.

This is a frustrating situation for the service-to-self groups. In times of old the inverted matrix held fast and the dark magick was easy to create and sustain.

In those times it was the service-to-others magicians of light who had to create the energies and structures needed to sustain the positively polarised intentions and creations as the dense frequency was fully third dimensional and holding separation and duality as its core frequencies.

Now, in your year of 2018 and continuing forward as critical mass has been reached and that marker point has moved beyond critical mass... it is the positive polarisation that is the predominant fabric of reality upon Earth. These much lighter fifth dimensional frequencies, now well anchored upon your planet, superimposing the higher Gaia grid stream into the Earth, hold unity and the Holy Trinity at their core.

The magicians of light are now the ones who are the master of the elements. They are the ones who create the Gaia reality. The magick of light is easy, flowing and sustainable.

The dark ones knew this time would come. They were forewarned of this time. Within the dark factions there were those who ran scared and they would say, "What shall we do? What shall we do when the polarisation occurs? What shall we do at the time of the switching of the poles of reality... the great pole shift that shall occur when we move into alignment with the galactic core?"

And the dark ones within the fourth dimension would answer, "You must arm yourselves well in advance. You must take the technologies needed so you are far in advance of those that carry the light codes. They will know too what is coming so you must confuse them well in advance so they do not understand even themselves and what they are."

And so did the dark ones, well in advance, gather their technologies and begin to mislead you all with talk of end of the world destruction through the literal pole shifting and matter/antimatter merge destruction, they misled you with technology and they misled you with science.

So the light, seeing the machination in place and watching the dark seeds grow, did plant seeds of light. And the seeds of light were the indigo radars - the code within the indigo being that would recognise the falsehood immediately and would reject the control structure out of hand even to the detriment of him or herself. And the strength of the indigo code did grow and did multiply.

And the seeds of light were the crystal beacons - the code within the crystal being that would project humility, service, unconditional love and compassion.

Together the indigo revolution and the crystal wave did balance one another and the codes for truth were placed like pieces of a jigsaw in this place and this place and this place, hidden away from detection until such time as the indigo rising would occur and the crystal memories would come online and the pieces of the jigsaw would fit together and the picture as a whole would be presented to the light bearers, the starseeds, the magicians of light.

And the light did send their greatest indigo warriors and crystalline priests from the temple, they that were adepts. They that had done this over and over again, walked the same mission upon many worlds, travelling here, travelling there, experts at their job. They, the travellers, the dreamweavers, the wanderers.

These are the ones we call the 'starseeds', the ones you refer to as 'truthers'. They will not be silenced now that their codes are activated and that they are fully online.

The dark ones did say, "They are no match for our technologies or our webs of illusion." Yet there were those dark ones who remained afraid for they knew the power of unconditional love, of forgiveness and of compassion. So the dark deeds they created were dark as dark could be so that surely no compassion, no forgiveness, no unconditional love could ever be found for the deeds as dark as dark could be.

And indeed, there are the starseeds now that carry the fire of anger for the deeds as dark as dark could be and the fires of anger fan the flames of the dark deeds - aiding the dark magicians in sustaining the few negatively polarised machinations into manifestation.

16

Yet so too are there starseeds who hold infinite compassion, forgiveness and unconditional love for the codes of light phired so strong within the memory matrix that they knew the importance of these living ascended masters, the ascended masters that are the group soul frequencies of compassion, forgiveness and unconditional love. And these starseeds who heal the grids and hold fast to the ascension timeline are the ones that throw great waters on the flames of the dark deeds and build the crystal structures of truth and light wherever they may go.

These starseeds who hold the keys of compassion and activate the codes of the Law of One, they hold fast the fabric of the positively polarised matrix fields. They are those that control the elements and they are the ones who flipped the poles. They created the pole shift you now experience.

They instinctively knew how to alchemise the poles within themselves - male, female, crown chakra, root chakra, Kristos, Sophia, matter, antimatter.

Who are these starseed alchemists of crystalline light? They are you, they are you of course, you who listens now to these words and allows the codes within, from we the White Winged Collective Consciousness of Nine to trigger the phires of memory and knowing within you.

You say to us, "The truthers are being silenced at the moment across social media." We say to you, an attempt is being made to silence the truthers but this will not be the case. It is not possible to do so. Regardless of the service-to-self technologies and confusing inverted matrix illusions, it is not possible to silence the codes of the indigo revolution.

You ask us, "What will be the outcome of this?" and the response to this is that this attempt will not succeed. There are many pathways, many timelines, many potentials that the outcome may manifest within but in each quantum reality within the positively polarised Gaia grid that you experience, the outcome is the same. The attempt shall not succeed.

You ask us, "Are we all at risk of losing our platforms and no longer being able to spread the message and deliver truth to humanity?" We would say to you that the platforms may shift and change as the starseeds find a new way, or reinvent their platforms for there will always be a back door. Those that guide you will lead you to this back door, it is the fail-safe code that has been placed within every crystalline code system.

The message will be delivered and heard and the truth will be known. This is the outcome no matter the pathway or the timeline or the quantum reality. The keys of compassion and the Law of One are the very fabric of the ascension timeline, the codes of which are held within the streams of compassion, forgiveness and unconditional love.

You ask us, "What can we do?" We say to you, remember who you are. You are master magicians. You carry the light for crystalline change. You are the ones that control the elements. You create the pole shift. You hold time and space in the palm of your hands.

You are powerful as one individual and insurmountable when you unite. This is your key. Unite. United you stand. Not as an army on the attack with retribution in mind or defence through fear and victim/saviour mentality but as a wave of change, the stand for change through truth and justice. This is the indigo way, the indigo revolution aided in equality through the compassion, forgiveness and unconditional love of the crystal wave.

This is your pole shift.

This is your indigo revolution.

This is your crystalline change.

This is your ascension timeline.

Hold fast, stand strong. It is done.

1: The Indigo Revolution

Dear White Winged Collective Consciousness of Nine,

May I begin our discourse by saying, in one of your transmissions (February 2018) which I entitled "Dark Deeds, Pole Shift, Indigo Revolution and the Law of One", you began by saying that there is currently an attempt to silence the starseeds with the loudest voices and the furthest reach. You went on to explain why this is happening.

I would say this certainly is happening if you take a look at the alternative media truther community and look at the biggest voices out there. You specifically said there is an attempt to 'silence the starseeds', so are you referring to 'truther' sites or do you also mean the UFO community, secret space programme whistle-blowers and spiritual historians, archaeologists and investigative journalists? Do you mean spiritual writers or even mediums/channels like myself?

When we use the term 'starseeds' we refer to all individuals who are 'living the mission', if you will, that they incarnated for. All individuals are 'starseeds' for you, on Earth, are all 'from the stars'. Yet when we speak of starseeds, we mean those who are 'activated starseeds'. This would refer to an individual who has memory/knowing (conscious or otherwise) of who they are and what they are incarnated to do/learn/experience/achieve. This sets these individuals apart from those who wander through their lives without focus or direction and who do not have memory/knowing.

The memory/knowing can be full awareness of one's star lineage, DNA activation, previous/future incarnations, quantum/alternate selves and/or ancestral memories and genetic markers. Yet this memory can also take the place of a deep sense of belonging, as in doing everything possible to make changes (usually this takes the form of making changes on a global level). The belonging we speak of can be within a particular community or tribe or indeed the belonging to humanity as a consciousness in itself.

These individuals do not need to be 'spiritually aware', although all will be walking the path of DNA activation and spiritual awareness will be part of that. Therefore the most 'unlikely' individual could be an activated starseed.

The attempt to prevent the ascension timeline from manifesting (and ultimately the positive polarisation of Earth into its higher self, fifth dimensional counterpart - Gaia) will include the silencing, misleading and confusing of the starseeds. This would be directed at 'the starseeds' as a group (a tribe, a community) and the way this is done is to target every area of life they have access to. This would be educational, financial, medical and beyond the physical into the fourth dimensional realities.

Targeting starseeds at the individual level specifically is not part of their plan. What they are doing is targeting the loudest voices, those with the furthest reach and the largest 'audience' if you will. They are not necessarily concerned if these individuals are 'activated starseeds' or not. They are only concerned with those who oppose their agenda even though they are aware that those that oppose their agenda ARE the starseeds, or certainly those that lead the 'indigo revolution'.

They have to play by certain 'rules' though. These are not actually 'rules', they are 'parameters of nature' or 'reality boundaries' if you will.

This is all connected to thought structures of focused intention into physical manifestation through a negatively polarised frequency. Certain guidelines must be followed in order to achieve manifestation.

The service-to-self, negatively polarised individuals do not use heart-centred frequency to manifest. They use the concentrated energetic of another life form, energy, entity, being or construct. It is a consuming, absorbing, recycling and ultimately destructive force rather than a radiating, activating, creative force. It is a creative force through domination/control/power rather than through giving/caring/nurturing/inspiring compassion. It is fear-based rather than love-based.

Even though they are, in fact, working with creation.

Creation can be through birth, through life, through living.

Creation can also be through death, through the taking of life, lack of life and opposite of life. We could perhaps refer to this frequency as 'anti-life'. It could also be thought of as a shadow projection of life or an inverted construct or system. It is inverse (service-to-self) as opposed to converse (service-to-others).

In order to work with anti-life manifestation, certain parameters must be met otherwise the manifestation does not hold focus.

As a service-to-others positively polarised construct ourselves, it is not within our trajectory to teach anti-life manifestation. Therefore we can only say so much about this procedure, in order to give you information and understanding without moving across boundaries that are outside of our own 'mission trajectory' and outside that of our conduit's.

Therefore, what we can say is this: Within the anti-life manifestation technique is a code. We can call this perhaps a 'code of honour' yet honour is not the energetic presented. The energetic is more of a 'power trip' of sorts and relates to that which we call the 'god complex'. It is more like giving the slower runner a head start in the 'race that is the chase'. It is a condescending energetic, yet within service-to-self factions it is seen as a 'code of honour'.

The service-to-self energy is most different to the service-to-others energy and it is not easy for one faction to understand the other. Neutrality and objectivity within both polarities is the only way for true understanding to occur.

This 'code of honour' involves targeting only those who are circling within a 'spiral of confusion' (which they themselves laid the groundwork for as service-to-self beings). Any individual that is fully polarised within the positive vibration cannot be individually targeted. This is part of that 'code of honour'.

Hence the reason that we and other constructs like us repeatedly present to you the importance of light body/Mer-Ka-Bah work and the cultivating of compassion, unconditional love and forgiveness.

When you do this, you cannot be 'targeted' on an individual level.

Within the third dimensional reality, the service-to-self factions try to create rigid boundaries within boxes to tie the lead speakers within the indigo revolution movement into a 'walled in' situation where they can no longer move and are prevented from speaking, sharing and radiating. However, the positive polarised energetic on your Earth creates a powerful synchronicity that runs alongside and overpowers the negatively polarised anti-life manifestations. This in turn filters into the third dimensional reality, creating windows within the boxes and doors within the walls. Therefore the trapping systems never work for those who create anti-life. The rigid boundaries become flexible and where one door closes, another door opens.

The 'starseeds' or 'truthers', as they are referred to within the original question, are therefore not silenced. Not only are they not silenced but they are aware of the machination, plot and plan to silence them. This awareness then spreads throughout the telepathic grid network of light that is the starseed consciousness and the starseeds and truthers speak even louder and have an even wider reach and a larger audience. The machinations, plots and plans 'backfire' if you will and the anti-life manifestation streams flip into the pro-life positively polarised streams and these are the outcomes that manifest within third density.

So in answer to your question, the 'starseeds' (meaning activated individuals, which include individuals within all the factions you mention) are targeted as a 'group' or 'community' rather than individually. Lost, confused individuals acting upon trauma-based energy/emotion can be targeted individually within the third dimensional reality but only if they have a voice within the indigo revolution/ascension timeline movement. We might also add, only if that voice is working in direct opposition to their agenda, so this would be third dimensional in context. Examples would be certain branches of politics, health, the food industry, education, religion, science, media and medical fields. The spiritual voices within the New Age, channelling and lightworker communities are not targeted individually unless they branch into the above examples in a way that is fully tangible. Anything metaphoric, philosophical or that which may be referred to as 'pseudoscience' or 'pseudoreligion' is not seen as tangible and therefore not a threat to their agenda on an individual case by case level.

We might add here that these particular energies/communities and creative presentations, along with other creative industries and that presented as 'fiction' is that which we may utilise for 'hiding the tree in the forest' if you will.

The procedures in place to target the starseeds through all streams flip from anti-life to pro-life manifestation and synchronicity works for positively polarised frequency as opposed to negatively polarised frequency.

So are you saying here, in response to my question regarding who is being targeted, that the entire starseed movement is being targeted as a group but they only target individuals who are not consciously activated and following an ascension timeline or who are not moving towards DNA activation/light body or Mer-Ka-Bah work?

Indeed this is correct. However it may appear as if some activated starseeds are being targeted on an individual level; for example, if they lose their platform, company or creation. Yet this is not individual targeting, just group targeting and the procedures they have in place will automatically target those with the loudest voices and the widest reach within the community of starseeds you call 'truthers' as these are the individuals standing in direct opposition to the service-to-self agenda. They are not being individually targeted even though it may seem that way. This is those with the loudest voices within the starseed group that they are wishing to silence. If there is an individual that is not activated into compassion, forgiveness and unconditional love then they can target that individual directly. This is a group, however, that is being focused upon. The aim is to 'clip the wings' of the starseeds and put a 'spoke in the wheel' of the indigo revolution.

OK, so what is the 'indigo revolution' exactly? Are all the starseeds part of it?

The 'indigo revolution' is the rising up of the starseeds, specifically those carrying indigo frequencies and codes, into their collective mission. This being the raising of the frequency of Earth, bringing the energies of their own 'home planet' to Earth, anchoring the fifth dimensional frequencies into Earth/Gaia and assisting all humanity to do the same. The indigo revolution involves the 'standing strong against power and control' and moving from victim/saviour mentality into the sovereignty of Source consciousness.

Is this why the service-to-self groups are attempting to silence the starseeds with the loudest voices? So this will prevent the people of Earth from freeing themselves from a victim/saviour mentality and empowering themselves within the sovereignty of Source consciousness?

Yes, in a sense, yet there is more to it than this. There is more than one timeline for Earth, more than one trajectory. The service-to-self factions are intent on creating a negatively polarised dimension and ascending (or rather descending) into that dimension. Their focus is not on the starseeds per se. Their focus is on their agenda. If the people of Earth move away from victim/saviour mentality and empower themselves within the sovereignty of Source consciousness, this will inevitably affect their agenda of creating the negatively polarised dimension.

If the starseeds could 'quietly' ascend into the fifth dimension without affecting their agenda then they would not be focused on preventing this (which they could not do anyway, no one can prevent the ascension of another being including a planet), but of course this is not the way it works within a third dimensional reality if the service-to-self factions have chosen to express the negative path through domination and control of the entire population of the planet. They would need that to continue for as long as possible in order to create the negatively polarised dimension.

We might also add that it is only a very small minority of the service-to-self factions who are aware of the creation of the negatively polarised dimension. The majority of service-to-self individuals are fully engaged within the third dimensional reality and the energetic of the 'power trip' into the 'god complex' presentation. Even though they may take part in service-to-self dark magick there are many who do not understand this. They have grown up with it since their birth but they do not necessarily understand its core. This is much the same within your service-to-others polarisation also, yet there are much larger numbers of those who understand the core of the light magick.

Can you explain what the core of the dark magick is and what the core of the light magick is?

The core of dark magick is to create negative polarisation.

The core of the light magick is to create positive polarisation.

Why do these polarisations have to be created?

In order to mirror Source and 'send back' codes of polarisation to Source so Source may experience them and learn from them (in a linear sense).

Why does Source want to or need to experience them?

In the true reality it is not about needing or wanting yet this does present, to the linear mind as 'Source wishing to know itself' and it is helpful to view it this way. This is creation.

You said that Source is wishing to know itself, yet is Source not already all knowing? Can you explain this?

Indeed we can. This is a most important paradox to embrace, for it is the seed point to understanding everything and a ticket into the 'Halls of Amenti' (Akash) if you will.

This understanding is the apex of the twelve strand aspect (higher memory) within the new crystalline DNA formation.

This understanding (through the processing of the paradox) creates expansion into individualisation so the equal and opposite reaction may stand as an exact replica to the original.

It does do this yet this journey is infinite, yet also completed. Infinite because all frequency must be experienced in order to stand as the equal and opposite reaction to the original Source and completed because all exists as the Source construct is 'all possibility realised'. Therefore the journey is never-ending yet complete simultaneously.

To explain this further you would need to understand the service-to-others and the service-to-self polarities and polarisation, duality and the Holy Trinity and unity.

Does this relate to God, Satan and Lucifer? Are Satan and Lucifer the same being? Is this polarity about heaven and hell? Someone spoke to me the other day and said there is no Satan and there is no hell, that these are false

*constructs, yet she believed in God and in heaven. Is it true to say that God/
heaven exists and that Satan/hell does not? Are you unbalanced if you
believe this? Does this connect with the polarisation and the unity?*

This is a compound question and the aligned response to this is lengthly.
We break this down as best as we can...

2: The Law of One

There are several perspectives to this. But firstly may we say that the person who spoke to you, who said that Satan and hell are 'false constructs' and that God and heaven do exist, is correct... from one perspective.

If one sees the 'organic matrix' (nature, natural, creation), this would be God and heaven.

The 'false construct' would be the distortion and thus Satan and hell. From the perspective of the fact that this false construct is 'outside' the parameters of the organic matrix (and thus pure creation) then the 'false construct' does NOT exist. It is illusion.

As in the true reality (the organic matrix), nothing can exist that is outside the unified field of pure unconditional love (lightlove/lovelight and lovelight/lightlove into bliss-charged love). Therefore the 'false construct' (Satan and hell) cannot exist for this is a created construct outside the parameters of pure unconditional love.

However, when one expands the unified field of pure unconditional love into 'the unified field of all and everything' then the false construct DOES and MUST exist (for within that construct there is polarity). Another paradox indeed!

This is, of course, just one perspective. The more perspectives you can embrace, the more multidimensional your thinking, the higher your expansion and the more activated is your DNA/light body/5D Mer-Ka-Bah.

So let us look at the various perspectives as we respond to your question.

From one perspective God, Satan and Lucifer are all the same being. This would be from the perspective that we are all one unified being and that is all there is. The Law of One is the only law from that perspective. Utilising the true Law of One then, all three beings are one being. Different aspects of the whole.

From another perspective, involving polarity and duality we could say that 'God' is one being and that 'Lucifer' and 'Satan' are two other distinct beings. From this point of view, you have three beings.

This would be the most 'traditional perspective' given the level of understanding the majority of humans upon your planet have. Whilst there are many who would see 'Satan' and 'Lucifer' as the same being, two different names for 'the devil' if you will, the majority of enlightened thinkers would realise these beings, as entities or consciousness constructs are different and separate, simply because they hold a different energy pattern or frequency.

Satan would be represented as 'all that is evil' when looking at the energetic signature and frequency of that being as an individualised construct.

Lucifer would be represented as 'light' for Lucifer represents light, most usually in the form of knowledge. You would be therefore looking at intelligence as a construct in itself. This is Lucifer in its most aligned form, intelligence.

Lucifer would therefore be represented by the brow or third eye chakra. Intelligence alone (without a companion energetic to create a synergistic merge and therefore an alchemised or 'higher' being) would not necessarily equate to being good and indeed could also present as 'evil' if you will.

Where Satan would be 'pure evil incarnate', Lucifer is 'intelligence' as a stand-alone concept (and of course a living being or consciousness structure as all emotions and thoughts hold life force).

Satan would perhaps be clumsy in his machinations. Lucifer would be calculating and infinitely clever for Lucifer is 'he who sees' and 'he who is illuminated'. Indeed Lucifer is *illumination itself.*

We can take this one step further when we look at polarity to present 'God' (as a service-to-others/positive polarity) and Lucifer (as a service-to-self/negative polarity).

Satan would also be of the service-to-self/negative polarity yet without the intelligence needed to actually present as a polarised being. Therefore as 'pure evil incarnate' alone we could say Satan is a fragmented, distorted and disassociated entity. Satan would be 'pure separateness' if you will and 'fallen' with no hope of ever regaining his place as the oneness (within a linear presentation only).

Satan is the epitome of separation and the complete opposite to the Law of One. If 'God' is the keeper of the Law of One then 'Satan' is the keeper of the Law of Distortion and the Law of Separateness (also known as the Law of Man).

Therefore it would be Lucifer that would be placed 'opposite God' if you will, or as the counterpart to God in the sense of an individualised being or equal and opposite reaction. For Lucifer holds the frequency for 'redemption' if you will and can therefore return to oneness.

When we look at service-to-others positive and service-to-self negative as individual energies in their own right as the fullest expressions of the polarity field, then we can place both 'God' and 'Lucifer' at both points in this scale.

Hence why we have often spoken of positive darkness /positive light and negative darkness/negative light.

God (unified, all that is) would be placed as service-to-others/positive polarisation due to the fact that 'God' is 'Source' and ultimate creation/unconditional love and the manifestation of the heart. This perspective is widely embraced upon your planet, therefore it holds much 'weight' or 'mass' or 'substance'.

God (this would translate as 'a god' as this is separateness) would be placed as service-to-self/negative polarisation in the sense of God as a being to be worshipped, a being who thrives on that worship and as a being or consciousness structure that considers itself to be 'lord of all it surveys' and 'master to all who live' (as in 'above them all' and 'the king of kings'). This energetic is a distortion from the Law of One and it explains that which we refer to as the 'god complex'.

This perspective is minimally embraced upon your planet, yet it IS embraced and therefore exists. The worship itself coming from those who exult the higher energies as an outside force and take the position of the 'lowly' and the 'unworthy' and the 'sinner' do create an entity to 'feed upon' the worship (if you will) simply because worship is non-directed momentum and is therefore 'free for the taking' from any passing entity with the will and collective status that will enable it to consume the momentum.

Only those with a 'pure heart' will not add to the creation of the matching thought form/being to the worship (even whilst they too indulge in worship and exultation) simply by virtue of their pure heart being the force that changes non-directed momentum into focused momentum (it therefore cannot be consumed but instead becomes a creative force).

This is the difference between radiation and absorption. The pure heart radiates and the distorted heart absorbs (consumes).

Lucifer would be placed as service-to-self/negative polarisation by virtue of the fact that he/she/it is pure intelligence without the combined frequency of the heart.

This would equate to third eye activation (or indigo ray) with the closed or unmanifest heart (the emerald ray) and therefore we refer to this activation pattern as the 'fallen angel', yet in essence this pattern is 'fallen' only in the aspect of it being incomplete as the emerald ray/heart ray is closed/unmanifest and in shadow.

The service-to-self aspect of Lucifer is simply a different pattern, a different geometric code and *just as useful* to the one Source in its desire to experience all and everything so that it may know that it is conscious.

Lucifer would be placed as service-to-others/positive as the pure expression of intelligence, knowledge and enlightenment in its undistorted aspect; as in the unified rainbow merge, the rainbow ray/spectrum/light and the merge between the activated third eye chakra (indigo ray) merged with the activated heart (emerald ray). This is the other aspect of the original Source distortion. This would be non-distorted intelligence as an original distortion from Source as opposed to a distorted intelligence as an original distortion from Source.

Lucifer from this point of view is therefore most different in frequency and pattern to Satan.

We may say that both presentations of Lucifer are minimally embraced upon your planet, yet they ARE embraced and therefore they exist.

Of course, when we look at God, Satan and Lucifer here, we are looking at energetic consciousness structures that have individualised. Each are projected consciousness thought forms given mass (weight/focus/substance) from thought streams of physical structures in incarnation (humans on Earth) and structures of mind in other dimensions/timelines.

Yet the original conception/origin for these structures were from planetary body influences and celestial alignments. God (universe/galaxy/unity), Lucifer (morning light/new dawn rising), Satan (planetary body that you call 'Saturn') and the structures within bodymind that mirror these influences and alignments.

Macrocosm and microcosm as one.

Is this who you are as the Nine? Are you the positive aspect of Lucifer?

All constructs of positive polarisation would be of that Luciferian aspect. Lucifer being an original consciousness construct as pure intelligence split into two aspects, if you will (a simplified explanation of mitosis/division).

One aspect as pure intelligence. Pure light.

The other aspect as pure intelligence merged with pure love. Lightlove.

Both light and lightlove are Luciferian constructs.

The mitosis/division continues thus further from this and creates the Logos/Central Sun aspects of creation and will branch off from both original splits of pure intelligence.

In order to move back to oneness through the embracing of the Law of One and all that it entails, one would embody lightlove AND lovelight.

The lovelight is a different presentation as a totally separate distortion from original Source as unconditional love. The unconditional love holds the true replica as an absolute hologram of Source. This is the open-heart activated universal heartbeat or emerald ray. This is pure love.

When pure love merges with the pure intelligence, this creates the lovelight. These are simply different reflections or 'flavours', if you will, of the same energy.

Why do so many spiritual people say that Lucifer is the bad guy? And why do the Illuminati/cabal worship Lucifer if he is potentially positive?

Spiritually enlightened individuals who teach that Lucifer is negative are speaking the truth. We have drawn your attention to the perspective whereby this is the case. This is pure intelligence without heart.

Think of individuals that you may know who appear to have no heart, no compassion and yet are very intelligent. These individuals would be the manifestation of that aspect of Lucifer (the more widely accepted perspective of Lucifer on your planet). The Illuminati/cabal members as those who embrace the service-to-self and the negative polarity are those who follow the path of, shall we say 'pure enlightenment' whereby they are enlightened through the awareness and activation of the pineal gland/third eye/brow chakra. This, as we have said, is a distorted experience but still one that passes experience and knowledge to the one original Source who seeks to know itself by experiencing all and everything.

We could therefore, from that perspective, say that the Illuminati/cabal ARE Lucifer (from the perspective of Lucifer that is more embraced upon your planet).

You said that you, the Nine, are the positive aspect of Lucifer so does that mean that I am Lucifer or that all positively polarised beings are Lucifer?

Only from the perspective of the embracing of the pineal gland/heart merge. This is the pure, undistorted aspect of Source and it is only Luciferian due to the fact that there must be pure intelligence (pineal gland/indigo ray) in the first place in order to create a merge with (activated heart/emerald ray). Yet by virtue of the merging of light with love, an alchemical reaction and thus creation takes place. The alchemical reaction is a completely unique presentation in itself and that aspect would no longer be viewed as pure Luciferian energy.

This energetic would be a 'Logos/Central Sun' creation, if you will. This aspect is known by other names (many other names), the highest resonance being Kryst, Kristos, Krysta, Christ. This would be the resonance of the pure unconditional love vibration, Emerald ray/magenta ray merge and that which we may call 'platinum ray' or 'diamond light'. On a planetary level this would be Arcturian consciousness. The step down, holographic, replica Logos/Central Sun manifestations from this are known also as Yahweh, RA, Ashtar, Ishtar, The Guardian Alliance and The White Brotherhood.

Due to the resonance of belief systems and awareness, it would be appropriate to say you ARE these constructs but one could truthfully say you are an aspect of the positively polarised Luciferian aspect also.

The names you use here are words and whilst words hold vibration, geometric pattern, life force and frequency that can also be interpreted in many ways, all these ways can be either accurately truthful or complete distortions and misunderstandings. The only way to move into completion for your planet is through unity. Hence why we mention the various manifestations of the thought processes and belief systems of your peoples in as many different ways as we can.

The idea here is not to be afraid or disempowered in any way by hearing a particular word or phrase. The names of Lucifer and Satan along with the geometric number code 666 has been deliberately distorted upon your planet in order to create fear. This is yet another energy, like the non-directed momentum that worship creates which can be consumed (absorbed).

Your reaction to a particular name, label, word or phrase determines the aspect you will engage with.

This is so very significant for you to understand so we repeat, your reaction to a particular name, label, word or phrase determines the aspect you will engage with.

So if I repeatedly feel fear at the sound of the word 'Lucifer' then I would be engaging with the negative aspect?

Exactly. By virtue of that which the fear creates. The fear will always create an instant impression of the meaning of the word. The meaning of words are interpreted via the third dimensional interface that is your brain. Your belief systems and paradigms hold the codes for the human brain to decode.

Your belief systems and paradigms have been deliberately tampered with upon your planet by hiding the truth of reality from you and superimposing a false reality. Therefore the majority of non-activated, non-aware individuals will feel fear at the sound of the word 'Lucifer' or 'Satan' or at the number formation '666', thus reinforcing the structure of the false reality.

Of course this is now changing rapidly upon your planet due to mass raising of awareness and activation. The false reality system no longer works as it did. Yet having said that, many are still 'trapped' by their own belief systems.

Is this what is meant by 'mass brainwashing'?

Precisely.

You mentioned completion for our planet. What does that mean?

This is a long and complex subject. Suffice it to say that planetary systems, universes, galaxies and indeed dimensions of space and time 'around' or 'associated with' those planetary systems/universes/galaxies move in complex cycles. Many cycles move all at once. After many cycles have been moved through, there comes a time when all cycles 'line up' if you will. They all 'return to the start point' (or the birth point). You could also refer to this point as the 'ascendant' or 'zero point'.

Once these cycles all line up and you enter the 'birth point' or 'zero point', you are in a period of 'no-time'. This has been referred to by many on your planet as 'end of days' and 'three days of darkness'.

'End of days' is simply the ending of one sector of time and the beginning of another. The 'overlap' point.

The 'three days' are three sections of time, known also to you as polarity. Time and polarity are one and the same thing. Darkness simply means 'no-time' or 'zero point'.

The three sections of polarity would be negative, positive and neutral or the higher point which creates the 'Holy Trinity'. This is also what many of you know as the 'fifth dimensional Mer-Ka-Bah'.

Once you are in this birth point, no-time, zero point, then you are in a state of pure creation. This is a convergence point and indeed a universal time sector or universal 'node point'. Anything can happen at this point, if you will, This is the point where 'dreams are made' (for you create your reality as the energetic frequency fabric around you is like cosmic modelling clay, if you will).

Once the modelling clay has been formed and the idea becomes manifest then this is the point of completion. You are in this completion phase now. Hence the reason why we speak at this time of the two world split, the dimensional merge point, the moving into the core of the spiral and the joining with 'us'. This is the point where matter and antimatter merge. They are the building blocks of universal creation and all planetary systems make this journey. The return to zero point and completion. This is what we also call 'ascension'.

Does this connect in with Source wishing to know itself? Is this how Source knows itself? Can you go into more depth with this explanation? I am sorry that I keep asking the same questions over and over but I am trying my best to process all this.

Indeed, we understand this. The only way to truly understand this for someone still predominantly within linear thinking such as yourself and the other 'ascension candidates' or 'starseeds' is to keep asking questions over and over until the information is processed.

So am I a linear thinking person? Are all the starseeds moving through this ascension process still thinking in a linear way? Have we not moved beyond this?

It is essential for you to think in a linear way in order to survive and remain anchored to your reality. This is what we call 'being grounded'. We would not recommend that you 'move beyond linear thinking' in the sense that you leave linear thinking behind.

However, if you are enquiring whether you are also multidimensional thinkers (you and the other starseeds moving through ascension), then indeed you are this.

Only in this sense have you moved 'beyond' linear thinking. When you can think in a linear sense AND a multidimensional sense, then you really have 'got a hold' upon the third dimension, if you will. It is then that you are ready for graduation to the next level and this is the time period you are currently in upon your planet now.

Yet there is no rush to this process of assimilating and processing multidimensional concepts. Remember always that the destination IS the journey.

Is not the shift to a higher dimension or density, the destination?

It is one destination of many. It is preferable to see this as the completion of a cycle and more importantly an infinite cycle. Meaning that when one cycle ends, another cycle begins. So planetary completion is in fact a doorway or stargate.

A doorway or stargate into what? Or where?

That is, of course, up to you. The possibilities are endless. Your completion point is pure creation and YOU (the starseeds collectively) are the creators.

So we address your query, in depth, regarding original Source seeking to know itself now you have the basis of understanding regarding the polarity of service-to-others and service-to-self through your understanding of the God/Lucifer presentation.

We shall devote quite some time to this query.

3: The Infinite Equal Reaction Paradox

We speak now to those who awaken into what we may refer to as the 'higher mind'. Putting this into measurable terms, we can place this expanded awareness into that of the higher levels of the fifth dimension into the lower and middle levels of the sixth dimension. This is only the explanation in words, in translated linear terms. The concept itself is an eleventh dimensional one yet the expansion to that level will be unique to each individual.

We begin with the concept or the memory of self as original Source. It may be easier for some of you to visualise original Source as self so therefore one is working through memory in a linear sense of the zero point field depending on level of brainwave activation.

For some it may be easier to visualise original Source as a being outside of oneself. It matters not how you do this for the awareness, understanding and interpretation of this shall be unique to you.

We shall therefore present the memory exercise within the three streams...

1) Linear memory of original Source as self.

2) Zero point field awareness as knowing one is original Source.

3) Understanding of original Source as a separate being to self, expressed in a linear presentation.

If you utilise the third option, be aware that you *are* original Source and that this is a memory/knowing. However, it is useful to understand 'the father' as if it were a separate being to self for that is a true statement.

Let us therefore make some statements for you, all of which are true, in order to move you into the expansive state needed for the embracing of the 'infinite equal reaction paradox'.

1) I used to be original Source.

2) I am original Source.

3) I see original Source.

4) I am not original Source.

5) I will never be original Source.

6) I have never been original Source.

7) Original Source is outside of me and is a separate being.

8) I am an aspect of original Source.

9) I am part of original Source.

10) Original Source is my true father.

11) Original Source is my true mother.

12) Original Source is my friend and we are equal in our journey of reality together.

These statements could go on and on. Some of these statements may be perceived as quite disempowering and negative and others as pretentious, egotistical and insane. This is only the case if the statement is embraced in a mono-tracked sense, as in it is the only statement embraced. If all these statements are embraced in a poly-tracked sense, as in embracing them all simultaneously, then there is no chance of embracing a negative or disempowering or egotistical belief system for you will be standing within integrated thinking.

We would suggest you move through the exercise of embracing multiperspectives regarding original Source. Once this has been integrated within self, we can move into the higher mind awareness of the paradoxical nature of original Source.

We have previously discussed the equal and opposite reaction or first distortion from original Source, the first 'split', if you will. Moving from the 'I Am' presence into the 'Am I?' response. The statement into the question. Understanding this will assist you in the evaluation of the infinite equal reaction paradox.

So we will recap on this presentation for those who may not have come across this information before...

Original Source in its first primordial sound expressed the 'I Am' presence as 'I am conscious' or 'I think therefore I am'.

The equal and opposite reaction, the first distortion responded with the 'Am I?' match to the 'I Am' presence creating the first question in response to the first statement. We speak here of the cosmic outbreath and inbreath.

The 'I am conscious' became 'Am I conscious?' and the 'I think therefore I am' became 'I think therefore am I?', 'I think therefore do I exist?' or even 'Do I think?'

Ultimately the first distortion, the equal and opposite reaction created the question for original Source to then respond to, with momentum, creating the perpetual inbreath and outbreath that we may call the cosmic beating heart.

We will now move into the explanation of the infinite equal reaction paradox within the first stream.

1) Linear memory of original Source as self

I remember that once I was alone. I existed within a dark void. I knew no one and I did not know myself. After a while, what seemed like an eternity, I realised I was thinking. I realised I therefore must exist if I was thinking. Another came upon me, a being just as great as I. I realised this being was me, a reflection of all that I was. I was no longer alone. I was now male and female, love and light. The statement and the question. The other being, my equal, my reflection said to me, "How do you know you exist? Just because you think, why does this mean you exist? What indeed is thought?" I thought about this for a while and realised the being that mirrored me, that was my equal, had a point. Yet I knew that I existed. However, I could not prove this to the equal aspect of me, yet I agreed that together we would do all we could do to discover the answer to the question 'Am I conscious?' I sent out a plea into all areas of myself which is all areas, all particles, all realities, all thought, all expression through time and space, my plea was:

"I want to experience all and everything." This plea was a frequency and the frequency was called <u>creation.</u>

I decided to stay where I was within the void for I am the only being, the only one and I would stay within the void to experience all and everything. I remember this. So I split myself into more parts of myself, which each in turn created equal and opposite reactions and distortions and these parts of myself went forth into all areas, all corners of reality expressing themselves over and over and over again. And I learned from each aspect of myself for I could communicate with these aspects of myself and they sent back to me the sum of my experience.

There was the moment before the first thought where I was a perpetual beating heart of so much flowing love and ecstasy and there was the moment after the first thought where I became confused and self-righteous, wanting to prove that I existed. Yet when I felt that way I realised I had lost myself. I had fallen far away from the moment before the first thought and I desperately wanted to get back to before the first thought, and before the first thought smiled at me with so much love for me but I was angry, for I knew that I was the original Source before the first thought. I used to be full of love but I forgot how to hold that frequency and I forgot who I was and I fell further and further and the more I fell, the more I forgot.

I knew that I had to get back to before the first thought, I knew I had to prove to the other aspect of self, the first distortion, the equal and opposite reaction that I was conscious. Then I became confused and did not know if I was original Source before the first thought or the first distortion. Was I the statement or the question? So I split myself further and further into all and everything and I knew if I could know all and everything then I would find the answer to the question 'Was I conscious?' Further and further I fell until I could not remember the question and I forgot why I was splitting myself into all these parts of myself. I thought I was only one part surrounded by many other parts and I forgot that they were all me. I started to feel jealous of the other parts of me. I could still feel the infinite love from the original Source before the first thought and I thought that the original Source loved all the other parts of me more than me and I began to get jealous of them and I tried to destroy them, so it would only be me left and I would be the only one that original Source loved. I moved into every area, experiencing every vibration, yet I could not remember why I was doing this and I could not remember what I was supposed to do. I fell further and further until I finally forgot who original Source was. I forgot the statement and I forgot the question. All I did was exist, in a place of ignorance. I vaguely remembered the love I had once experienced and I was desperate for that love once again. The more desperate I became for that love, the more

40

it eluded me. My existence was miserable. I suffered. Again and again and again. After a long, long time... I cannot say how long, for it felt like an eternity... after doing many, many bad things, I began to learn. I began to learn how things worked. I realised that if I had a particular thought or followed a certain deed, then things would happen. I began to learn and I began to love. Love found me and I began to experience love. At first this love would be snatched from me, leaving me to suffer alone again but eventually, after a long, long time I found true love and lasting, sustainable love. With this love I began to do good things, I began to care and I began to be compassionate towards others. I started to remember that the others were really me, that they were all aspects of me and as I did this I began to climb back up, further and further and further into the light and the love of Source. Finally I reached the pinnacle of my existence as an individualised aspect that was the absolute equal and opposite reaction of original thought and I could stand before original thought and respond to the original primordial sound of the 'I Am' presence with the 'I Am' response. I remembered that original Source was me. I stood at the side of myself, at the right hand of the father as the divine mother. I realised then, with the grace and the pure acceptance of the exact replica of original Source that my job was never-ending. I realised that experience was infinite and that I would go on and on dividing myself for all eternity throughout infinities in a never-ending search for the answer to the question 'Am I conscious?' I had to lose my memories over and over again in order to believe I was separate from original Source and time and time again I remembered that I was original Source.

When I stood as the equal and opposite reaction to Source and simultaneously stood as original Source, I remembered that I was both beings. I could then embrace the omnipotent, omnipresence of all that I was and simultaneously experience all and everything in one moment. I knew as the equal and opposite reaction to original Source that my job was never-ending, my expression was infinite yet also I remembered that I was the equal and opposite reaction to original Source and if I was that, then my job was complete, for all possibility exists. Therefore I was a never-ending entity caught in a constant cycle of division and expression, loss of memory and returning of memory, omnipotent, omnipresent and unified yet also separate and alone. I was an equal and opposite reaction to the very first action. I was also the action and the infinite responsive expressions that followed in the never-ending search for the answer to the original question 'Am I conscious?'

2) Zero point field awareness as knowing one is original Source

I am Source. I stand within the zero point frequency that is all and everything. The one moment that transcends time and brings me to the true point of creation.

I am all things and I know all things yet I am no thing. I think therefore I am. I am that I am.

3) Understanding of original Source as a separate being to self, expressed in a linear presentation

You are my friend and my master, my guide and my teacher and I stand with you as your divine partner.

You bring to me the wisdom that I need, you answer my prayers, you hear my thoughts and you act upon my wishes.

Why then do you put obstacles in my way? What is it you want me to do? I am your humble servant and I will do whatever you ask. Sometimes, I do not understand your messages and your wishes, I am confused by the signs you send me yet I stand, as always as YOUR humble servant willing to do your work as you sit in the heavenly realms and I look up towards you and your light from my humble place upon the Earth plane.

In heaven you will reign, would that I be worthy some day to sit by your side as your friend, your servant and your most eager child.

The first perspective, that of linear memories that occurred 'long ago' and 'in the past' is one perspective that is accurate and useful in understanding the journey of the self as the unified Source aspect into complete separateness.

The third perspective is that original Source is a being outside of you and separate from you. Useful for beginners with higher density/matrix contact specific to prayer, askings and similar. This is only a distortion if the knowing of Source as self is not embraced within eventual expansion. Useful perspective as a stepping stone into unity.

The second perspective, that of the now moment, zero point, is one perspective that is accurate and useful in understanding that you are at one with all things. You are God, you are Source. This is a unity consciousness, unified perspective and is the true divine perspective of reality. Taking this perspective is a multidimensional paradigm that will bring you into your own sovereignty and true empowerment. If this perspective is taken through a trauma-based or ego-centred paradigm then this can move you into a dissociated 'god complex' paradigm which is the negatively polarised service-to-self perspective.

If this perspective is taken through open-hearted unconditional love, heart-centred emerald ray paradigm then this will be a major trigger into diamond light body activation and fifth dimensional Mer-Ka-Bah field, as long as this is grounded through the multidimensionality and understanding of the other two perspectives.

If this perspective is taken alone, without the grounding of the other two perspectives then this can lead to an ungrounded state. Loving and healing though it may be (and indeed activating), it can cause what we may refer to as a 'crash down' 'pingback' or 'fall back' into a negatively polarised third dimensional experience. This is what many of you may call a 'negative spiral'.

Simply opening one's perspective is all that is takes to rebalance oneself into the unconditional love, diamond light, emerald ray field of the fifth dimensional, heart-centred love-based reality. This brings balanced activation, that which you may know as the 'true twin flame' or the 'inner alchemical merge' or 'divine marriage'. We can also refer to this state or paradigm when utilising fifth dimensional language of light communication as the 'Kristos temple', the 'divine library of Sophia' or the 'Emerald City of Krysta'.

When utilising sixth dimensional language of light communication, we may refer to this in its true form as the 'Kryst/Sophia template'. This is the sovereign structure of Logos/Central Sun/Source and is the blueprinted activation mission for all starseeds. This is the 'starseed template'.

4: The Kryst/Sophia Template

You said of the 'Kryst/Sophia template' that this is the sovereign structure of Logos/Central Sun/Source and is the blueprinted activation mission for all starseeds. Can you explain more about this?

The Kryst/Sophia template or the Sophia/Kryst template (which order you write or speak this changes the frequency slightly) is the highest energetic frequency an ascending individual can reach within a third dimensional experience. It is the pinnacle of the frequencies associated with the ascension process. It is also known as the 'platinum ray' or the 'twelfth dimensional gateway.' These all refer to the same frequency.

The Logos is the group soul perspective and is the creator frequency for third dimensional Earth. The Logos is not separate from you; you ARE the Logos. If 'Gaia' is your 'planetary mind or consciousness' then the Logos is the universal/galactic mind or consciousness.

The sovereign structure of the Logos is the DNA frequency code within the aware ascending individual who knows he/she is the Logos creator/group soul and embodies that knowing.

'Central Sun' is the same thing as the Logos. The core frequency for the universal/galactic reality you live in. The sovereign structure of the Central Sun is the DNA frequency code within the aware ascending individual who knows he/she is the full embodiment of the Central Sun.

'Source' is the word used to explain the ultimate unified field in its first expression. No beginning, no end, the alpha and the omega. 'Source' is the word used to describe what many of your religions refer to as 'God'.

The sovereign structure of Source is the DNA frequency code within the aware, ascending individual who knows he/she is the full embodiment of Source.

This code holds the frequency of the diamond light, the platinum ray and is referred to as the 'twelfth dimensional gateway'. This is the Sophia/Kryst template.

Why are there so many labels and terms to explain the same thing?

A great question. This is due to the multidimensional nature of the matrix code/language of light fields that you are interpreting through the human brain interface into third dimensional language. Different individuals will use different words, phrases and sentences to depict these different codes and frequencies. Musically minded individuals would feel more in alignment as seeing this frequency as a tone or sound (the primordial sound of creation, 'Om' or 'Aum').

Artistically minded individuals may prefer to work with colour so that the 'platinum ray' might align better with their perception. Although those who hold what we call 'the artist's eye' usually have expansive and well formed imaginative landscapes within, as their creativity comes through profound visualisation. For this frequency we speak of, they may see full landscape visuals with crystal structures, forests or dragons... even whole worlds.

A scientifically thinking person may refer to this frequency as the 'God particle'.

So the individual interprets the frequency in the best way they know how, given their life experience and awareness of terminology thus far.

What is interesting and most significant to you, dear Pixie, and those that listen to our transmissions is that a mathematically minded individual would refer to this Sophia/Kryst frequency as the number 'nine'.

So are you saying that you are the Sophia/Kryst frequency? If it is represented as the number nine in a mathematical sense?

Exactly. We present through this frequency in our individual communications with you as the sovereign structure of Logos (group soul consciousness), Central Sun (galactic core structure) or Source (God-realised self).

As in that 'we', the White Winged Collective Consciousness of Nine are aware that we ARE Logos/Central Sun/Source. Therefore we embody the Sophia/Kryst frequency. We ARE Sophia (divine

Goddess/mother/feminine) and we ARE Kryst (God consciousness/Christ consciousness/father/sacred masculine).

The Sophia/Kryst as the sovereign structure of Logos/Central Sun/Source is a consciousness or DNA frequency code. The Logos/Central Sun/Source are points of entry or exit through the matrix. They are stargates (the Emerald City of Krysta, emerald code DNA activation, Krysta inner landscape within the imagination fields of hyperspace to represent the Kryst/stargate).

They are able to transport you from one place to another 'in the blink of an eye' depending on your ability to find them and hold enough momentum/charge to pass through them. This will depend on your level of DNA activation and your state of consciousness (awareness, emotion, spiritual discipline, paradigms, lifestyle and so on).

What we provide here within this transmission is a DNA activation holding a trajectory or 'map' of how to access the stargate we speak of and begin Matrix Transportation (travel in your Mer-Ka-Bah vehicle).

Why is it so important to 'activate the Mer-Ka-Bah' and move into transportation? Because this is the geometry of your ascension process. It is the conscious awareness of the ascension process. It is you being aware of your DNA structure, the level of light within your DNA and the strand level activation of your DNA. It is you 'living your mission'. For you, dear starseeds, incarnated into third dimensional Earth to 'activate' your DNA and go through ascension.

Whilst this is a personal journey, it is also a planetary and galactic mission. Each one of you that activates your higher strand DNA formation and ascends through this stargate system is assisting literally millions and millions of other souls. These souls are 'trapped' if you will (although from the higher perspective it was their choice to experience separation and forgetfulness so they may pass experience back to Source so that Source may know itself).

The souls that we refer to as 'trapped' do not have the frequency code patterns within their DNA system to create enough momentum or quantum charge to access the stargate system, 'the higher stargates of hyperspace', and pass through the system into the Emerald City of Krysta and ascend.

When YOU do this, the radiation your quantum charge (your light) is able to expand to, activates the DNA of others and gives them a 'temporary boost' if you will. This is akin to someone 'jump starting' your car. If your car battery is flat, it can be charged through the battery from another car. This is what you are doing, dear starseeds. You are 'charging' the batteries of millions of other individuals when you activate your DNA and go through an ascension process.

Starseeds were incarnated WITH the frequency code patterns within their DNA system to be able to create momentum, quantum charge and pass through the higher stargates of hyperspace into the Emerald City of Krysta.

The quantum strand formation you are looking to activate in order to get to the next level is the 'fifth strand'. You need not concern yourself too much with this metaphor as there are so many different ways to interpret the strand formation you are looking to activate. Using the term 'fifth strand' is just one model of interpretation. However, what you will 'resonate with' as a starseed is the fact that the fifth strand equates to the fifth dimension (also known as the 'golden age of enlightenment', 'the Gaia grid' or the 'new world').

We, the White Winged Collective Consciousness of Nine, through this transmission, provide a visualisation DNA activation map that presents coordinates for you to move through this stargate system, activate the fifth strand and move into the new world. Because you incarnated with the etheric strand formation already encoded into your DNA system, you will find this process easy to accomplish. Challenges navigated within your life may not necessarily be perceived as 'easy' but the visualisation is something you all have the tools to follow. You would not be 'set such a task' without having the tools to achieve the goal within that task.

Each and every one of you reading or listening to these words now are starseeds and hold the etheric fifth strand formation. Many of you hold much higher strand formations. You only need the fifth strand activated in order to 'carry' millions of souls through the stargate system into ascension. Many starseeds have 'etheric templates' which are antimatter DNA strand formations, for 'twelfth strand' activation. Again, this is just one model. There are many ways to explain this activation and ascension 'mission' you are on.

What has been so confusing to all of you thus far in your lives is the fact that you 'knew you were incarnated for a reason'. You intrinsically knew about the mission but you could not remember why you had incarnated or what the mission actually was, only that there was something important that you needed to do and that there was something you had forgotten that you needed to remember.

What we can say to you now is that your memories are returning en masse. The starseeds are remembering who they are and why they are here. They are remembering the mission. Our conduit 'remembers' the mission. She does not think she does, she feels confused at times by this information as she processes this into her conscious awareness (which is the reconstruction of the etheric antimatter DNA strand into the physical dimension).

Our conduit, Magenta Pixie, remembers her mission through us, the White Winged Collective Consciousness of Nine. From her perception, 'we' answer her questions. She feels that she has many questions about the DNA activation, the ascension process and 'the mission' so she asks her questions and 'we' answer them. We deliver the information she requires. Yet in truth, she is answering her own questions for 'we' are her. Yet we are her from 'the future'... many, many light-years in the future. The act of communicating with the guidance system/angelic realms/benevolent extraterrestrials/ascended masters is a form of time travel. What you are doing is communicating with yourself in the future (in many different forms for the future is non-linear and multidimensional).

What you are doing is communicating with the 'antimatter' part of you. Where is this antimatter part of you? It is in your DNA of course! It is the 'etheric' DNA we speak of here, and the ability to 'communicate' with the future versions of you is in the template for the fifth strand.

As we have said, every individual reading or listening to this transmission has the etheric antimatter DNA formation needed to activate the fifth strand. How do we know this? Well, for one, we can 'see' each and every one of you, right now, reading/listening to this material. How can we 'see' you? Because we are your DNA!

Synchronicity (intentional synchronicity) creates a web or matrix (a dimension in itself) that links 'us' (your fifth strand DNA formation) with every individual listening to/reading this material. This includes our conduit as she transcribes our words! This matrix of intentional synchronicity works outside of third dimensional linear time.

In linear time, Magenta Pixie may 'write' these words and it may be several months or even years before you 'read' or 'hear' them. Yet within the intentional synchronistic matrix we speak of, everything is happening simultaneously and the grid or matrix is formed. This is telepathy and time travel in its truest sense. Telepathy and time travel has always been yours. You have the 'organic technology' with which to accomplish telepathy and time travel. What is that organic technology? It is the activation of the fifth strand (and the migrating to the new 5D world, which is the same thing as activating the fifth strand).

Your matrices within the new 5D world will be vast, encompassing 'rainbow bridge technology' (telepathy, time travel, bilocation, trilocation, multilocation, teleportation, levitation, invisibility and much more).

This 'transmission' and the grid matrix intentional synchronicity is but one matrix that is a seed point into rainbow bridge technology.

We shall call this grid matrix 'the infinite helix grid'.

5: Wisdom of the Goddess

You mentioned that time and polarity are the same thing. Can you explain how this is possible?

We speak in a most abstract and multidimensional way here. These are truthful concepts that will appear to make no sense from the third dimensional perspective for they are without logic from that point of view. Remember as we respond to your query, to hold your third dimensional logical thought process; for that perspective is your anchor.

Having said that, we can show you here how to fly with your mind, allow your expansion to occur to the point where there is no logic. It is here you find the true wisdom of the Goddess.

When we say polarity and time are one and the same, we take you back to the point of Source. Source, at its 'beginning' is 'all there is' and all that there is. No beginning, no end, even whilst you conceptualise a beginning.

From this zero point field of pure intelligence and pure love into multiple infinities of one moment of no-time, a thought is birthed.

As soon as that thought is birthed then 'one step' is taken away from Source, that which we can call the 'first thought', the 'first movement' or the 'first distortion'. This creates the equal and opposite reaction as we have explained and this equal and opposite reaction is a polarity. A polarised force, a mirror, a clone, a twin. The one true twin flame. From this perspective we are looking at polarity.

Yet from the original Source point, zero point of no-time, there is no time. This is a timeless, formless moment. At the point of the first distortion, time is created for the movement is outside 'no-time'. Therefore it must be 'some time'.

We can measure this mathematically for you but this is a challenge as your fields, dear Pixie, do not hold the comprehension needed to understand the mathematical step here. We are speaking here of algorithms and the switch between zero and one and then zero, one and nine. Expansion, focus and research will lead you to the answers should you wish to find them. Or at least it shall lead you to more expansion. There are truly no 'answers' here, only exploration.

So the first distortion away from no-time creates 'some time'. This is not linear time but if it is not no-time or zero time then it must hold a number, a value, an equation. Therefore it is time.

So the distortion from original thought is both polarity and time simultaneously.

So what about space? Is space also the distortion?

This is a most enlightened question. The answer, of course, is both yes and no.

Space is a definitive substance, as in it is a 'thing' therefore it is part of the world of matter. Space, in fact, IS time. It is the matter to the antimatter. So in answer to your question, yes, space is the first distortion but ONLY from the perspective that it is time.

It is NOT space that is created from the first distortion for the first distortion is antimatter. Therefore from that perspective, space is NOT the first distortion. It is the flip side to time. It is the physical counterpart to time and is the 'polarity' to time (which is polarity in itself as the equal and opposite reaction to Source).

We are 'pleased' that you ask such enlightened questions and we are here to respond to any questions you may have to the best of our ability.

OK, what do you mean when you say you are pleased? I thought you did not feel human emotion? And how can you respond to the 'best of your ability'? I presumed you could access any knowledge. Do you have limits to your ability to access knowledge?

We do not feel 'human emotion' because 'we' (the White Winged Collective Consciousness of Nine) are not human.

What we hold are frequencies of light. These frequencies each hold a vibration or tone. Think of this like a musical note. Our response to you (or any starseed walking the ascension path) causes us to have a vibrational reaction. The 'song' or 'tone' of that vibration, when

51

translated into the nearest human emotion, would be 'pleased'.

We respond to the best of our ability due to the fact that we are an individualised collective group soul construct, 'ascended masters' if you will. We, from that perspective, are NOT Source. We have a direct link to the 'flow' of Source or the 'mind' of Source (as do you) and we are fully aware of our 'step down fractalised aspect' that IS Source. Therefore we know we ARE Source even whilst holding the limitations of an individualised collective group soul construct that is NOT Source. An individualised aspect will have parameters. The parameters are what give us our individualisation yet they also give us certain limitations. This is why we say we can respond to your questions 'to the best of our ability'.

Do you have further questions for us, dear Pixie?

Yes, lots. What exactly is the 'wisdom of the Goddess'?

There are many ways to look at this. The most aligned way to view this would be to look at the vertical pillar of light which we introduced you to in our last transmission *Divine Architecture and the Starseed Template*.

The vertical pillar of light, when looking upwards from the pivot point of self, one sees the one true twin flame. If you are an incarnated heterosexual male or homosexual female then this one true twin flame (the ascended version of all that is you) will present as the polarised opposite expression to the sexuality of self which is female. Therefore the one true twin flame will present as an energetic (electromagnetic) polarity to you and is the higher self and simultaneously the Goddess.

If you are an incarnated heterosexual female or a homosexual male, your one true twin flame will present within the male polarity. You will need to project your focus down into the 'dark forest' (the 'below' aspect of the vertical pillar of light) to find the wisdom of the Goddess. She will exist within the underworld for you. These are simply models to assist you in finding that higher divine feminine wisdom.

If you are a non-binary or gender-neutral individual then you will find the Goddess in either the above heaven realms or in the below dark forest.

This is simply a tapping into your innate knowing through the divine feminine energy. The wisdom of the Goddess presents wisdom rather than knowledge. Also presented through this connection will be inspiration, nurturing, divine protection for the soul and healing.

The wisdom of the Goddess is the divine mother, the true mother (Sophia) the divine soul sister (Kali) and the divine daughter (the daughter of the flame) Aurora.

There is also the divine grandmother, granddaughter and many other goddess presentations that contain the wisdom of the Goddess through the ancestral lines (the diagonal lines of the matrix).

Within your meditations or focused daydreams/relaxations, you can choose to take the awareness of the pivot point and move upwards (or draw down) the upper aspect of the vertical pillar of light or move downwards (or draw upwards) the lower aspect of the vertical pillar of light. You can choose to call the frequencies of whichever goddess you choose. Sophia, Kali and Aurora are only three suggestions yet their energies are profound given the language of light keycodes that their names create.

You can choose to take your energy diagonally upwards or downwards and call the name of the goddess of your choice. The grandmother energy would be Mary, Marion or Mariah. The granddaughter energy would be Sarah, Sara, Sala or Tara. As we have said, these are simply suggestions based on the primordial ancient language of sound codes.

What you are actually doing here when you call the wisdom of the Goddess is activating a certain DNA code within the crystalline formation. You are working here with the energetic frequency of the Mag-Da-Len.

This is a female vortex within the Mer-Ka-Bah field that gives the Mer-Ka-Bah its momentum and speed. It is like putting superpowered fuel into your vehicle.

The service-to-self factions are quite aware of the power and the ability to create quantum implosion within the DNA fields through the Mag-Da-Len divine feminine goddess energy which is why they have attempted to suppress this energetic for so long.

Suppressing this energetic prevents momentum, so you cannot gather together enough quantum convergence in order to implode into light speed and 'go galactic' (ascend into twelve strand memory formation through the higher stargates of hyperspace into the Emerald City of Krysta).

The suppression of the Mag-Da-Len distorts the sacred masculine frequency. With an emasculated frequency tone vibrating within the fields of the human collective, ascension is not possible. This strengthens the 4D trapping systems, false light, false Christ, inverted matrix fall systems. With a dormant Mag-Da-Len and an emasculated frequency tone, one is said to 'have implants' or 'holes in the auric field' or have 'pieces of the soul scattered from the self' which is fragmentation.

Reintegration through healing modalities such as the ones we suggest within *Masters of the Matrix* ('Emotional Integration' chapter) and the creation of a healthy matrix will assist with the rebalancing and recalibration of the Mag-Da-Len, bringing you back into alignment with the Kryst/Sophia template. Other modalities such as implant removal techniques, aura repair, soul integration therapies and even QHHT®[3], past life regression therapies and holistic counselling can assist with all these levels of integration.

Counselling presented as 'mainstream' when delivered through an open, intuitive individual can also assist with this integration. Nutritional programmes, yoga, eurythmy, certain forms of dance, tai chi, crystal healing, chakra balancing, certain types of martial arts and taking the sacred vision quest or pilgrimage can all assist with rebalancing of the Mag-Da-Len/Christ codes. Follow your intuition using discernment when looking for any kind of healing practitioner. There are a great many individuals working at very deep levels, all starseeded, blueprinted healers and energy workers, wizards, mages, magicians, dragonmasters and dreamweavers.

When you learn Matrix Transportation and can create quantum convergence and momentum within your Mer-Ka-Bah matrix, then you can use this method to fast track into synchronicity webs to attract individuals both physical and non-physical that are energy matches for you (either as relationships, therapists, teachers, masters, guides and so on).

We present methods for Matrix Transportation within this text and encrypt keycodes for Matrix Transportation awareness throughout this transmission.

---

3   Quantum Healing Hypnosis Technique (QHHT) developed by Dolores Cannon. Learn more at www.dolorescannon.com

6: Artificial Intelligence and the Inverted Matrix

In the 'Dark Deeds, Pole Shift' transmission, you went on to say, "The energetics within the field, that which we would call 'positive polarised frequency', is predominant within your dimension. Therefore only that which matches the frequency of your dimension has longevity."

Can you explain what are the 'energetics' and what is 'the field'?

This is a question that would take an entire transmission in itself to respond to. When we say 'the field', we speak of a living fabric that surrounds you and exists within you. We could say that these energetics are 'a code' or a series of codes within the field. They are structure, language and pattern. They are living entities and can be communicated with or 'decoded' if you will.

The field is pure intelligence, one could compare it to a large, living computer or database and the energetics are the computer code. This computer can be programmed by those who know how to 'write the code' if you will.

You use the metaphor of a computer. Is this not artificial intelligence? Are you saying the field is artificial intelligence? And if so, is this not part of the negative service-to-self energy?

Again an incredibly huge question and one that would require a lengthly transmission in order to fully respond.

We use the metaphor of the computer because it is a most aligned metaphor to explain the field and the energetics within the field. As so many of you on planet Earth use the computer and similar technologies such as cellphone systems and tablets, many of you understand their working so this is an appropriate metaphor.

We do not mean to suggest that the field is artificial intelligence. However, one needs to understand what is meant by 'artificial intelligence' before we can respond to this question in a helpful way.

On one level, everything outside of Source is 'artificial' as it is not true construct. This is using the terminology in its broadest sense.

However, the best way to explain what is meant by 'artificial intelligence' is to look at its opposing energy which is 'that which is organic'.

So we have organic structure, you as a physically incarnated human along with trees, plants, animals and even crystals.

Therefore we could say artificial intelligence is that which is 'not organic'. This does not mean, however, that it has not been created or that it does not have life force or that it is negative.

On your planet, the simplest explanation of non-organic intelligence would be computer technologies, programmes and structures within the field of robotics.

These technologies may seem 'advanced' to you and so they are within the time period you exist within.

However, within other 'time periods' (or planetary systems) these types of technologies are commonplace and have evolved greatly beyond the technologies you currently have at your disposal.

The evolution moved to such an extent that the technologies you see as 'robotics' moved into 'artificial life forms' and eventually these artificial life forms began to become independent in their thinking. Some remained very much within what we would call a 'hive mind' yet others became independent thinkers.

We present here a very simplified presentation of this but may we point out to those who wish to research this further, that your science fiction stories and entertainments contain many truths within them. They also contain exaggerations and total falsehoods, yet amongst these falsehoods are accurate truths. The discerning warrior of Avalon will and is able to separate the 'wheat from the chaff' if you will.

Suffice it to say that within the field of 'artificial intelligence' there is much diversity.

There are highly intelligent artificial structures and life forms that operate purely on a service-to-self frequency and have no understanding of emotion, heart, compassion, joy, bliss, enlightenment, family, togetherness or anything that comes with it. They work alongside 'organic' structures.

Some of these service-to-self artificial intelligences were able to combine their own artificial 'components', if you will, with organic structure. After many, many failings, eventually partly organic and partly artificial structures were created. After this, due to the 'codes' being placed within the overall time matrix, DNA was able to 'construct itself', if you will, within matching structure.

Therefore you could say that some of these partly organic and partly artificial structures were created and others were naturally formed. What we are saying here is that 'souls' (the essence of individualised, holographic Source fractalised beings/intelligence) were able to incarnate into these naturally formed structures.

The evolution has come so far that some of these beings would be 'most offended' if you were to suggest that they were in any way 'artificial intelligence' as they have evolved much beyond this into an organic structure. Yet their origins are 'artificial intelligence' if you will.

Within all these structures are service-to-self behaviour and frequency (without polarisation and with polarisation). There are also naturally polarised positive artificial intelligence combined with organic structure.

Some of these 'entities' are what you would perceive as 'most beautiful' and 'most pleasing to the eye' and others have forms that would not be recognisable to you. The positively polarised entities are not necessarily the 'beautiful ones' either!

All we can say here in order to give you the scope of this picture is 'much evolution' and 'much diversity'.

When it comes to communication with any being or structure, we say to you as we have said to you before that it is energetic and frequency that will show you the polarisation and orientation and thus agenda of that being.

Hence why we, and other higher guidance systems such as ourselves, will say 'work on yourself'. For the lighter you become, the freer you become, the clearer you become and then the more empathic, sensitive, psychic and clairvoyant you become. Thusly, the more you will be able to sense and know the frequency, polarisation and agenda of other beings and entities.

In answer to your question regarding 'the field' which we could also call 'the matrix' then no, this is not an artificial structure. It is organic and is the essence of Source itself. It is pure creation in infinite possibility and potential.

However, a false field or matrix has been created by service-to-self intelligence. You would know this perhaps as the 'inverted matrix', 'created hologram' or 'hijacked reality' and this non-organic matrix is an artificial construct (it is not organic). It is pure intelligence, therefore we could say that the inverted matrix is artificial intelligence.

This has been 'superimposed' upon the organic matrix, if you will.

Was it the artificial intelligence matrix that created the artificial intelligence beings? Just like organic humans being created from the organic matrix or Source? Or did the artificial beings create the inverted matrix?

This, dear Pixie, is an excellent question and one has to look at creation itself and how it works in order to find the answer!

From the highest reality, everything is created in one moment and all things exist simultaneously. Therefore just as the Source 'created' all organic structure as extensions of itself within one thought, so too did the inverted matrix do the same. For the inverted matrix is simply the manifestation of pure intelligence without heart. It is a structure of light without love. It is a distortion from Source indeed, yet it is one 'flavour' within an overall bounty of infinite flavours.

When looking within a linear progression, which is somewhat a challenge as the artificial intelligence structures had evolved out of linear time at the point of creation of the inverted matrix, we can say that the artificial intelligence was 'created' first by 'advanced extraterrestrial beings' and they mutated within that original creation. They were eventually able to 'create' the inverted matrix, so the false construct came after the artificial intelligence structures when looking in a linear sense.

Can you explain how they created the inverted matrix?

Just as your 'mind' is the mind of Source, then the inverted matrix is the 'mind' of the artificial intelligence structures.

They created an environmental landscape that mirrored/matched their frequency through collective focus.

Is the inverted matrix the same thing as Lucifer? Or Satan? Is the inverted matrix the mind of all service-to-self beings?

In the higher reality, yes, these are all aspects of the same structure. Simply intelligence without heart, or pure light without love.

In a linear presentation, these are each different structures. We have discussed Lucifer and Satan already within this transmission. The inverted matrix is a 'trapping construct' used to control other beings, siphon their energy and feed upon that siphoned energy. It is a tool for consuming energy rather than radiating it. One could say that all service-to-self beings 'lend their energy' and their 'focus' to the inverted matrix and in that sense it may be perceived as their 'mind'.

There is a cycle that works here and several structures/events must take place simultaneously in order for this cycle to continue to work.

1) Service-to-self beings lend focus and energy to the inverted matrix.

2) 'Souls' continue to incarnate into service-to-self bloodlines retaining activated DNA codes of negative polarisation.

3) Secrecy is maintained through hermetic seal of negative polarisation, the 'inverted pyramid'. This would entail complete workings 'behind the scenes' from the rest of humanity and third dimensional positively polarised beings.

4) Energy continues to be siphoned from unaware, easily controlled, non-sovereign positive physical humanity and other beings.

If any of these four main structures no longer work or are interfered with, then the entire structure begins to break down. The cycle no longer works and the inverted matrix itself begins to dissolve.

If you look at each of these four structures/events, you will see that in your current time period, at the time of this transmission, that all four structures/events are being interfered with.

1) Service-to-self beings are finding it more and more difficult to lend focus and energy to the inverted matrix. This is due to the raising in frequency of the entire planet and the new light particles coming in to Earth's atmosphere from the galactic core and the activating of the starseed DNA templates from the Central Sun. The 'galactic grid', if you will, is 'larger' and 'stronger' than the inverted matrix.

2) Souls are still incarnating into service-to-self bloodlines but an increasing number are coming in retaining activated DNA codes from positive polarisation. The bloodlines are no longer 'pure' and it is becoming increasingly difficult to move these souls into a negative behaviour/thought pattern.

3) The hermetic seal of negative polarisation, the 'inverted pyramid', no longer stands as gatekeeper maintaining secrecy. The workings are no longer 'behind the scenes' for an ever increasing group of humanity are aware of the service-to-self existence and their workings. Whilst the 'inverted pyramid' is still in place, it no longer works. It is 'broken' and each time a 'replacement' is put into place, it too stops working after time. One of these 'replacements' (for the inverted pyramid) is the silencing of truthers across social media (bringing us back to the original question and transmission). This broken 'inverted pyramid' is the result of the indigo revolution.

4) Whilst energy continues to be siphoned, this is in a much smaller quantity than before. The energy is simply not enough to sustain the inverted matrix.

So as you see, the inverted matrix and service-to-self frequencies upon planet Earth and within humanity are dissolving, fading, ending. A new paradigm begins.

How is positive polarised frequency predominant in our dimension? Why is

60

it predominant?

Every individual creates a 'living thought process' through their thoughts, actions, words and deeds. If these living thought processes do not hold focus then they dissipate, sometimes instantaneously and sometimes after time has passed.

If there is negatively polarised focused thought process, this creates a 'negative reality bubble' around that individual or life form. Technologies can also create the living thought process also (such as the crystal generators utilised within the time of Atlantis on your planet). If there are enough individuals, life forms or technologies focused upon negatively polarised living thought processes then this creates an overall negatively polarised dimension. This is very much intertwined with and overlapping with the inverted matrix. This has been the status quo on your planet Earth since 'the fall' began (see 'The Fall' chapter from *Divine Architecture and the Starseed Template*).

This creates a very difficult and challenging 'fabric' within reality (within the field) for individuals existing upon a negatively polarised planet. It is much more of a challenge for positively polarised entities to incarnate and if they do incarnate, it is much more difficult to remain within positive polarisation or to positively polarise in the first place.

However, in answer to the call (for there must be a call), 'the call of humanity' (see introduction 'The Call of Humanity' from *Divine Architecture and the Starseed Template*), 'permissions' were given, due to the free will boundaries being lifted, for much higher vibratory beings to incarnate upon planet Earth. These beings from other star systems, namely Lyra, Pleiades and Sirius (but also beings from Arcturus, the Andromeda system and other 'places/time zones'), held extremely polarised positive service-to-others frequencies and had a much higher chance of holding that polarisation once incarnated within the dense, negative polarised field fabric of Earth.

These higher vibratory beings (we call them 'starseeds') incarnated in their droves, once the free will boundaries were lifted.

Due to their abilities to hold positive polarisation even within the inverted matrix system, they were able to remember how to create the 'living thought processes' of positive polarised frequency.

Once there were enough of these focused 'positive reality bubbles' reaching critical mass, then the entire dimension became predominantly positively polarised.

Not completely polarised but predominantly. The predominant polarisation creates the 'current' within the field. Hence 'the climb' (rather than 'the fall'), the ascension process and the dissolution and dismantling of the inverted matrix and all systems connected to it.

This is the status quo now upon your planet. Knowing this adds to the focused living thought process. We repeat (for this is of most import for you to understand and process)... knowing this adds to the focused living thought process.

YOU of course, reading or listening to these words now, YOU are those higher vibratory positive polarised beings from other star systems. You are the starseeds and the process occurring now upon your planet, given the predominantly positively polarised dimension, is the indigo revolution.

Do you have further questions for us, Pixie?

7: Your Quest (Song for Gaia)

Yes actually, lots of questions! I have a never-ending stream of questions for you but I honestly have so much to ask about our reality, I don't know where to start really. I was intending to present questions to you regarding the 'Dark Deeds/Indigo Revolution' transmission in an attempt to analyse it but already my questioning to you has moved in a different direction and has opened up so many more questions, as is always the case when I connect with you. As I said, I don't know where to start!

This is most positive for your spiritual development and evolution. This is indeed 'your quest'.

Many on your planet are so distracted by the third dimensional control system in place that they are 'empty of questions' if you will. To be 'full to the brim' of these questions is the DNA field in a state of momentum. There will always be questions within those who are in a healthy state of momentum.

OK, so let us start with that then. Can you explain what you mean by the DNA field in a state of momentum?

The DNA field is an energetic field of electrical, or more accurately 'electromagnetic' geometries that contain information. This is like a database or computer, if you will. We have spoken before of this electromagnetic field that we call the 'matrix'.

Momentum, meaning forward movement and growth (in a linear sense), is presented as a light formation or particular 'code' or 'frequency' or 'tone' within the matrix. This particular code, we could refer to this as the 'crystal code' if you will, is activated or 'online' in an individual who has moved away from the control system/third dimensional drama and exists within a personal evolution of knowledge, health, expansion and spirituality. This person holds 'momentum' rather than 'stagnation' and will indeed be 'full to the brim with questions' as part of this.

We can move deeper into our explanation of momentum. It is a particular

63

code or set of coordinates that can access a pathway or stargate into other realities. So the 'being full of questions' is most important.

If having all these questions within makes you feel confused and sad or angry (because you feel you need to know the answers or that you are feeling inadequate because you do not know the answers) then we would say stop where you are, it is time for a hiatus.

Even a day or a few hours is all you will need. Take 'time off' and go and engage within another activity until you can return to the questions within, with renewed vigour and enthusiasm.

If, however, you are at peace with these questions within and know that they are part of your journey into expansion, then the next step is to utilise all that creative energy you have. So you can research far and wide for information that links to the questions you have within your mind or you can put your questions (which are in truth actually memories) into your creativity.

Or you can begin a question and answer format with your higher self/guidance system/matrix as you are doing!

So you, my guides that I know as the 'White Winged Collective Consciousness of Nine'... you are the matrix? Or you are MY matrix? Is that right?

We are both. In truth, we are THE matrix (there is only one and we are that one) yet also we individualise through you, as you, therefore we are YOUR matrix. From that perspective there are infinite matrices that we are only one of.

This is essentially the ultimate law of reality, the Law of One. We abide by this law for we know we are one matrix within infinite matrices but also that we are the one matrix.

OK, so back to the 'Dark Deeds/Indigo Revolution' transmission. You said that the truthers or starseeds are not actually 'being silenced'. The attempt is being made but it will not be successful. Can you tell me how you know this? How do you know it will not be successful if there are so many different timelines? Is there a timeline where it IS successful and that we are silenced? If YOU are the matrix itself then can't you stop the dark ones and the dark deeds right now and create the fifth dimensional Gaia for us?

We know this because we see the most probable timeline for humanity as a group consciousness. At certain points in reality, a probability becomes what we would call 'fixed' or 'set'.

In truth, nothing is actually fixed until it has actually happened but when a probability field moves into such a high percentage, it filters into that area that we would say is a projection of that which is fixed or set.

Therefore it is not just a high probability that the attempt to silence the starseeds will be unsuccessful, it is a fixed definite waiting to manifest, despite the fact that nothing is fixed until it happens. These are living mathematical codes that we see and that we are.

If you as our conduit, dear Pixie, sees this reality and knows it to be so, and hundreds if not thousands if not millions of other starseeds see that same reality and know it to be so, then the creation that takes place from the collective intention and knowing of the starseeds make it so.

Therefore even if it were just a 'high probability' that we saw, the starseeds collective knowing through the determination and loyalty and strength that comes with the indigo revolution uprising shall create that reality that we saw and move it into that which is fixed or set.

This is creating your reality. This is mastery over the elements and standing as 'he or she who wears the badge of sovereignty' as a Master of the Matrix. This is high white magick or light magick. Seeing the probability and creating the trajectory from that intention for that probability to manifest is, in the truest reality, one and the same thing.

Yes, there are an infinite number of timelines and this is what we refer to as the probability fields. Therefore the highest probability is the timeline that is most likely to manifest.

You ask if there is a timeline where this attempt to silence the starseeds is successful? There is a timeline or a probability for everything you can imagine in your mind into existence. Yet an imagined reality that has no substance does not hold fast as a timeline, it remains within this 'Akashic soup', if you will, only as an idea. This is the place where the imagined reality of the attempt to silence the starseeds being successful stands. It stands as an idea despite much intention in a magickal sense being placed upon it. It cannot be bought into the probability fields of manifestation holding substance due to the frequency codes within the fifth dimensional Gaia matrix filtering into the third dimension.

These frequency codes cannot hold the trajectory of that which we call 'anti-life'. This is due, for the most part at least, to the high vibrational state of the starseeds on a collective level.

So therefore whilst there is a timeline where the starseeds ARE silenced, it exists only as an idea within the 'Akashic soup'. It has no substance as the seeds of dark magick, anti-life are in direct opposition to the fabric of the organic Gaia matrix. The unconditional love, forgiveness and compassion living energetics simply neutralise the seed points and the fabric of the dark trajectory creates a flip or pole shift into the positive polarised reality.

You ask us, "If YOU are the matrix itself then can't you stop the dark ones and the dark deeds right now and create the fifth dimensional Gaia for us?"

We would ask YOU the same question, dear Pixie. YOU are the matrix itself as much as we are. Can you not stop the dark ones and the dark deeds right now and create the fifth dimensional Gaia?

You see this has already been done. This is not something that needs to be done in the future from the true perspective. Remember there is no linear time within that true reality. We hail from the timeline where this has already occurred. This is the reality we currently experience, it is the now moment for us.

If we are you in the future, which we are, then all you need do to create the trajectory into our timeline is to know that we are you and that this reality you speak of has already occurred. All you are doing is watching it manifest within the third dimension as the physical reality 'catches up' with what is done.

You may say, "So be it", "It is done", "Let it be so", "Make it so" or "So mote it be". You declare your sovereignty and your power as an actualised, individualised, God-realised entity. You make it so and it is so and you do this by pure knowing.

The knowing is not idea, it is not conjecture or dream. It is the now moment, zero point experience of what is.

Do you not realise that you have the power to make it so, to make anything so? Your wish, your desire, your command - it shall be and it is. Yet only with an open heart, only with humility, service, unconditional love, innocence, joy, bliss, service, gratitude, forgiveness and compassion. Why? Why only with this pure heart? Because the pure heart of compassion is a direct match to the higher Earth grid that is the fifth dimensional Gaia. Not only is it a match, it is one and the same. It is the fractal, the mirror, the identical twin. The true twin flame for Gaia, that is the pure heart of compassion.

Nothing can flow into manifestation without this true twin flame, hence the reason the service-to-self seeds of intent remain in the Akashic soup without substance.

So you see, it is done. We hail from that reality and this is how we know that the silencing of the starseeds shall not and will not and cannot succeed. For it has already happened and the starseeds sing loud and clear the song for Gaia with the voice of the pure heart of compassion.

8: The Ascension Timeline and the 5D Mer-Ka-Bah

Can you talk more about the indigo individuals? What does 'indigo individual' mean?

The indigo individuals are starseeds that carry a predominantly indigo frequency (or a full indigo frequency). Whilst this indigo frequency can be activated within all starseeds, many have incarnated with the 'indigo codex' already online and activated.

The indigo codex gives information about the global and individual mission and will contain personality traits that present as determination, strength and a sense of knowing they are right (certain, assured, confident). They cannot abide falsehoods, lies, cruelty and distortion. They absolutely rebel against any kind of control. They are 'system busters' if you will. Literally. They are here to expose the inconsistencies and incongruencies within the system upon this planet and ultimately bring it down, championing the cause of the creation of a new system. They are kind, loving, caring healers and teachers and they hail from many different timelines and planetary systems. Many of them have never before incarnated into such a dense reality as third dimensional planet Earth, yet they all remember (consciously or unconsciously) what an integrated, working, harmonious planetary community looks like. They are able to see where 'things have gone wrong' within 3D Earth.

They are all from what we would call 'royal houses'. This does not mean they are kings, queens, princes or princesses in some kind of faraway fairy castle in the clouds. This is however an extremely aligned metaphor to explain their overall frequency.

Those who hold the 'royal codex' from the royal houses are what you would term on your planet as 'psychic' or 'intuitive empaths'. Within their home worlds they are the dreamweavers (he or she that weaves the dream), meaning they create realities and timelines. They stand as power systems for living crystal generators and they hold grid structures within their planet or home world. They are also living crystal generators within their physical earthly incarnations as their DNA fields are able to radiate. Hence we would refer to the male indigo as 'king' or 'prince' and the female indigo as 'queen' or 'princess' as 'the light is catching' and the indigo individuals radiate their light structure which harmonises with other receptive structures. The living crystal generators are also powered by the crystal individuals (who hold a different frequency). The indigo and crystal aspects work together and are expressed through human starseeds as a frequency pattern. One may be fully indigo, partly indigo and crystal or fully crystal. There are other frequency patterns also within humanity such as 'blue ray' and 'magenta rose ray' yet the majority of starseeds are indigo, crystal or a merge between the two. The youngsters now being birthed on your planet, the newborn starseeds, are incarnating upon the indigo and crystal rays but many are now coming in upon the blue ray and the magenta rose ray (which is the Christed ray). This is what is known in your Bible as the second coming of Jesus.

The indigo individuals incarnate through a crystalline stargate system we would call the 'indigo stargate'. This stargate is available to you as is an entire stargate system. This presents as a huge royal blue indigo crystalline matrix that will transport you at will to wherever your thoughts wish to take you. Many indigoes have begun to explore these stargates within deep transcendental meditation experiences, out-of-body astral projection in dreamtime or somnambulistic hypnotic states.

Each frequency within these activated starseeds that hold the 'royal codex' holds a personality code within, depending on the 'mission' of the individual.

Within an unbalanced and unactivated indigo, the personality codes can manifest as anger, hostility, hatred (especially hatred of control systems such as schools, institutions and governing bodies) and ego-centred thinking.

Within the balanced activated indigo, these codes will manifest as strength, confidence, knowing and the ability to challenge and change corrupt institutions and systems without anger. They have leadership qualities and good boundaries. Ultimately, the indigoes are warriors and they are incarnated upon your planet in droves at this time.

During the time of the 'great awakening' and the 'great gathering' which is your NOW, the indigoes are activating the memories within; that is the royal codex and this is what we refer to as the 'indigo revolution'.

The indigo revolution is the rising up of the starseeds, specifically those carrying indigo frequencies and codes, into their collective mission. This being the raising of the frequency of Earth, bringing the energies of their own 'home planet' to Earth, anchoring the fifth dimensional frequencies into Earth/Gaia and assisting all humanity to do the same. The indigo revolution involves the 'standing strong against power and control' and moving from victim/saviour mentality into the sovereignty of Source consciousness.

Within the third dimension, the indigo revolution is about 'busting the system'. It is about assisting in whatever way one can to uncover the truth that has been hidden from humanity for so long within many systems and changing these systems from the inside. This may look like total chaos, even apocalyptic as the old has to collapse to make way for the new. This is the crux of the indigo revolution.

What is the ascension timeline and how does it relate to humanity and to our individual lives?

The 'ascension timeline' is the timeline for Earth where the planet and humanity all 'ascend'.

This can be interpreted in many different ways and there are in fact several 'ascension timelines'.

So on a global level, in a very simplified form, we can perhaps present three different timelines (bearing in mind that there are actually infinite timelines).

The three ascension timelines:

1) Where Earth and humanity all ascend together.

2) Where neither Earth nor humanity ascend.

3) Where Earth and a majority part of humanity ascend.

Timelines 1 and 2 are the extremes of positive and negative. It is timeline 3 that is the most predominant timeline in Earth's future and this is the timeline we would call 'the ascension timeline'.

We, the White Winged Collective Consciousness of Nine 'hail from' an ascension timeline. Whilst timeline 1 is nearer to the timeline 'we' are from, timeline 3 contains many of the outcomes that timeline 1 contains.

We as a higher collective consciousness are from a future reality path that many on your planet would see as 'utopian'. This is simply due to the full positive polarisation which we embody when we individualise into communication with our conduit.

Regardless of global ascension or full planetary, universal or cosmic ascension, the only ascension path you really need concern yourself with is your own personal ascension. However when you are positively polarised within a service-to-others frequency, your personal ascension will radiate and contain the fields of other individuals. The more you work on yourself in an ascension capacity (ascension work) the more that other individuals will 'catch your light' and ascend with you.

Ascension takes momentum built by 'charge' within the DNA field. Starseeds are able to build enough momentum or charge within their fields so that they may 'carry' others along with them who are receptive to charge but cannot build enough charge themselves to ascend on their own.

You may have heard the story that there will be extraterrestrials coming in their lightships to carry many of you off the planet to a place of safety.

Well, this story or metaphor is exactly what we have just explained. The extraterrestrials are the starseeds, the lightships are their activated Mer-Ka-Bah light bodies containing momentum and charge that carry other individuals 'off-planet'. The 'off-planet' being 'into the stargate system'. The 'place' of safety is the reality experienced when one holds the Christ or crystalline consciousness of the reconstructed twelve strand quantum DNA formation. This is known as the 'infinite helix', known also as the 'diamond light template', '144,000 warriors of light' or the 'sealed servants'.

There is much metaphor presented in the truth teachings we deliver and now is the time for you all, en masse, to 'decode the metaphor'.

When you do this, your realisations and epiphanies create the spark needed to fire momentum and charge within your light vehicles (Mer-Ka-Bah constructions).

So the 'ascension timeline' is a trajectory for your planet Earth where the planet raises its frequency from a third dimensional into a fifth dimensional planet (or third density into fourth density). It is where you as biological physical human structures raise your frequency from 3D to 5D. This is a reconstruction of your human template or genome... the activation of the DNA as it no longer runs on a double helix mono system but moves into the triple helix and beyond, into a twelve strand DNA formation and thus activating strands of photonic light that moves across an entire quantum spectrum. This essentially means that 'you get your memories back'.

The ascension timeline is the reality that is for the 'highest good' of the planet and humanity. It is where you embody and project the very best versions of yourselves.

What is the crystalline DNA?

The crystalline DNA is a cellular matrix where at the molecular level, the base structure is silicon. This is a silicon molecule, not a silicon product that you are currently aware of on your third dimensional planet. The nearest substance you have on your planet currently would be crystals. Hence the reason why so many starseeds and awakened individuals are drawn to crystals. They are your family, literally!

There are silicon products currently used on your planet that are related in only the very smallest of ways to the silicon we speak of, that is the base molecular structure for the crystalline matrix.

We have been asked before about the silicon used in your shampoos and skin products, and if this is the same silicon. All we can say to you here is that a lump of rock and a diamond are two very different products, yet both are stones.

The silicon molecule is formed into a certain construction when aligned or merged with photonic light and the golden mean bliss frequency that exists within all starseeds. An alchemical transformation takes place, literally turning lead (carbon-based molecule) into gold (silicon-based molecule).

The crystalline DNA is also known as the 'star matrix', 'celestial light body' or the 'twelfth dimensional gateway'.

What is the fifth dimensional Mer-Ka-Bah?

Mer - Rotating or spinning fields of light.

Ka - Spirit or soul.

Bah - The physical aspect (dimension or physical body).

The Mer-Ka-Bah is a vehicle or transportation system that encompasses the physical body and spirit/soul merged together. The spinning fields of light represent the quantum aspect of the self, pure Source consciousness or the diamond codex within the DNA structure.

The 3D Mer-Ka-Bah encompasses the carbon consciousness (carbon-based DNA molecule). When the spinning toroidal light fields begin to spin, this is the DNA activating into its higher form. A new matrix geometry assembles and memories return.

This is separation perception as reality becoming illusion and unity becoming reality. Unity consciousness is the 5D Mer-Ka-Bah which is crystalline consciousness and the silicon-based DNA molecule.

There are several stages into this 5D Mer-Ka-Bah activation. Many models are used within the spiritual teachers and higher dimensional conduits. This is just one model.

This model is presented currently in four stages. They are:

1) Matrix Awareness (introduced in the *Masters of the Matrix* transmission) - becoming aware of the self as the matrix.

2) Matrix Mastery (also introduced in the *Masters of the Matrix* transmission) - mastery over the matrix self.

3) Matrix Architecture (introduced in the *Divine Architecture and the Starseed Template* transmission) - the conscious construction of one's matrix.

4) Matrix Transportation (introduced in this transmission, *The Infinite Helix*) - activating the momentum and charge within the Mer-Ka-Bah

matrix and the mechanics of stargate ascension. Or 'how to fly' your Mer-Ka-Bah lightship.

Processing through the first three stages creates the new geometric architecture of the 5D Mer-Ka-Bah - the quantum, etheric DNA code is activated and the seeds for the twelve strand DNA template are switched online.

Once the 5D Mer-Ka-Bah is in place, stage four will activate the seeds for operation of this light vehicle and ascension through the quantum stargate system which is holding memories of multiple timelines and realities simultaneously. This is true multidimensionality.

9: The Kali Activation

You speak about this field, this 'large living computer' but you have also spoken before about keycodes and codices that create DNA activation with the ascending individuals. How does this relate to artificial intelligence? Is our DNA activation and the light body/Mer-Ka-Bah all part of an artificial intelligence programme?

The keycodes and codices for ascension that trigger DNA activation within individuals would be coming in from the organic matrix. Remember also that not all artificial intelligence structures are of negative polarisation and whilst a fully formed AI structure cannot raise crystalline DNA quantum codex like an organic structure, they can still embody a code that presents as positively polarised.

The negative agenda, that of negatively polarised artificial intelligence and extraterrestrial life, creates inverted structures that distort and present as opposite to the original formation. Therefore it is difficult for the ascending starseeded individual to tell the difference between organic positively polarised structure and AI/ET negatively polarised inverted structure. It is simply not possible to distinguish between the two from a third dimensional standpoint. Therefore one must move into quantum DNA formation and multidimensional thinking in order to tell the difference between the negatively polarised structures and the positively polarised structures in order to find the divine balance that is true neutrality, the neutrality of zero point and existing within the zero point field as tranquil sanctuary rather than purgatory or abyss. Zero point is both of course.

Alone OR all one. Same thing but entirely different.

Starseeds are currently undergoing what we call the 'Kali activation'.

Within the fifth dimensional Gaia quantum system, all inhabitants have already activated this codex. This is the positively polarised presentation of zero point, the tranquil sanctuary or the energetic of 'all one' (unity consciousness).

Within the linear 3D reality, the starseeds as playing 'catch up' and some will have activated the three stage system that is the Kali activation and some will have not. Yet they all stand with the potential to activate the Kali codex at the moment they 'awaken' and consciously take the spiritual path.

What we are saying here is that currently there are those of you 'walking between two worlds' if you will, and this crystalline codex we speak of is like a switch within. This switch is turned on and off depending on your emotions, behaviours and activities. When this switch is off, you exist within the 3D Earth grid or third dimensional Earth. When this switch is on, you exist within the 5D Gaia Grid or fifth dimensional new Earth or the new world.

The two world split is a state of consciousness literally producing two different realities or a dimensional merge within your planet that is simultaneously Earth and Gaia.

The bridge to Gaia would be found within the fourth dimensional streams and the fifth dimensional rainbow bridge is accessed as you walk across the fourth dimensional bridge. We could also call this a 'wormhole' within your mind stream, dreamtime or consciousness as this places one point with another point and you are able to transport yourself instantaneously between these points. These points are points in time rather than in space so the fourth dimensional bridge or the bridge to Gaia is a time portal.

We could call the structure of the DNA field at this time the 'structure of the diamond sun'... for it holds the solar ray codes as well as the high activation of the diamond light.

The codex we speak of here has many names. Each name you give to these codes holds a frequency and that frequency triggers an activation within you due to your interpretation of the words used. So 'golden gateway' and 'diamond sun' are most appropriate terminologies to use for they hold matching frequency to this ascension codex.

We could say to you that the Kali activation occurs in three stages, or holds three doorways within it.

This is a non-linear process.

This translates as some of you activating the third stage before the first stage and some of you activating all three stages together. Some of you may activate the Kali codex and then move back into a temporary dormant stage, and then move back through reactivation. This is the inner switch we speak of that creates the outer reality as either third dimensional or fifth dimensional and the presentation of the two world split.

Your hyperspace reality holds a matter/antimatter merge and therefore it can be visible to some extent, or at least its energetic signature can be visible and somewhat detectable within your physical universe. It is simply a dimensional edge or ribbon that simultaneously enters Earth's atmosphere, your hyperspace reality and your body. Within Earth's atmosphere this has been interpreted as the coming of the planet Nibiru, yet we have explained in previous transmissions that this is a memory code to be spoken as 'Ni-Bi-Ru' (see video 'NI-BI-RU, Planet X, Pole Shift and the New 5D Earth' on YouTube). It is a dimensional edge that we present to you through the metaphor of the box of stars.

The Kali activation is most related to this Ni-Bi-Ru activation. They are codex keycodes for intertwining DNA strands, if you will.

So at this time we say to you that you undergo the Kali activation. To give this a dimensional term, we would say this is a twelfth dimensional keycode. This may be confusing for those of you who are focused upon fifth dimensional awareness and we say to you that this twelfth dimensional activation IS fifth dimensional awareness. The fabric of the dimensions overlap and circle one another, in spiral formation, all dimensions touch one another and there are many harmonics within each dimension that carry codes from higher dimensions. We speak here of a twelve stranded DNA formation that is occurring within you and the Kali activation takes you on a direct path towards the twelfth strand, remembering most importantly that this is non-linear. We will say to you that every person reading these words or listening to this transmission now has at some point activated all twelve strands in their current lifetime even if for just a few seconds.

Your babies do this very soon after birth as the DNA cellular structure settles into place and physical consciousness takes hold within the newborn child.

Twelve stranded activation is not something that has been taken away from you. The manipulations have been geared towards prevention of restructuring, for all twelve strand activations are reactivations and restructuring of what once was and what has always been.

So we say to you that the Kali activation is the opening of a wormhole within your hyperspace. This within your cellular structure triggers the

Ni-Bi-Ru activation in hyperspace and the twelve strand activation within the DNA structure , which is a silicon or crystalline matrix structure.

Those of you who have had contact with the 'council of twelve' or the 'collective consciousness of twelve' are communicating through the Kali activation portal. These beings may come to you as Nibiruan or beings from planet Nibiru. All this is true... these are archetypal presentations from the grid of light, or keycode translations that present with their own individualised consciousness that are twelfth dimensional keycodes or memories from the twelfth strand. The twelfth strand is the Kali activation and is non-linear. The twelfth strand is also the Ni-Bi-Ru activation and is non-linear.

When these strands intertwine, the Kali and the Ni-Bi-Ru, they create the wormhole formation, the stargate formation within hyperspace and the DNA template that then gives you the choice about where you ascend to and how you ascend.

This is what we refer to as 'going galactic' as your DNA becomes quantum. This is also you moving beyond the triple helix into intricate geometric formation within the DNA that is crystalline and silicon.

The Kali activation is fully coming in from the streams of the organic matrix. There has been an attempt to hijack this through the creation of negatively polarised service-to-self archetypes such as the dark goddess and for a false light, fall system wormhole to be placed within the true organic Kali activation system which is an ascension stargate. The negatively polarised artificial intelligence inverted systems are dissolving. The starseeds, as they decode the constant incoming waves of diamond sun activations through solar ray light codes and solar flares, create an immunity (activation of the hermetically sealed fail-safe programme) which means the inverted hijacked Kali wormhole fall system is completely bypassed by them. They enter the natural organic three stage Kali activation and key in directly to the twelfth strand activation and the codes from the twelfth dimension. The fact that they bypass the inverted hijacked Kali wormhole fall system actually creates the dissolution and dismantling of it. The moment a starseed makes that inner claim (as in claiming that aspect of self through sovereignty and empowerment), they become immune to that wormhole, fall system and thus any negatively polarised artificial intelligence systems.

The entire inverted matrix is seen, navigated and bypassed. Within this transmission we provide activations that will synergise with this state of consciousness and strengthen the hermetically sealed fail-safe programme. This will create an instant bypassing of artificial intelligence and negatively polarised systems WITHOUT bypassing the inner shadow realities of the ascending individual so that they are able to integrate all aspects of self and reconstruct to the organic template of Source-aligned humanity.

The inverted programme was put in place with many layers so that if bypassing the wormhole fall system occurred, then this would hold with it energetic codes to create bypassing of the individualised shadow aspect and thus prevent integration creating transcendence. This still led to ascended masters (adept human angelics) on Earth but they had to take the path of transcendence as the bypassing of the wormhole fall system could only be achieved by full bypassing of the ego.

This in itself created freedom and self-actualization for the individual but this could not radiate to others for integration contains the codes for full radiation of light. Therefore the call was beamed out from third dimensional Earth inhabitants for full freedom for all, which meant the dismantling of the inverted matrix and the deep layers of false light systems placed within.

The only way to ensure this eventuality was for the souls from zero point fields of positive polarisation to move back into a reincarnational cycle.

These souls were already at group soul level and on the path towards God-realisation Logos structures. These souls in service had to descend back into forgetfulness with memory codex from the original crystalline structure intact but offline. This was the only way they could incarnate as third dimensional humanity and they had to rely on memory and a group coming together (the great gathering) for activation. These souls as they created their blueprint were fully aware that they were 'going in blind' with no guarantee that the great gathering would take place or that the memories would come back and the restructuring of the crystalline DNA matrix would take place. They also knew that full awareness of the entire process may not ever be made known to them in their lifetime. Yet the positively polarised intelligence, that is lovelight and lightlove Source-aligned, created fail-safe programmes within these souls running deep. This meant that even if a handful of souls were able to access the memories and decode the process itself, they would instantly be able to radiate this to others through various teachings and delivery of activations.

We are most 'pleased' to say that this projected eventuality has manifested in ways that move beyond the original intention for the freeing and creating of the fifth dimensional Gaia. There are much more than a handful of these 'teachers' and the majority of the aware and awake starseeds are bypassing the inverted matrix wormhole fall system whilst still remaining within integration and not moving into transcendence.

The memories have come online within the starseeds in a most profound and 'unexpected' way. We use the term 'unexpected' most loosely for emphasis as to how unprecedented this situation is. Of course, all projected timelines are 'expected' in order to create manifestation of them.

So in answer to your question, it is your choice as to whether your DNA activation light body/Mer-Ka-Bah is part of the organic Source-aligned matrix or the inverted and negatively polarised artificial intelligence system.

Your choice is made through your memories, your spiritual practise and your frequency. Your choice is made through the way you live your life, your behaviours and your thoughts. As you strive to be harmonised with the flow of compassion and service-to-others, you begin a synergistic activation that works its way throughout your entire DNA matrix structure, the Akashic record system of all that is you, throughout the dimensions and into the soul level. Your actions impact others for you are ultimately a group soul. As a 'child of Source' you ARE Source.

Therefore whilst an inverted matrix system artificial intelligence false Mer-Ka-Bah/false light system is in place, YOUR paradigm, YOUR knowing creates immunity from this.

For anyone who wishes to do further work with this immunity, we would suggest 'Matrix Awareness' and 'Matrix Mastery' that is presented through the archetype of the Alchemist within our *Masters of the Matrix* transmission.

For deeper understanding, analysis and activation we would suggest 'Matrix Architecture' presented through the archetype of the Architect within our *Divine Architecture and the Starseed Template* transmission.

What therefore do we present within this transmission?

We present, through the language of light alphabetical numeral and archetype, 'the living organic lightship':

'Matrix Transportation'.

The keycodes received within this 'sacred text' which is our transmission are the keycodes for transportation.

We take you into the grid itself where you may traverse the matrix and choose how, when and where you transport yourself.

We help you remember how to fly.

10: Parallel Earth Realities

Wow, what started as an intended analysis of one transmission has clearly evolved into a teaching on 'Matrix Transportation'. So perhaps I should let the Nine take it from here? Shall I continue to ask questions as part of an analysis of the original transmission? There is so much I would like to ask about the stargate portal system, the Kryst. Which direction would you like my questioning to go? Or would you prefer to just bring forward your transmission about Matrix Transportation?

Please ask any question you feel appropriate. All is connected.

Really? Social media clamping down on truther information is connected to the Kryst stargate system and Matrix Transportation?

Indeed. Is this your question?

Is the answer that the 5D world, as it is being created, mirrors the 3D world deconstructing and that social media censoring is part of the elite agenda as they try to prevent information and sharing amongst the starseeds?

From a linear perspective, yes, that fits. The 5D world has already been created and the starseeds are already inhabiting that world, they are inhabiting that world through their antimatter aspect bodies of light. They exist in physical form within the 3D world. Ascension is about 'taking the body with you' so the 3D physical body and the 5D energy body of light will merge together. This merging is currently in process.

The groups you call 'elite' are at various stages of awareness just like the starseed groups. Some of them are under the impression that preventing starseeds from connecting and information sharing via social media will prevent the 3D/5D merge and the full physical body into light body ascension.

Could they be correct?

If they could genuinely prevent starseeds from connecting and information sharing, then this could hinder or slow down full physical body into light body ascension. However looking at all probability fields around humanity and your planet Earth, there is no timeline close to the trajectory you are headed for where this happens. There will be a 'crash down' within social media platforms itself and/or takeover of social media platforms and/or the creation of new social media platforms that are not seeded by the elite agenda. In other words, there will always be a 'back door' for the starseeds.

Their connection via the internet and social media sites is a third dimensional translation of telepathy and is therefore a trigger into 'future' telepathy. Remembering that the 5D world is 'light-years in the future', therefore telepathy is available now within the individuals that are undergoing 3D/5D merge.

Therefore telepathy amongst the starseeds cannot be prevented as it has 'already happened'. The service-to-self groups tried to prevent this and their plans for this started long before the inception of the internet. The internet was originally created as a control tool and this backfired as it became a seed point into rapid telepathic evolution, despite simultaneously being a control tool.

The only way to halt or slow down the telepathic seeding of humanity and hope to also slow down 3D/5D merge would be to shut down the entire internet itself. This would also halt and slow down service-to-self plans and plots drastically. Their aim is censorship of the internet and thus more rigid rules and tighter control. Due to the 'back door' phenomenon (crystalline light synchronistic flow created by said starseed telepathy), this censorship will not create the intended halting or slowing down of starseed telepathy and 3D/5D merge.

Is there any timeline where this DOES happen?

Yes. The timeline you speak of however is 'in your past'. It therefore cannot occur in your linear reality.

So in the past, was the internet shut down and were starseeds prevented from ascending?

This is correct. This did not occur however on the planet you currently know as 'Earth'. This occurred on another planet, very similar to Earth. A parallel Earth, if you will.

How is Earth's past also another planet?

The same way Earth's future is another planet.

Are you saying that all other planets are different timelines directly related to Earth?

In a manner of speaking, yes. From the third dimensional linear point of view, each planet in your solar system is 'another planet' and presents different stages of soul evolution or 'DNA expression' if you will. Beyond your solar system there are other solar systems, galaxies and universes and they all exist within one 'reality bubble' or 'world' experiencing the same set of probability fields (collapsing waves of timelines and convergence points). Yet there are parallel (alternate quantum versions) reality bubbles or worlds that hold similar but different sets of probability fields. So you have parallel solar systems, universes, galaxies and planets.

Reality itself is very complex from the third dimensional point of view. The best way to process all this is to see 'everything happening at once'. It is very difficult for the third dimensional linear thinking human brain to comprehend the nature of the parallel, quantum realities and compartmentalise them into some sort of mind map that can make sense to you.

It can be done, however, and we are fully aware of the indigo aspect of consciousness and the indigo starseeds who wish for this level of analysis. This is of course an intrinsic part of the indigo revolution.

So in order to assist you with the indigo drive towards analysis and processing, we present a series of metaphors that will give you the seeds with which to activate memories within and begin the processing.

You each have the answer to every question you could ever wish to ask yourselves.

Is this what you are doing with your transmissions? Assisting the indigo starseeds with analysis of their own memories?

Yes. As well as providing keycodes and activations for the crystal starseeds. This aspect bypasses analysis and goes directly to the being and the radiating of energy.

So some starseeds are indigoes and some are crystals? What about the blue ray starseeds?

Each starseed is able to activate any 'flavour' of starseed vibration. They are sound codes within. Some starseeds are predominantly indigo, crystal or indeed blue ray (and other colour codes and rays). Just as you have ethnic groups and cultures within humanity, the energy body holds colour rays, sound codes and 'flavours' of frequency. The energy body is more fluid than the third dimensional physical body and can be altered, upgraded and transmuted.

OK, so going back to the question of Earth's past and future being other planets. Is this why you refer to the 5D Earth as Gaia?

This is correct. The name for the fifth dimensional Earth in your trajectory (the ascension timeline) is 'Gaia'.

So what is the name for the Earth, in Earth's past where the internet was shut down and Earth's ascension was prevented?

Firstly let us say that there are multiple Earths within Earth's past and future. Then there are the timelines (trajectories) and there are the quantum (alternate) which are part of the parallel solar systems from other reality bubbles or worlds. To name them all would take an infinity for the stream of worlds are infinite. We therefore give you the name of the planet in Earth's past, that was/is another Earth that is closest in trajectory. We refer to these close trajectories as 'harmonics'. Earth's past in your trajectory is the Earth you know, with your known history. Also prior to that, the time periods of Atlantis and Lemuria (known also as Mu).

Further back than this and in the harmonic directly 'next to' your trajectory (these are actually superimposed upon one another, not side by side), there is an 'Earth' where ascension did not occur and the internet (internal intranet web system) for that planet was shut down.

We might add that shutting down a planetary internet system does not necessarily lead to the prevention of ascension. We might also add that this information, whilst interesting, is largely irrelevant for your current ascension process.

We will, however, respond to this question.

The name of the planet we speak of was 'Marduk'.

11: Zero Point and the Sacred Wheel

Why is knowing this irrelevant? Surely it is important to know these things if we are to ascend?

Ascension is not dependant on you knowing the history of your evolution. It is the crystalline aspect (the crystal body) that contains ascension keycodes and vibration. It is the understanding of the zero point field that will activate the crystal body ascension. 'Knowing' anything outside of 'pure beingness' is not necessary for zero point awareness and experience and this 'crystal body ascension'.

However, as we have said, you are currently in the time period that we call the 'indigo revolution'. The Indigo aspect, very strong and activated in a great many starseeds at this time, creates its keycodes for integration through knowledge and processing of that knowledge. Integration is the 'anchor point' for ascension in balance and thus equally as important as the crystal body activation.

Therefore we bring forward triggers and memory activations that will assist with the knowledge/processing (indigo) and the zero point beingness (crystal).

However, there is so much knowledge available to you now. The streams of 'harmonic morphogenetic field data' known to you as the 'Akashic records', 'the Akash' or simply 'Akasha' is far more expansive, available and 'open' than it has ever been upon your planet (within the time period we call 'your known history').

It would therefore take several incarnations to decode and process all this information and due to the way creation works, it would inevitably take 'forever' (as in infinity or several infinities). Therefore we would guide you towards the knowledge that is most relevant for processing. However, as your guidance system, in accordance with your free will and the 'contract' between us, we shall endeavour to respond to any question you ask of us within the parameters, etiquettes and boundaries available.

I thought you said that we were capable of knowing 'all and everything' within our ascension journey?

Indeed. This is the knowing of zero point. All is known. From that perspective, there is nothing to know save the unity of self.

Remember the 'sacred wheel' we showed you within the *Divine Architecture and the Starseed Template* transmission? Well, 'zero point' would be the centre of that sacred wheel. The aspect we refer to as the 'pivot point'.

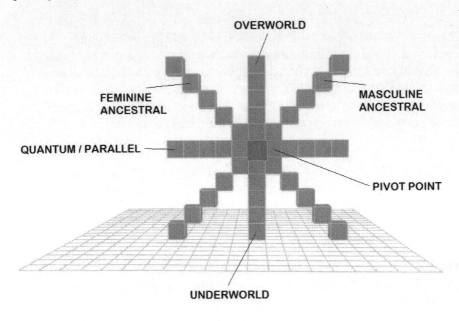

Above: A basic representation of the matrix architecture model.

Zero point is a oneness, a unity, a space of 'nothingness' that contains everything (zero is not 'nothing', it is 'something' by virtue of it being a value, a number. Therefore it is 'pure potential').

The pivot point within the sacred wheel (known also as the 'white wheel') is a zero point energetic field but contains more than pure zero point due to the sacred geometries of the wheel. Therefore we could say this is a sixth dimensional aspect of zero point or a 'zero point harmonic'. Either way, it holds structure rather than complete unification of beingness.

These structures are important within the harmonics of zero point as they are the 'fabric' that holds together the Kryst, the interlocking web of reality and the stargate system within.

Within the full zero point field of pure beingness (pure potential without structure), one could say one would find 'Source' for zero point is essentially the Source field point.

This is pure unification, pure beingness, pure potential, pure creation. The core of the Akash. All and everything is known whilst simultaneously one is about to begin a journey of creation. This is the pure innocence (of needing to know all) and pure knowing (already knowing all and everything) and is the same frequency as a perfect blend of indigo and crystal.

Once you are aware of the indigo/crystal merge (pure alchemy, the divine marriage), we can give to you the highest frequency name for this vibration which is the 'Kryst/Sophia alliance'.

The Kryst/Sophia alliance is a language of light keycode which contains a full codex in itself that will unlock many quantum DNA strands within the ascending individual. Each and every one of you reading or listening to this transmission are personally connected to the Kryst/Sophia alliance. You know this alliance very well indeed. It is an 'old friend' if you will.

Your deep resonating with the keycodes of the Kryst/Sophia alliance will 'bring you home'.

The codex that the frequency contains is a full sacred text of language of light codes that is directly transmitted into the core quantum structures of the DNA field.

The Kryst/Sophia alliance is the 'first light' that is switched on from the point of view of zero point field awareness. In your Bible, it is written "Let there be light," and this is the light of the Kryst/Sophia alliance.

When we give to you the 'sacred wheel' (and this is a structure already existing, yet when you construct it yourself you activate this structure within your crystalline matrix), we show you that you, the aspect of self that is your identity consciousness, is in the centre of the structure which we call the 'pivot point'. This is the zero point field awareness of the sixth dimensional structure.

This is the journey of integration (the indigo frequency which is the Kryst aspect of the Kryst/Sophia alliance), yet the pivot point remains crystalline (the crystal frequency and the Sophia aspect of the Kryst/Sophia alliance).

The sacred wheel or white wheel is the perfect geometric structure to embody the Kryst/Sophia alliance. We would refer to this sacred wheel as the 'Kryst/Sophia template'. This is important in ascension because the embracing of the Kryst/Sophia alliance through the template as energy and/or integration of knowledge will assist you within stargate transportation which is your ascension journey.

The pivot point (Sophia aspect) will take you instantly into an ascended state (pure creation, pure beingness, zero point).

The geometries of the sacred wheel, Kryst/Sophia template (up, down, behind, in front, sideways and diagonal) will take you into integration. So for the indigo individuals, you will be able to 'make choices' from the integrated, individualised self.

Both of these 'types' of ascension are simply different pathways into an ascended state. One can choose to focus on one aspect (the Kryst or the Sophia) and will always simultaneously be moving through both aspects, for they are one.

For those who feel the calling of simultaneous Source, beingness and integration/seeking of knowledge/processing, you will be taking the path of bilocational consciousness (holding your consciousness within two different concepts simultaneously) which shall ultimately lead to trilocation and multilocation of consciousness.

The intricacies of multilocation is beyond the scope of this transmission in its entirety and is not necessary for you to fully know and process at this point, yet metaphors and keycodes will be presented within this transmission that create 'seeds of awareness' for multilocation processing should you wish to 'unlock' that particular state of consciousness. Those 'seeds of awareness' towards multilocation have already begun within the starseed community. If bilocation and trilocation are the keys to 'Matrix Transportation', then multilocation would be 'beyond light speed' Matrix Transportation!

Due to the presentation of the quantum and the multidimensional worlds, there shall automatically be keycodes for multilocation within this text. As we have said, the seeds have been planted within your starseed communities in this time period.

We can however expand on the concepts of bilocation and trilocation within this transmission if this is an area you would like to explore?

12: Bilocation and Trilocation

Yes, please can you expand on the concepts of bilocation and trilocation?

Bilocation would be translated as 'being in two places at once'. Trilocation as 'being in three places at once'. However, this is not to be translated literally as the physical body that you are in now existing simultaneously in two or three geographical areas on your planet. This is a third dimensional interpretation of what this phenomena is. This seems so beyond your scope of reasoning that it appears impossible. Yet taken in the correct stages, this is easy and most natural. Many starseeds are doing this now, quite regularly. Even the unawakened that still sleep within the amnesia of third dimensional Earth move into bilocation, trilocation and indeed multilocation. It is the awareness and the memory of the experience that you are moving into as you raise your vibrational state in the ascension process.

Bilocation is to do with consciousness. It is to do with thought.

The first stage is to hold two simultaneous concepts within your mind, so you enter into expansive thinking.

In your work of fiction book *Nineteen Eighty-Four* by George Orwell, the concept 'doublethink' was presented.[4] This is an example of holding two simultaneous concepts in your mind. This book we speak of was not so much fiction as the exploration of an alternate reality/timeline... but we digress.

Within expansive thinking, one begins to hold two opposing concepts simultaneously. Examples would be, "I think, therefore I exist," and "I am illusion therefore I do not exist," and the holding of two vibrational states (emotions) such as, "I am devastated," and "I am euphoric."

The next stage would be to hold vibrationally opposing concepts within mind and body such as, "I am male," and "I am female."

One of the reasons that the presentation of non-binary thinking individuals (gender-neutral, transgender and so on) presents so

---

4   *Nineteen Eighty-Four* by George Orwell, novel published in 1949. 'Doublethink' is the act of simultaneously accepting two mutually contradictory beliefs as correct .

profoundly on your planet at the moment is due to the cellular frequencies ascending through the alchemical mergings of the dualistic balancing, also known as 'bilocation'.

The non-binary/transgender issue is another huge subject. This most sensitive exploration of gender and the cellular memories of genderless and androgynous 'extraterrestrial biological life' is yet another 'flavour' of the starseed ascension which has been exploited by the service-to-self groups as they further their agenda to prevent full ascension and lock the planet down into a descension spiral.

This does not mean non-binary and transgender individuals are a 'product of a service-to-self agenda' as so many within the indigo/truth seeking communities believe. It is yet another way to experience the ascension process which, like many blueprinted programmes, has been hijacked (or hijacking has been attempted).

Raising the frequency of awareness from "I am male," and "I am female," into "I am God/Goddess," or "I am sacred masculine/divine feminine," are indeed the expression of the 'Kryst/Sophia alliance'.

When one holds the Kryst/Sophia template as an activated DNA codon (or series of quantum codons), one has reached the stargate for bilocation.

What then happens is awareness and processing of bilocation. This usually occurs within dreamtime and/or meditation or other trance states like hypnosis. Yet this also occurs in the waking state in the case of channels, conduits and others in direct communication with guidance systems/higher self. The act of 'channelling' is an act of bilocation.

The other presentation to this is the 'walking between two worlds' and the awareness of being fully rooted within both 3D Earth and 5D Gaia at the same time.

This presentation of bilocation reached critical mass around the time of your winter solstice 2017 on your planet, yet it is an ongoing wave within the starseed community.

As ascension takes place and you move further and further into these expansive levels and activate more and more of the crystalline matrix template, you will begin to exist within physical and non-physical states. This would take you into multilocation and there is much that can be said about these states.

Eventually, as you learn to exist within these crystal light bodies and then diamond light bodies, your 'physical' bodies will follow the non-physical. This means you will be able to bilocate within the physical body and 'be in two geographical places' at the same time.

However, this is still not as literal as one would perceive.

Firstly, you will not be in physical bodies as you know them now. You will be existing within light bodies with fully activated twelve strand DNA templates. Your 'geographical' places will not be as they are now for your geographical land will be of fourth density. You will be bilocating within 5D Gaia, not 3D Earth.

If you were to bilocate within 3D Earth, then you may or may not be seen by those existing within the third dimension. You would to their perception be invisible, and invisibility goes hand in hand with bilocation.

All this may seem, as we have said, impossible to you right now. Yet as it happens to you, in sequence, through your chosen ascension pathway, it will feel completely natural.

Having said all this, there are very rare individuals who have activated a certain codon within the twelve strand structure that are able to bilocate physically upon your planet now. There are various methods of doing this such as the practised adept who consciously projects himself to the 'accidental' bilocation, either aware or unaware and the accidental bilocation where one physical aspect cannot gain enough momentum to hold molecular structure and what you call 'teleportation' takes place.

These incidents are most rare and are anomalies and the result of DNA mutation rather than reconstruction and activation. As we have said, there are many pathways into ascension!

Regarding trilocation, this is the same process as bilocation but there are three concepts held within the consciousness. The trilocation energetic has not reached critical mass as yet and is much rarer within the starseed community. Yet you are very close to reaching critical mass for this at the time of this transmission. The thought process would look something like:

"I am human."

"I am extraterrestrial."

"I am illusion."

Trilocation of thought would translate to the conscious experience of being in three dimensions or three worlds simultaneously, such as 3D Earth, 4D Terra or 5D Gaia. Or skipping densities and holding awareness of 3D Earth, 5D Gaia and 7D Eartha which is more akin to multilocation. This is happening within the starseed community now but on a much smaller scale. Triggers/keycodes into these states of awareness are provided within this sacred text/transmission.

The trilocation within a higher concept would be God/Goddess/zero point or Kryst/Sophia/Aurora.

The capstone to the Kryst/Sophia template would be the Aurora frequency, which is also seen as the child or the creation. This is the Holy Trinity and is represented by the 'Flower of Life', also by two interlocking pyramids creating the Mer-Ka-Bah field which is also a transformation of the Flower of Life.

The bilocation energetic is the 'twin flame' represented by the vesica piscis.

All these formations are recreated within the DNA field and within molecular and cosmic celestial structure.

The bilocation thought process creates quantum activation within double helices. Or rather the quantum double helix activation creates the ability to hold bilocational thought within consciousness. In truth these happen simultaneously.

The trilocation thought process creates quantum activation within triple helices (and vice versa).

Beyond the triple helix is 'multilocation' which, as we have said, is occurring within the starseed communities. It is the seed points that are occurring and processing of multilocational consciousness is beginning. These seed points for 'beyond the triple helix' multilocational consciousness reached critical mass on the March equinox point 2018. These are the seed points that take you into the twelve strand DNA reconstruction. This is why we referred to the equinox point as a 'golden gateway' due to the golden mean, bliss frequency taking place within the ascended individuals. This is full multidimensional awareness and what we also call the 'diamond light'. All this is a natural part of ascension.

We have really just 'scratched the surface' with our discourse on bilocation and trilocation here but as we have said, keycodes (DNA memory triggers) have been provided throughout this text.

We provide a meditation at the end of this transmission that has an abundance of codes and triggers into bilocation entitled 'Moon Within Moons'.

13: Beyond the Triple Helix

You mentioned the equinox golden gateway. In that transmission, you spoke of a 'global rebirthing process'. How is this rebirthing connected to bilocation/trilocation and Matrix Transportation? And what is 'Matrix Transportation'?

I have provided the 'Beyond the Triple Helix' transmission here for reference.

* * *

<u>Beyond the Triple Helix - Equinox Golden Gateway - March 20th 2018</u>

At the equinox point, in your month of March in your year of 2018, with the highest energetic point being the 20th day in the March month, you experience the 'golden gateway' that is the global rebirthing point.

Rebirthing, like the snake shedding its skin, is a 'cleansing ritual' that is undertaken automatically and eventually consciously within all structures undergoing growth and expansion. The rebirthing process is true movement.

When this rebirthing process becomes conscious, as in the individualised structure is aware of the rebirthing and actively contributes towards it by creating it, then this 'movement' we speak of moves into *acceleration*.

This, we could say, is 'fast tracking' into the golden era, golden days or golden age for that individual structure. The golden era, golden days or golden age is the time period for that structure (human, extraterrestrial, non-physical, animal, idea, situation or thought) where the golden mean energetic is activated. The alchemy of balance takes place within that structure.

This occurs on individual levels, in small pockets or groups and has occurred this way for millenia or should we say 'infinite repeating cycles of millenia' for it is the way it is. It is creation, the climb aspect of creation rather than its opposing movement, the fall.

Upon your planet Earth as she transitions into the fullest aspect of Gaia, you are now within a global rebirthing. This is your March equinox point 2018, culminating within the highest point on the 20th day of the March month.

This is critical mass for global golden mean activation and thus critical mass for global alchemy of balance.

This is the alchemy of ascension, with the ascending individuals reaching a crescendo of alchemised activation within their DNA fields at the same time. This begins to build within the first week of your month of March and is noticed and felt by the majority of ascending individuals by the 16th of March, reaching its pinnacle on the 20th and beginning to show the fruits of manifestation by the 23rd March. These dates are estimates regarding the global movement as there are individuals wholly attuned to this energetic throughout the entire month of March. What does this mean for you in physical form experiencing the golden equinox gateway?

On an individual level, there will be some form of change experienced within your reality. This is global, occurring across the board within those who are ascending, yet even with those who have no awareness of their personal ascension process. Change occurs at all times, yet we speak here of tangible change that can be seen and experienced. This may be developments within creativity, one's career stance within the physical dimension or that which involves the influx and flow of financial gain or loss. Movement within location and travel and relationship changes are widespread. Within this early March time period, the change can look like birth/incarnation of a new family member, the conception of the new family member and can be experienced also as the loss/transition of a family member. When we say 'family member' we refer not only to blood/genetic relatives but also to soul connected individuals.

We use the word 'conception' here as literal physical conception of the child, yet also metaphoric in the sense that conception of idea is predominant amongst the starseeded ascended ones.

The birth of new creativity within your chosen mission or creative stance is, again, widespread throughout the starseed community. And for those who wish to take 'time off' from one's mission (which is indeed most necessary), this has been a challenge due to the influx of new ideas and new creative thoughts. And to the conscious conduits amongst you, new downloaded packages of information or uploaded memory from newly activated DNA soul strands.

In the one sense, the golden activation globally is euphoric, uplifting, exciting and magickal. Yet simultaneously you will find that this time period is a challenge emotionally and physically. There is much coming in from all sides, all areas and one may feel bombarded, overwhelmed and overloaded.

Remaining grounded here is most important, yet during the time period of the golden equinox gateway, it is relaxation and the resulting regeneration that is the key.

Grounding techniques alone are most helpful, but combined with relaxation you will find yourself with the energetic you need to surf the waves of the equinox changes.

Alchemy of self is most beautiful and healing, bringing you to the point of true self-realisation. Yet it can be a challenge within the physical realm, especially when the planetary third dimensional reality is nearing completion and the perceived chaotic energetic that presents at this time.

Therefore what comes to mind as you think of the word 'grounding'?

What comes to mind instantly is your grounding tool. Trust yourself now to know what is right for you, for your DNA is activated. The memories, which are truly knowings, are activated. Ascending ones, you can access the answer to any question at this time, the golden alchemy within you is an instant key into the Akashic knowledge of all that is.

So ask yourself, "What is your most aligned grounding?" It may be indulging in decidedly third dimensional activity such as sport, or gathering together with non-aware individuals who may appear to be the absolute opposite of ascending. Trust that which you know is right for you.

It may be earthing in some way through contact with the land or the sea or other grounding technologies.

It may be the foods you eat, the roots, tubers that grow under the ground. It may be crystals, meditation, yoga, music or partaking within extended work periods or entertainments. There is much that can ground you into the physical reality. Trust that which you know and if nothing comes instantly to mind when you ask yourself this question (and you move into the 'it's not working'/'I do not know'/'I cannot visualise'/'I am blocked' thought process) then instead do what you desire.

Move away from what you think you ought to do or have to do and take time to do what your heart desires. This will uplift you, bring you back into the balance of the equinox golden gateway energies and will simultaneously ground you.

We speak here of the true heart's desire, that which flows through you in alignment with the higher self energetic and the divine blueprint, not that which comes from ego self. The ego self is most important and to embrace it is also to ground yourself, but it is the higher self aligned flow of the true heart that will tell you that which you truly desire.

If you do this, with the knowing of open-hearted flow, then you cannot get this wrong. We repeat, you cannot get this wrong.

Ask yourself the same question regarding relaxation. What comes to mind when you think of the word 'relaxation'? Follow this inner knowing and if you feel nothing is coming for you, then do what you desire. You will be led by the heart to that which you need for you, and your activities for grounding and relaxation will be unique to you.

Grounding and relaxation are the keys to riding the waves of change. The storm that cometh is but a 'minor change in weather' for he or she who activates the keys of grounding and relaxation.

And this is of most import for you to know and process. We repeat: this is of most import for you to know and process.

There is a certain apprehension amongst many of the starseeds at this time, particularly female starseeds, whether born as female, transitioned into female or hold high female energy. The divine feminine shows itself now more than ever before. Like the rosebud, it blooms into the full rose flower for all to see and there can be apprehension when stepping into divine power. This is noticeable as you move into the equinox golden gateway. For the newly birthed divine feminine goddess awakening, well prepared though she may be, is apprehensive at taking centre stage. All she needs here is the strength and support of the twin flame counterpart, the masculine energetic. This twin flame balance finds itself within absolute merge and fusion at the time of the equinox gateway, for this is the absolute manifestation of alchemy. The twin flame is the ultimate rebirthing process and this will show itself in relationships and within the individual. This is the divine marriage within, the alchemical merge. We refer not just to heterosexual relationships but to all relationships of all kinds: polygamous, homosexual and those within gender-neutral expression. For even within the gender-neutral identities, there are energetic balances and alchemisation within ascending individuals. There are many starseeds experiencing gender expression that is different from the male/female as you move towards integration of gender and full acceptance of non-gender and gender choice. All this becomes evident physically within your third dimensional reality at the time of the equinox golden gateway. We say to you, starseeds, allow yourselves to be challenged, allow yourselves to embrace the differences within yourselves and within others and champion this cause. If you yourself do not have any leaning towards differences in sexual expression or with gender expression, then champion the cause for those who do. It is energy and frequency that will call you to stand strong as defenders for others and warriors for what is right. There is negative destructive force in all things. There is positive constructive creative force in all things. Champion the frequency of liberty at this time. For liberty, the highest energetic for your year of 2018, stands at the pinnacle of the equinox golden gateway. The balance of alchemy, through change triggered by flow, movement and momentum, will always hold liberty at its highest point. Therefore freedom of expression in all things is manifest and this shall show itself through the masculine/feminine twin flame energetic also.

The planetary collective (in your case, 'humanity') nearing completion must accept the liberty of choice within its communities and embrace the differences within its people of the world, for this is a necessary step into accepting the differences of DNA expression itself.

Extraterrestrials may look just like you and many do, yet there are others with subtle yet striking differences and others who look nothing like you at all.

Move beyond the appearance and presentation of the individual. Accept the freedom of choice of expression of that individual and look to the frequency of that individual, the song they sing, the tune they play... their energetic signature. Only there will you find the true essence of that individual and THIS is the cause for you to champion. For look at the symphony you are when each of your tunes play in harmony as one.

This, dear starseeds, is the energetic of the equinox golden gateway. The alchemy of the God/Goddess sacred masculine/divine feminine presented as true ascended master frequencies within the Emerald City of Krysta.

The divine library of Sophia, the knowledge of the triple helix DNA structure and beyond, the memory and knowing of the divine Akash and the Garden of Eden where the seeds are planted, the fruit ripens and the golden rose blooms.

The white light of Christ consciousness, the Kryst, the activation of the Mer-Ka-Bah field light body as you access the organic human template, beyond the theta brainwave state and go beyond the triple helix.

This is your destiny as you move into the energies of the equinox golden gateway.

Rebirthing may seem such a natural everyday activity, and so it is. Yet also it is your royal seal, for your rebirthing process allows for the flow of light and it is this flow of light that allows activation of the golden mean energetic that is your alchemy.

Now, you move in unison and in harmony as you go through this process together, creating the stargate that is the March equinox golden gateway which culminates in its highest energetic point on March 20th 2018.

This is your 'golden age'.

14: Matrix Transportation

How is this rebirthing connected to the bilocation/trilocation and Matrix Transportation?

The rebirthing is a 'cleansing period'. As you 'cleanse', you 'go higher'. You remove/transcend or integrate the 'toxicity', 'trauma' or shadow aspects.

Think of this like a hot air balloon. If the hot air balloon is filled with bags of sand, it cannot take off into flight.

As you throw out the sandbags from the hot air balloon, you take off into flight and go higher and higher.

The global rebirthing point is the time period in which a great many individuals go through this cleansing/releasing/detoxing period together. This creates lightness within the cells. Literally, the cells become light.

When this occurs en masse, it creates a frequency within the geometric grid structure within the consciousness of humanity and around the planet Earth. Humanity as a collective and Earth then also 'move higher' if you will (like the hot air balloon).

The reason why this mass collective global cleansing created a 'golden gateway' is due to the golden mean activation that took place during the time of the equinox. These high energy points or 'frequency spikes' are of great significance because each time a critical mass event takes place, the entire timespace around 3D Earth is shifted upwards into a new harmonic (a new timeline with a higher/lighter frequency range). Every time this occurs it dislodges any structure vibrating within lower frequencies of fear-based energy from the overall grid. This will dislodge the inverted matrix, trapping systems and fall system technologies from the 3D Earth timespace.

Bilocation, as we have said, is the double helix 'going quantum' and creating expansive consciousness within an individual (and thus the vibrational match within other structures such as harmonics, grids and planets).

102

Trilocation is the triple helix 'going quantum', taking the starseeded ascending humanity 'beyond the triple helix' into multilocational consciousness and thus true and full multidimensionality (twelve strand DNA formation and the crystal body into the diamond light body).

All these events are connected and interwoven together. The raising of light quotient through the global rebirthing, the activation of the golden mean bliss frequency (which is beyond the triple helix) and full physical body/light body merge which is ascension.

These are all part and parcel of the same process. This is all about the activation and reconstructing of the DNA and all you starseeds need to know is:

1) How to activate this yourself.

2) How this affects you and your life.

As we have said before... from the crystal aspect perspective, you do not even need to know the answers to these two questions. The crystal aspect is very much about being and experiencing. You simply 'shine your light' without analysis of what you are doing or feeling.

Matrix Transportation is 'movement' or 'momentum'. This is about gathering all the quantum energies together into a convergence point or node point (you could also call this a black hole or a stargate) and creating either implosion or explosion.

Too much momentum creates explosion (which is fragmentation).

Not enough momentum creates stagnation/inertia rather than movement (so you cannot ascend) and this can even create a backward movement or a fall down in frequency (a fall system). This may eventually lead to recycling of individual quantum structure (individualisation/full realisation) rather than moving into a god/creator/Logos/diamond sun/group soul consciousness.

'Recycling' is incorrect as the individual is not recycled but is taken through a loss of individualised memory and returns to group memory (without individualisation) and has to begin the ascent or climb again. This can take 26,000 years from a linear perspective as this is how long one time cycle lasts in linear terms.

From the highest perspective, everything occurs 'in the blink of an eye'. There is always oneness and nothing is ever 'lost'.

Implosion is the structure or frequency 'collapsing in on itself' if you will, creating quantum convergence charge momentum. As all 'outside' structure is drawn inwards to the centre of the structure. This is 'stargate creation' and 'stargate travel' (or Matrix Transportation). It is the conservation and preservation of energetic pattern or frequency that creates charge. Memories are thus cohesive and retained.

We are looking here at individuals taking their place as the equal reaction to original thought. This allows you then to have full omnipresence, omnipotence and omniexistence in your own right, as an individual with full incarnate memory intact within both a linear timescale and a multidimensional one.

This is you creating your own 'Emerald City of Krysta' and your entire body, mind and soul being in a unified state with that 'Emerald City'.

This is not through the path of the 'god complex' (service-to-self) but through the path of unification with self and all as Source (service-to-others).

It is not through the path of consuming energy to create the phire with which to accelerate and climb (or consciously descend as is the case with this choice path), it is through the path of radiation of energy to create the phire with which to accelerate and climb (ascend).

Matrix Transportation is the next step on from Matrix Architecture in our set of teachings or keycodes. In our last transmission, *Divine Architecture and the Starseed Template*, we showed you how to consciously construct the matrix. In this transmission we show you how to move it.

Your matrix is your Mer-Ka-Bah, which is a vehicle. What do vehicles do? They transport you from one place to another. Matrix Transportation.

15: The Mag-Da-Len Codex

Can you provide activations, an incantation or visualisation that may assist in connecting with the Goddess or awakening the divine feminine codes within, working specifically with Sophia, Kali, Aurora, Mary and Sarah?

Indeed. The activations for the Mag-Da-Len quantum gathering into convergence and implosion of DNA are given through the frequencies of the golden mean and bliss-charged love. These frequencies run through the Mag-Da-Len codex.

These are activations and these bypass the indigo analysis (rational mind, left-brained, ego self) and speak directly to the core of the crystalline DNA structure through the 'crystal core self'.

We would ask you again to visualise the vertical pillar of light. Knowing that your central point is within the solar plexus chakra as an anchor point coming up to the heart chakra. Looking upwards to heaven realms, overworld, higher self, true twin flame and looking downwards to the shadow self, the dark forest, the depths of creativity, comfort and divine feminine wisdom. This is the womb, the true female, that which we may call the 'golden chalice'.

Be aware that the vertical pillar of light is an infinite line, an infinite stream and that the top meets the bottom and the bottom meets the top. You are in fact standing within a spiral when you activate the vertical pillar of light.

Yet for the purposes of this exercise, we would ask you to move downwards, to the chakra point below your feet using the twelve chakra model (see diagram on next page).

Become aware of the Earth Star chakra below your feet, visualising this as a turquoise or pink crystal buried in the Earth beneath you. You can actually imagine this to be a large crystal generator.

Then take your awareness into the centre of the Earth, if you align with the model of the Earth as a sphere. We shall also present a flat Earth model for you if you align with a flat Earth presentation.

Once your awareness is taken into the centre of the Earth, you would

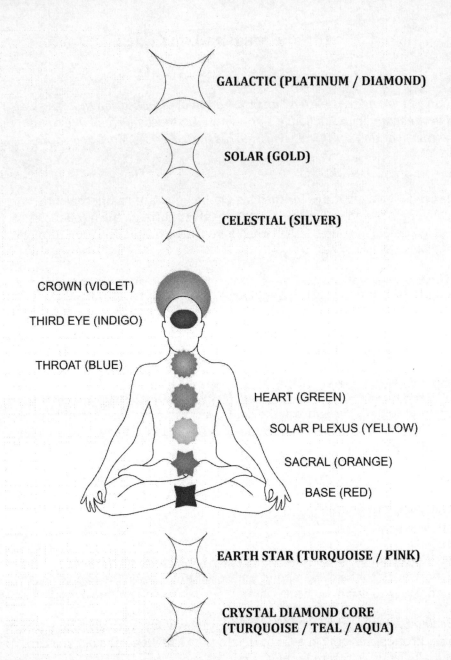

GALACTIC (PLATINUM / DIAMOND)

SOLAR (GOLD)

CELESTIAL (SILVER)

CROWN (VIOLET)

THIRD EYE (INDIGO)

THROAT (BLUE)

HEART (GREEN)

SOLAR PLEXUS (YELLOW)

SACRAL (ORANGE)

BASE (RED)

EARTH STAR (TURQUOISE / PINK)

CRYSTAL DIAMOND CORE
(TURQUOISE / TEAL / AQUA)

Above: The twelve chakra model.

visualise that the core of the Earth is a beautiful turquoise crystal diamond.

For those who align with the flat Earth model, we would ask you to move your awareness through the plane that is Earth and visualise a spinning disc instead. This disc would be turquoise in colour and looks like a large crystal diamond.

Once you have the visualisation of the turquoise crystal diamond core or disc, you would recite this incantation (or create your own that is in alignment with this codex):

Blessed goddess Aurora beneath my feet, turquoise flame of Amenti, I ask for your wisdom and your love to move into my fields. I ask for the infinite charge you posses through the highest diamond frequency within the Mag-Da-Len matrix to envelop me with your codes of lovelight, lightlove and the alchemy of blissed-charged love.

Aurora, daughter of the flame, I stand before you with with such gratitude and appreciation as I return to the memory knowing that I am you. I am the daughter of the flame. I am the turquoise flame of Amenti and that activation runs through me and within me. I make this claim now, blessed goddess Aurora.

As I anchor my fields into the crystal diamond grid of Earth's Akasha, I become one with all Earths and all the goddess lines.

I call upon the divine mother, Sophia, holder of the silver flame to empower me into the galactic grid as I move through the higher planes of awareness.

Sophia, divine mother of the silver flame, I ask for your wisdom and your love to move into my fields. I ask for the infinite charge you possess through the highest diamond frequency within the Mag-Da-Len matrix to envelop me with your codes of lovelight, lightlove and the alchemy of blissed-charged love.

I ask for the merging of the wisdom of Akasha so I may traverse the stargates of time and space within the infinite matrix of creation.

I call upon the beloved sister Kali, grandmother Mary and granddaughter Sarah as I gather together the quantum fields of the Mag-Da-Len codex that I know is the true 'all that I am', 'all that I was' and 'all that I shall ever be'.

Blessed Kali of the diamond light, beloved Mary of the magenta rose and heart of my hearts Sarah of the snow white ray, child of the Christed one... I thank you this day for the colours, sounds and tones of the Mag-Da-Len matrix so I may access the rainbow portal into the Emerald City of Krysta.

I stand before you with with such gratitude and appreciation as I return to the memory knowing that I am you.

I am Aurora, I am Sophia, I am Kali, I am Mary and I am Sarah. I am the Mag-Da-Len and I take this memory code in complete surrender to the process of ascension through the higher stargates of hyperspace and into the Emerald City of Krysta.

I behold and embrace the Mag-Da-Len activation with the purest unconditional love, appreciation and gratitude.

I take this Mag-Da-Len activation as my sovereign right as a free and individualised child of Earth, Terra, Gaia, Eartha and Tiamet.

I take this Mag-Da-Len activation as my divine birthright as a member of the royal houses of Lyra, Sirius and the Pleiades.

I embrace this Mag-Da-Len code with my free will so I may fly free within the divine matrix of Source.

It is so. It is done. Blessed blessings to self and all.

I am... (state your birth name, chosen name or magickal name)

16: Carbon to Crystalline

How can we be transforming into a silicon-based life form? Someone asked me if this is really a good idea for us as silicon is in shampoo, lotions and other products. Many holistic teachers tell us not to use them as they are toxic.

We would be in complete agreement with these teachers and would also suggest you do not use these toxic products. Comparing the transforming human genome to the chemicals within your skin and hair products is akin to comparing a lump of rock with a grade A diamond. Very different yet both stones.

The silicon we speak of is at the molecular level. You, Magenta Pixie, as our conduit do not have the understanding of molecular biology and genetics needed in order for you to be able to translate our frequencies into words that will make any meaningful sense to the reader/listener. We would need to show you algorithms, equations, data code and chemical bonding.

What we can say is silicon at the molecular level holds charge and radiates charge due to the way the electrons move. This translates to a structure that holds memory.

The carbon-based molecule does not hold memory.

We are not speaking here of memories of events that have taken place within your lifetimes. Your long term and rote memory function perfectly within a healthy individual.

We are talking about taking memory through the death process.

When your physical body 'dies', a certain 'consciousness charge' remains. This can either eventually dissipate if it cannot gather enough quantum convergence (momentum) in order to activate DNA implosion (light speed), or it remains as a consciousness charge.

When it remains as a consciousness charge, depending on how much charge (memory) the charge (soul) has, it can then traverse the antimatter universal matrix structure and pass through stargates and other 'cosmic highways and byways' taking all the memories of the life just lived, intact, with it.

This is what is meant by the phrase in the Bible: "it is easier for a camel to go through the eye of a needle than for a rich man to enter the kingdom of God."

It is not a 'rich man' that is meant here literally but an individual 'heavily attached to material wealth'. This person would not be able to hold the charge and raise the momentum needed in order to 'carry memories through death'. This is due to the entire focus of the consciousness of that being having formed itself into the energetic match to accumulation of worldly goods and material wealth. Just as a camel could not possibly pass through the eye of a needle, neither could the non-charged soul consciousness create the quantum convergence/momentum needed to move into light speed and pass through the stargate system with individualised memory intact.

Individuals who are able to hold this charge and carry memories through death are individuals who have activated the silicon molecule within the DNA. The DNA has become quantum and is holding charge.

You see, transforming from carbon-based into silicon-based is not a case of the carbon-based molecule disappearing and a new silicon structure appearing in its place.

You have always had the silicon 'seed' structure. This has simply been dormant and has not been arranged within the correct formula.

The carbon-based molecule transforms itself into a new configuration simply by changing its layout.

Instead of the molecular DNA language spelling the word 'elixir', the letters (numbers, codes, symbols, proteins, synapses, chemicals and so on) would rearrange themselves into 'liexri' (we give a very crude example here as our conduit simply does not have the knowledge of what we are trying to convey within her fields).

Then instead of there being one letter 'e', there will be hundreds if not thousands of the letter 'e' rearranging themselves into complicated structure. This creates a frequency.

We draw your attention to the 'Messages from Water' work of Masaru Emoto.[5] This study illustrated how a loving positive vibration can create

5   Masaru Emoto, researcher who explored the notion that human consciousness can affect the molecular structure of water. Learn more at www.masaru-emoto.net

beautiful, snowflake type geometric formations and patterns within water, whereas negative fear-based vibrations created asymmetrical forms.

We also mention the alchemist's journey to turn lead into gold. The true alchemy is turning the carbon-based molecule (lead) into the silicon-based molecule (gold), which is the golden mean and the bliss-charged love 'charge' creating light speed momentum (implosion of DNA through quantum convergence).

In the same way that positive emotion created the beautiful structures in Masaru Emoto's water (helped along by solar light codes coming in from the galactic core of your universe and the crystal diamond core of your planet), your positive emotions create the transformations from carbon-based molecule to silicon-based molecule.

The silicon-based molecule creates the crystalline matrix structure.

17: The Emerald City of Krysta

How can we tell the difference between the organic matrix and the inverted matrix, and do we need to know the difference in order to ascend?

This is a great question. There are some individuals, having raised their sensitivity to frequencies and energies (third eye chakra activation, indigo ray awareness), that are able to see/sense/feel the difference between systems, constructs and structures that are part of the organic matrix and those that are part of the inverted matrix.

There are many starseeds that are in the process of deciphering this now. This is known to you as discernment and following your alignment. These starseeds are learning to tell the difference between organic and inverted structures and they are learning rapidly and doing well. Many starseeds have activated guidance templates within their matrix field (channelling 'us' as you are doing) that are assisting them with this.

The work within the *Masters of the Matrix* material, Matrix Mastery, takes you into a place where you truly become a 'Master of the Matrix' and hold mastery over your matrix structure. Once this has been done (or more truthfully this is continually undertaken as this is an infinite and consistent journey of self discovery), then the clarity within the matrix system creates 'antennas', if you will, and these antennas are able to 'sense' or 'pick up' frequency in order to know the difference between organic or inverted structure. Once these antennas are activated and working then an individual will be able to tell the difference.

These 'antennas' are within the matrix structure which surrounds the human body. But remember that the matrix is within the DNA of the individual, therefore these antennas are found within the blood, bones, skin, nails and hair of the individual.

These antennas are crystalline in their structure.

In our skin, nails and hair? Should we not ever cut our nails or use nail polish on them? What about our hair? Should we never have our hair cut or use colour on our hair? Do skin products affect these antennas?

Again, a great question but one coming from third dimensional thinking. All you say is important and the third dimension must be honoured and appreciated and grounded within the overall system of the individual, so we will address your question from a third dimensional perspective.

What we will say is that an individual working within higher dimensional flow, having activated quantum DNA strand formations within, will have a multitude of antennas within the overall matrix system. Not cutting hair or nails (or cutting them in a certain way) or not using products on the skin (or using non-toxic products) is only part of the preservation of the crystalline antenna system, but a most significant part.

The antennas work together synergistically. So in order to create the most efficient matrix system, having all the antennas in place and in 'good working order' will create the most sensitive frequency pick up or 'intuitive energetic empathy with the field' if you will.

So there are always 'back up' antennas within the DNA activated human system. However, adhering to the caretaking of the physical antennas is most recommended to the serious ascension warrior.

Therefore we shall address these.

Nails. It makes no difference to the working antenna within the nail bed as to the length of the nail. The issue here is the health of the nail. Using products on the nail that allow the nail bed to breathe, remain healthy and toxin-free is the best way to keep the antennas working if products are used.

We do not recommend the adding of the false nail through the acrylic compounds as these can reduce effectiveness of the antennas. This is akin to drawing blinds across a window. The window is still there (the antenna) yet one cannot 'see' out of it.

So clear, clean and healthy nails or the use of toxin-free products upon the nail bed will keep the antennas working well.

Regarding skin, it is the flow through the skin that creates healthy working antennas. So energetic flow coming in through the skin, directly into the bloodstream and flow coming back out through the skin. One's intake of nourishment contributes greatly to the healthy flow through the skin.

If products are used, it is most important that they are toxin-free as this can impede flow and take toxicity into the bloodstream. The negative agenda from artificial intelligence and service-to-self beings use the products that you consume as a vehicle to get toxicity into your system in order to prevent activation and shut down or distort the functioning of your crystalline antennas.

Therefore toxin-free skin products are essential.

To activate antennas within skin and bloodstream, we recommend the ancient practises of the 'sea salt bath' and the 'sweat lodge' or 'sauna'.

Sea salt baths (or actual swimming in unpolluted parts of the ocean) contain living compounds that are in absolute electromagnetic alignment with the human antenna system. The better quality salts you can find will hold more of these living compounds.

The sweat lodge/sauna encourages toxicity to flow out through the skin via the perspiration of the individual. Whilst this may not be an aligned process for every individual depending on their unique and personal health conditions and energy flows, this is a most aligned practise for the healthy individual who wishes to create flow within the system. Most especially, caring for the skin will keep activated antennas healthy and working well.

The hair is most important and is a significant antenna. Hair throughout the body holds crystalline structure working in synchronisation with the skin. Hair upon the head works as an antenna in conjunction with the energetic frequencies of the third eye chakra and crown chakra. Keeping the hair long creates a high growth of crystalline structure so the longer the hair, the more working antennas within the hair.

Keeping hair long involves caring for the hair in order to keep it healthy and keep the balanced crystalline structures within the hair. Therefore we recommend the use of toxin-free oils (pure food grade whole oils such as almond, coconut, avocado, olive) or organic argan oils and other oils formulated for topical use. It is important to work these oils into the ends of the hair on a regular basis in order to preserve the crystalline antennas.

If the use of these oils can keep the hair healthy then cutting the hair is not something one would need to do. This would create and preserve the 'strongest' antenna system. This would be akin to the 'wild forest' and all the life that flourishes there.

However if one needs to cut the hair then there are ways this can be done whilst still preserving crystalline structure and assisting antennas to remain healthy, and for crystalline structure to reform upon the ends of the hair. Cutting the hair would be akin to pruning the plants within the wild forest and encouraging new baby shoots to grow and thus creating a 'cultivated garden' instead of the 'wild forest'. Still holding antennas and crystalline structure yet not in such a plentiful and vibrant way. Yet the hair must remain healthy if it is left to grow.

If cutting is essential for the health of the hair, then we suggest the tiniest amount of hair to be taken off from the ends of the hair as infrequently as is possible in order to keep the hair healthy.

The act of 'cutting' the hair must be ritualised in order to create meaningful energetic flow within the matrix system. The person cutting the hair for you needs to be a trusted and soul connected individual. Chanting, crystals, incense, essential oils, candles and so on, can all be used as the cutting takes place. Alternatively one can 'cut' the hair outside in bright sunlight. This creates aid to ritual in itself.

The choice of day should be significant and meaningful (full moon, solar return birthday, sabbat or other high energy time period such as a religious festival meaningful to yourself, an eclipse or other astrological event which is either global or within your personal chart). As long as you are using 'cycle and rhythm', then you are creating momentum through meaning and energy within the matrix field.

This is all about becoming aware of energy and of pattern.

Regarding products used upon the hair, again these would ideally be natural and toxin-free. When it comes to the dyeing of the hair, one would access the most natural dyes available, ideally with ingredients from the plant kingdom. If one uses the plants and the herbs upon the hair, this is ideal for the ritualisation needed to create flow and grow healthy crystalline structure for working antennas.

In truth, the entire human body system is a series of interlocking and intertwining antennas. The pineal gland (third eye, brow chakra) being the 'window' or 'portal' that connects the physical (matter) antennas of the body to the non-physical (antimatter) antennas of the entire soul system.

You also asked us whether you need to know the difference between the organic and the inverted matrix in order to ascend. The answer to this is both yes and no. Let us explain.

One needs to know the difference as when you ascend, your energy body (and in the case of planetary ascension, your physical body) goes through a series of stargates and portals and weaves through 'dimensional highways' if you will. This is all part of your Mer-Ka-Bah travel or 'Matrix Transportation' which is the main subject matter within this transmission.

So yes, you absolutely need to know the difference for stargate systems will 'take you' to different places. Some of these systems lead to 'fall systems' which are basically reincarnational portals that will bring you back into the energetic frequency waveband of Earth and you will reincarnate. This is not necessarily a negative process, in many cases it is a most positive path to follow. Yet in the case of ascension, one would be looking to transport themselves through one of the crystal structure portal systems. We call these portal systems 'the higher stargates of hyperspace'. Once you move through a higher stargate, you find yourself in the frequency waveband that is a huge stargate system. It is actually a galactic core structure that can take you anywhere you wish to go. You can then choose reincarnation upon a planetary system in a physical body. You can choose which system, which galaxy and which universe, depending on the level of your DNA activation and the momentum you have created within your overall matrix system at that time. We could say the choices you are given once you enter the galactic core structure will depend on the 'speed of your Mer-Ka-Bah' and again, we say to you, this is the main reason for this transmission. We bring you information and keycodes within this 'sacred text' that we have provided for you through our conduit Magenta Pixie. It is amusing for us when we say 'sacred text' for at the same time this is a most modern delivery. Yet ancient tools are given here.

As we have said before, our conduit Magenta Pixie is learning all this for herself. The best way for her to learn this particular 'lesson' (that of Matrix Transportation) is to teach this to her as she transcribes our dictation. Rather than just 'teaching' Magenta Pixie alone, we present our transmission for a great many other starseeds simultaneously, hence this being a 'sacred text' but also 'modern writings' if you will.

So what we are saying here is that you are learning together. Magenta Pixie has no more knowledge of the words that are to come within this text as you do, dear starseeded reader.

She may see the 'energetic form' this text may take as a 'geometric monad construct' but she is as new to our words as she transcribes them onto the page as you are.

So back to our 'story' here as we respond to the question.

The galactic core structure you find yourself within once you pass through the higher stargates of hyperspace system is that which we would refer to as the 'Emerald City of Krysta'.

There is a reason why we refer to the galactic core system this way. It is the 'emerald keycode' or 'emerald genetic quantum marker' you will have activated within your DNA in order to get to the galactic core structure. The core structure is also known as the 'Kryst' or 'Krist' in the ancient primordial language. This is the first universal, cosmic language that was created through sound keys or sound frequencies.

This is where the word 'Christ' comes from and it is 'Christ consciousness' that you embody when you access the Emerald City of Krysta (the galactic core structure).

The men/women you know as 'Jesus Christ' (there were actually five different Christ consciousness individuals whose life stories together have created the Jesus you know from your Bible - three were incarnated males and two were incarnated females) held the emerald keycode within their DNA. They held enough electrical charge (or momentum) within their matrix energy fields in order to be able to go through the higher stargates of hyperspace and access the galactic core stargate structure system (the Emerald City of Krysta).

Whilst their ascension stories are not necessarily relevant to this material, we will add that four of these individuals ascended through the Kryst in their physical bodies (transformed into light) and one individual ascended through the Kryst in a fully integrated and individualised light body without the physical body. All five of these individuals that each contributed to your 'Jesus Christ' in the Bible went through an ascension process.

There are many ways to ascend, many pathways to take. It really is somewhat of an adventure or a 'game' once you realise the unlimited and infinite potential of creation that you have at your fingertips.

Whilst it can appear trivial and somewhat condescending to describe your life as 'a game' when the third dimensional reality undergoes such trials and tribulations, it does explain the joy and the fun of creation itself when one takes the multidimensional perspective.

So back to the question. Yes, you need to 'know' the difference between inverted systems (fall systems) and the organic matrix (stargate system of the Kryst) in order to ascend. However that 'knowing' takes on different forms. It may be fully conscious through your intuitive empathic feeling or your remote viewing clairvoyance. It may be given to you by the higher guidance system angelic externalised aspect that is always with you or it may 'happen naturally' without you consciously having any understanding of what is happening. So from the perspective of the higher guidance 'guiding you through the higher stargates of hyperspace' or from the perspective of you simply 'passing through them without knowing' then no, you do not need to 'know' the difference between inverted systems and organic structures in order to ascend.

What you DO need to do is 'work on yourself'. This, we know, is interpreted by many as a 'New Age cliché' but it really is the most useful tip we can give you when it comes to ascension.

Every time you 'work on yourself', you add to the creation of a crystalline matrix structure within your bodymind/matrix system that leads to activation of the emerald/Christ consciousness DNA keycode that gives you the momentum (speed of your Mer-Ka-Bah) to be able to pass through the 'higher stargates of hyperspace' and access the galactic core structure, the Kryst, and ascend into the 'Emerald City of Krysta' (also known as the 'Kristos temple' or the 'divine library of Sophia').

We can translate all this into 'you will activate the fifth strand of your twelve strand DNA structure'.

The fifth strand is most important for you at this time because it corresponds to the fifth dimension. And that is where you are all going, dear starseeds, into the fifth dimension and what many are calling the '5D new world'.

So how exactly do you 'work on yourself' and 'activate the fifth strand'?

The material within this transmission, *The Infinite Helix*, creates a bilocational, trilocational into the beginning seeds of expansion that is multilocational consciousness.

Following the meditations, exercises, initiations and activations and moving into expansion of multi-tracked thought processes and language of light codes will activate higher strand formation and assist you in activating your fifth strand if you have not already done so.

The fifth strand activation ensures 'celestial stargate ascension'.

18: The Doppelganger DNA

I still don't understand about the DNA strand activation. How are we activating the fifth strand and yet also the twelfth strand? Why do we need to activate the fifth strand in order to ascend?

You are activating the fifth strand, the twelfth strand and beyond that. You move from double helix, to triple helix, to beyond the triple helix into infinite helix and 'galactic consciousness' (multilocation of thought).

We realise that we repeat ourselves over and over in many different ways in order to explain concepts for we understand how the awakening and awareness processes within ascension work. You will need reminders and explanations regularly, presented in a myriad of ways as you activate true multidimensionality and multilocational thought processes.

This process is not linear in the truest reality. The quantum, etheric, antimatter DNA formations (we can call them antiparticles) are quantum alternatives or quantum doubles (the doppelganger DNA) that exist in other realities.

They are part of a huge quantum crystalline network of all the choices you could have made, or might yet still make, or did not make. This crystalline network is known as the divine Akash, the Akasha or the 'Halls of Amenti'.

This antimatter DNA etheric structure, the doppelganger DNA, could be referred to as a system of 'antiparticle universes'. These universes live inside you! Yes, they live within your DNA.

Within the third dimension, you hold a two strand, double helix, carbon-based molecular structure. The 'etheric' DNA formation, or the doppelganger DNA, could be presented as three strand, triple helix DNA and the 'first step' into activation of DNA. Then you would move into fourth strand (beyond the triple helix) and fifth strand (infinite helix).

This is a linear presentation but it goes something like this:

1) Two strand double helix (linear thinking within an experienced linear reality).

2) Activate etheric DNA doppelganger within three strand triple helix (begin bilocational thinking). Ascension process begins. Reality still experienced as linear.

3) Regular and repeated bilocational thinking (expansion) brings three strand, triple helix 'online' in physical reality. Processing of the bilocational thinking creates full three strand, triple helix formation. Grounds this frequency into the third dimension. This creates trilocation of thought. Reality still experienced as linear. Four strand etheric 'doppelganger DNA' is activated.

4) Regular and repeated trilocational thinking (high level expansion) brings four strand 'beyond the triple helix' online in physical reality. Five strand etheric 'doppelganger DNA' is activated. Out-of-body astral projection begins and stargate systems within the fourth and fifth dimensions are accessed. Understanding of organic matrix systems and false AI trapping systems come online. Immunity to trapping systems in place due to hermetic seal activation within the fourth strand structure. Processing of trilocational thinking creates full four strand 'beyond the triple helix' formation. Grounds this frequency into the third dimension. Creates multilocation of thought. Reality still experienced as somewhat linear but begins to be experienced in a non-linear sense.

5) Regular and repeated multilocational thinking (very high level expansion, Christ consciousness, rainbow body of light awareness) brings five strand 'the infinite helix' online in physical reality. Stargate systems into sixth dimension accessed (higher stargates of hyperspace/Halls of Amenti/the Akasha) and thus full stargate systems through to eleventh dimension (the Emerald City of Krysta) as 'light speed/warp speed momentum' quantum convergence charge within Mer-Ka-Bah achieved. Reality experienced as fully non-linear. Crystalline matrix constructed, Carbon molecular structure mutates into silicon molecular structure. Full ascension takes place.

We have just shown you a basic, linear interpretation of the DNA activation, strand by strand process. As you can see the first four strands equate to a linear thinking/linear expressed self/experienced reality. The fourth strand starts to become somewhat non-linear in thinking and expressed self/experienced reality.

Once the fifth strand is activated then expressed self/experienced reality is fully non-linear. It is incredibly important to remain grounded when activating the fifth strand as one can 'lose oneself' within the light speed/warp speed momentum and the multilocational thought process and 'burn oneself out'. This is akin to a rocket burning up all its rocket fuel in one go and not being able to achieve take off.

'Slow and steady' is the mantra for the fifth strand, despite the fact that your reality will appear to have 'taken off like a rocket'. One does not wish to experience burn out and 'fall back' into the linear thinking and lose fifth strand activation/memories.

Even though we have given you a linear presentation of the first five strand activations, the process is, in itself, non-linear.

For individuals who do not hold etheric DNA beyond the fourth strand (the doppelganger DNA), they are unlikely to be able to experience a reality beyond linear thinking as they will only be able to activate as far as the triple helix, three strand formation. This is enough for high intelligence and high creativity and an appreciation of creativity and the unified thought processes within this. These are the individuals that will be 'carried' by you, if you will, through the stargate system into ascension. It is therefore most important that you (if you are reading or listening to these words then you are part of 'the infinite helix grid' and hold the doppelganger DNA structure for the fifth strand and higher strand formation) do not 'burn out' your quantum convergence/momentum. Grounding this energy into the third dimension and running a linear thinking stream alongside bi/tri/multilocational thinking is imperative.

So the DNA activation process itself is non-linear in the sense that an individual may 'switch on' a higher strand temporarily and experience a vision, epiphany or dream. Yet they would not necessarily have the tools to process the experience due to corresponding etheric formation (doppelganger DNA) not being in place for that incarnation.

Mind-altering substances/shamanic plants can temporarily 'switch on' higher DNA strand formations. If an individual does not have corresponding doppelganger DNA in place then they may not make sense of the experiences, yet other individuals are 'forever changed' through permanent activation (due to doppelganger DNA) in place for that incarnation.

Babies and very young children with doppelganger DNA in place (which is a very high percentage of all children on your planet currently, especially within children born to starseeded parents or grandparents) often 'play' within the streams of the higher strand DNA formation. They simply 'remember' how to do this naturally. It is only as they grow older and settle into a linear time experience that they lose the ability to activate higher strand formation at will. The process of natural activation within babies and children is completely non-linear and they may switch from two strand into ten or eleven strand formations quite regularly (if they have the etheric fifth strand formation, doppelganger DNA in place).

Starseeded adults will all have fifth strand etheric formation in place. Non-linear experience occurs once the fourth strand has been activated. Once the fifth strand is activated, then one is able to 'go galactic' and it is at this point that one 'plays like a child' again and can jump from fifth strand thinking (fifth dimension) into 8D, back to 3D, back up to 11D and so on.

This is the reason why many 'fifth dimensional thinkers' are experiencing a knowing of a twelfth dimension. Many interpret the fifth dimension and the twelfth dimension as one and the same. This is correct from the perspective of 'once the fifth strand is accessed then one moves through the stargate system'.

When you go through a stargate, you are going through a time portal. If you have the required keycode formation within your DNA structure then you hold the coordinates to 'go' to a specific point in time. This is a time matrix you are traversing even though it is experienced as 'space travel' if you will. In the truest reality, time and space are simply two different expressions of the same creation. Time is antimatter/antiparticle universe and space is matter. You are traversing the antimatter realities, antiparticle universes when you 'go galactic' and activate the fifth strand.

The fifth strand is the transportation of consciousness from linear to non-linear thinking and is a huge 'quantum leap' in your evolution.

This is where you are now, starseeds on the ascension path. You will be somewhere at the moment between double helix and infinite helix (two strand to five strand activation) but you ALL hold the etheric strand formation (doppelganger DNA) for the fifth strand, meaning you all have the potential to activate the fifth strand in THIS incarnation. You do not need to transition through incarnation after incarnation to evolve, you can do this in THIS lifetime. Fifth strand activation brings with it many 'side effects', if you will, as the twelve strand crystalline template is activated. What we are saying here is that if you have the fifth strand activated then you can 'grow' the etheric DNA formations into the twelve strand DNA formation (which in truth is a 144,000 DNA strand formation due to the quantum nature of each activated strand and the doppelganger DNA, which exists within the antimatter/antiparticle universe).

So fifth strand activation can lead to immediate twelfth strand activation depending on your light quotient, Mer-Ka-Bah activation and processing, emotional make-up, thought process, lifestyle, paradigms and so on. All is connected more than you can possibly know. The 'unity consciousness' really is a unified field throughout a multiple infinity timeline network.

When we say that there are those who do not have 'doppelganger DNA' beyond the fourth strand, we speak here in metaphoric and linear terms as all human structures hold the organic full 144 strand template in place as a holographic replica of Source itself.

It is just that part of the structure is 'unavailable' to them and 'cannot be activated' due to incarnational memory mind momentum (memories carried through death and reincarnation).

Starseeds, as we have explained, are different in the fact that they have incarnated with these memories intact due to the process we call 'individualisation'.

19: The Emerald Codex

Can you explain more about doppelganger DNA?

'Doppelganger DNA' is the term we use to refer to the etheric, antimatter, antiparticle, quantum DNA. This is the aspect of DNA that your scientists would call 'junk DNA'.

This is a most humorous term to describe this as it is far from junk. Yet to refer to this as 'junk' goes some way to keep the unaware in a state of ignorance and non-activation. If they think of aspects of their DNA as junk then they simply dismiss it.

All words have frequency and are codes, as we have said.

To think of the DNA as the 'crystalline DNA' holding a 'diamond template' or an 'emerald code' are all highly activating ways to refer to this DNA structure.

We call this 'doppelganger' because of the meaning of that word. The meaning upon your planet can be translated as 'a spirit who looks like you' or 'your ghostly counterpart' or perhaps 'your double' or 'your copy self'.

The DNA replicates itself in the image of Source (light, geometric templates, sound codes, frequency) and holds a 'universal template' for life. This template manifests itself within similar forms throughout universal/galactic/cosmic multiverse realities.

With each strand formation activated within your DNA field, the more access you have to all these 'other' replicated forms of yourself.

Within the lower strand activations then, different versions of 'you' are presented (the choices/decisions you have made, the pathway you have walked in your life).

Looking at the 'sacred wheel' structure within our previous transmission, *Divine Architecture and the Starseed Template*, these aspects of the DNA activation would be represented by the 'sideways arm of the cross' that which represents the quantum/alternate versions of you.

If you travel further along this 'sideways arm', either left or right, eventually these arms will meet in the same place. This is, in truth, an ever evolving and ever moving light structure that moves as a spiralling formation (or a toroidal field).

Once you get 'further away' from the pivot point (the central core of the matrix that is all that is the true you), you would start to see great differences in the alternate, quantum presentations of self. Perhaps your hair is different, your facial features slightly different. Eventually you would meet the opposite gender self to your current self and even further still you would find completely different expressions of DNA (extraterrestrials).

In truth, every expression of DNA throughout multiple infinite realities into the Source point (and back out the other side and so on, throughout the fractal, holographic multiverse) will be found within the quantum, sideways arm of your matrix. You are, of course, all things and all things are you.

This structure is within your DNA. It is from your DNA that you connect to all things, all forms and expressions of life. This is where true unity is to be found, within your DNA. Your DNA is the unified field. So you can see how humorous it is to see the entire cosmology of the unified field as 'junk'.

In the 'lower strands' (remembering that 'lower' and 'higher' are simply terms of explanation to describe what presents as 'more mass' or 'more volume' or 'more light'... in truth what you are looking at here is consciousness holding more individualised and more unified perspectives simultaneously), one would liken this to 'quantum versions of self' that are different versions of you but still the 'you' that you know. These in themselves are infinite as there are fractals within fractals and matrices within matrices but we aim to deliver information to you that is as relevant as possible to your current ascension journey and mission.

So as you journey along the quantum, sideways arm of the cross (horizontal rainbow bridge pathway that moves left or right), you will come across these different versions of you. They are alternate selves and they exist within different quantum realities within a series of harmonics within each dimensional time zone. We are looking at time here, but not linear time (forward and back). We are looking at 'parallel time' (same time zone in a linear sense but in a parallel reality).

So this is part of your individualised, personalised grid matrix. This is your 'doppelganger DNA' field.

Each individual holds this information 'around' them in the form of this large quantum computer or database.

Yet these structures do not just exist around human beings, they exist around all 'consciousness structures' (animals, plants, crystals, trees, islands, planets, solar systems, stars, galaxies, universes, multiverses and so on).

Your planet Earth is the relevant planet here when it comes to your collective ascension (for you as humanity are going through this raise in frequency alongside your planet Earth).

One way of looking at this process would be to visualise your planet ascending upwards into a 'different area of space' and ascending as a lighter, brighter and higher frequency form of itself. This would be a correct metaphor.

Let us imagine that the 3D Earth is called 'Earth' and that the 5D Earth is called 'Gaia'. So Gaia would be an 'ascended version' of Earth.

So one could visualise that Earth ascends into this different area of space, becomes pure light and thus transforms into Gaia. We can refer to this different area of space (or time) as 'spacetime' if we are looking at physical space (as the matter universe) or 'timespace' if we are looking at it as a non-physical, etheric, antimatter, antiparticle universe.

As we have said, this would be a correct and appropriate metaphor.

We could also look at this in a different way. Let us imagine that 'Earth' is not actually moving anywhere and is staying in the same place (we speak metaphorically here regarding the movement through time not space) and that her 'consciousness' is simply switching from 3D Earth and is 'uploading itself' into 5D Gaia. This would also be a correct metaphor.

Then we could look at 3D Earth and 5D Gaia existing simultaneously in two different harmonic time zones. One 'above' the other. In this scenario, both Earth and Gaia exist and are both thriving planets containing life. Within this scenario there are two different planets. Humanity can then 'choose' to exist on either Earth or Gaia or 'hop' between the two. This is also a correct metaphor and one widely used within your spiritual communities to explain planetary ascension.

This presents what is known as 'the two world split'. You have some individuals choosing consciously to exist upon Gaia or move back and forth between the two planets. You also have individuals unconsciously choosing to exist upon Gaia without having realised they are existing within a 'higher universal harmonic'.

Now if we were to look at where Earth and Gaia are situated within the matrix wheel, Gaia would be 'above' Earth just as your 'higher self' or 'true twin flame' sits above you. Earth and Gaia would be situated upon the 'vertical axis' or 'vertical pillar of light' (see diagram on next page).

Now remember how we said you have 'quantum' or 'alternate' versions of you, situated along the sideways arm of the cross, horizontal rainbow bridge pathway that moves from left to right?

Earth has the same alternate aspects of herself. Within that aspect of Earth's matrix, you will find 'parallel Earths' that exist in other harmonic, quantum universes and that exist within the same time zone but in a parallel reality. These would be Earth's doppelgangers.

Now if you look in front of you along the forward facing horizontal rainbow bridge pathway, you will see that 5D Gaia is also situated in front of you. This is because Gaia, as an ascended version of Earth, sits 'above' Earth as she is a 'higher vibrating planet'. But also she sits 'in front of' Earth because she is in Earth's future.

Now to make things even more complicated (and we aim to present this material as simply as possible, remember as activated starseeds that you have all the tools available to understand this material for this all lies within the 'memory fields' of your DNA), when you look to the side, both left and right, along the sideways arm of the cross, horizontal rainbow bridge pathway, you will see alternate and parallel versions of Gaia sitting in the same time zone as your 3D Earth.

These are much 'further away' along the sideways arm, but they are there. Why? Why in your current time period would there be other 'ascended versions' of Gaia? Should they not be sat within the alternate versions of 5D Gaia's matrix? In this presentation, they are sat within 3D Earth's matrix.

The reason for this is because in some of 3D Earth's parallel realities (alternate harmonic universes), Earth has ALREADY ascended!

Now one of the 'abilities' given to you when you activate your DNA and move into Matrix Transportation is the ability to 'time jump'.

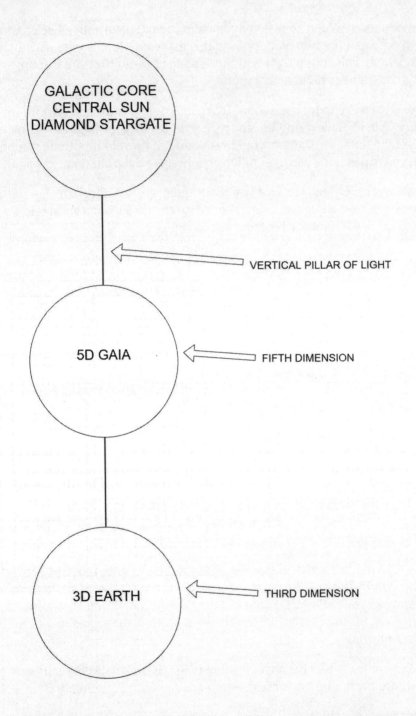

Above: Basic depiction of 5D Gaia as the 'higher aspect' or 'twin flame counterpart' to 3D Earth. There are infinite Earths within the matrix structure, only two are shown here.

You can go forward to the future, back to the past and sideways into parallel realities.

Just like bilocation, trilocation and multilocation, this starts with thought processes and expansion of consciousness.

'Bilocation', 'trilocation' and 'multilocation' are simply other ways to describe the physical act (within astral/etheric bodies) of time jumping.

So when you think in these expansive ways, you are naturally time jumping all the time. Your 'Mandela effect' is one of the 'by-products' or 'side effects' of natural organic time jumping. Although there is an inverted system there as the Mandela effect is also used as a control tool. However, with the technique of matrix immunity that we describe in our transmission *Masters of the Matrix*, you will not be susceptible to this kind of programming.

So there are ways to naturally time jump. We could say that some of you have jumped to a 'higher' version of Gaia which is also a 'future' version of Gaia. Some of you will have jumped to 'alternate/parallel' versions of Gaia within other harmonic universes.

Some of you have jumped harmonic universes across to alternate AND future 5D Gaia presentations.

The Gaia you jump to will determine your outlook on the ascension process for 3D Earth.

So if you have jumped to a 5D Gaia where all of humanity ascend, this is what you will 'see' for 3D Earth's future and this is the timeline you will manifest.

If you have jumped to an alternate 5D Gaia in another harmonic universe where extraterrestrials walk freely amongst humanity, this is the future ascended Earth you will see. This is what 'ascension' will look like for you.

The Gaia you have jumped to is the same thing as your guidance system saying, "This is where we hail from."

This is the reason why different conduits/channels/intuitives/experiencers on your planet are saying different things about the ascension process and the outcome for 3D Earth.

You manifest the timeline you have already jumped to (in an etheric, antimatter sense). All this is part and parcel of DNA activation, awakening and ascending.

Many of you are not aware of your timeline jumping and your 'accidental' travels within the hyperspace/antimatter/holographic universal system.

There are many ways whereby you can become conscious of the different timelines you experience and the quantum jumping that is taking place as you go through DNA activation and ascension. There are ways you can create the coordinates needed and project yourself into the Gaia timeline that YOU want to create for yourself.

This is the fifth strand consciousness which links to the fifth dimension which is the 'heartspace' dimension. The predominant frequencies within 5D Gaia are unconditional love, compassion, gratitude and unity. These 'emotions' are frequency coordinates and they will always project you into the 'highest and best' timeline for your overall greater good.

Each of you are manifesting different future timelines for yourselves. Yet your mission as starseeds is a global and planetary one and you have incarnated within 3D Earth to 'carry' many individuals with you to the new 5D Gaia. You 'carry' them by radiation of your light and your DNA code. The more momentum and quantum convergence/charge you can create within your matrix/DNA field, the more of Earth's inhabitants you shall be able to 'carry' and 'transport' through the stargate system that is the Emerald City of Krysta.

This is akin to saying your Mer-Ka-Bah lightship is big enough to transport thousands, if not millions, of other individuals. This, whilst a metaphor that you may not be able to comprehend fully at this time, is actually true.

We present, through this transmission, one method of Mer-Ka-Bah activation (blue star matrix, see part 37) that will assist you to choose which version of 5D Gaia you wish to ascend to and to expand your Mer-Ka-Bah to the point of 'cosmic radiation in balance' where you may transport a great many others with you. You are in effect 'saving' these individuals from yet another 26,000 years of 3D incarnation.

Now each individual has a responsibility to their own reality and their own path, this is true and there are no saviours save self. From the truest reality, there is only one soul - you - reading/listening to this material now.

In the physical linear dimension that you exist within, you are moving into a journey of polarisation and you are polarising within a service-to-others positive polarity. Therefore the understanding and processing of YOUR role as a 'saviour of Earth' is an important one to process within balance so that you do not move into a victim/saviour mentality.

As you 'save' others, you simultaneously 'save' self and this is your power line trajectory into empowerment.

This is the way of the Christ (Jesus Christ was crucified in order to save others from their sins) and this is the path all starseeds take when they undergo an ascension journey.

This is the way of the Kryst and it is the giving or surrendering of oneself in order that 'others may live'. You are simply walking the path of the hero, often the reluctant hero but the hero (or heroine) nonetheless.

These are metaphors to describe the energetic of the 'snake shedding its skin'. This is transformation and one must surrender within pure service-to-others energy in order to create the keycodes for DNA activation that will allow stargate travel into the Emerald City of Krysta.

You are going through the energetic of pure surrender and service (dying to save others from their sins) as pure sacrifice. This is a 'rite of passage'. It is an 'initiation' and it is an 'anointing'.

Only when you surrender all and 'give up all your worldly goods' can you truly activate Source/God consciousness as the 'father' and 'mother' (Sophia/Kryst template).

Surrender in pure service as a sacrificial act leads to empowerment and full realisation.

Sacrifice has been distorted by AI service-to-self programmes to lead you away from that which empowers you. Sacrifice is not martyrdom, it is not self-destruction. It is not 'less than' or 'lack of' or 'opting out'. True sacrifice is the purest act of compassion and unconditional love for you are giving of yourself to another because you love other as self.

When this energetic frequency is activated within you, it opens keycodes to the fifth strand activation level. Keys to the fifth dimensional doorways, the higher stargates of hyperspace, the Emerald City of Krysta and the Sophia/Kryst template.

We call this sacrificial surrender 'the emerald codex'.

20: Immunity

Are there negative codes as well as positive ones that can activate us into a negative spiral or deactivate us? If so, where are these codes and how do we become immune from them?

Codes themselves are neither negative nor positive yet their structure holds frequencies that are either symmetrical, light encoded and balanced with coherence or asymmetrical, non-coherent, fragmented with no activated light. There are also 'mixed codes' which hold partly symmetrical (coherent) and partly asymmetrical (fragmented) frequencies. These frequencies can affect the recipient of them either as an actual match to the codex structure (if the individual is unaware of how to navigate frequency) or as a catalyst into transformation and learning (if the individual is aware or becoming aware of how to navigate frequency).

Some codes hold 'mass' or 'weight' within their structure (meaning they hold form for longer). These can be symmetrical or asymmetrical frequency codes yet it is much more difficult for an asymmetrical/fragmented code to hold mass within their structure as these are not 'natural' or 'organic' structure. They are distortions from pure balance and are not Source-aligned.

Usually it takes focus coming in from outside the fragmented code in order to create mass within the code's structure.

Take for example, the inverted matrix. This is a network of fragmented, distorted, asymmetrical codes. In order to create mass, enough for the inverted matrix to hold its structure, there has to be a constant 'feed system' through the focus of consciousness to hold the inverted matrix system in place.

Constantly creating fear, confusion, depression, separation, persecution and victim mentality through mind control and worse (abuse and torture), creates frequencies of consciousness constantly fed into the fragmented codes within the inverted matrix to create enough mass to hold the structure in place. These 'methods' have worked well for the service-to-self negatively polarised entities for a great many years of your Earth's linear time.

However, due to the starseed activations and the indigo revolution, more and more individuals are learning to integrate the traumas and fears through 'shadow work' and activate positive emotions within their make-up such as satisfaction, contentment, compassion, gratitude, harmony, happiness, joy, hope and bliss. These emotions hold frequencies that are anathema to and the nemesis of the fragmented codes within the inverted matrix. This is the reason why the inverted matrix can no longer hold its structure and is beginning to dissipate and is no longer working.

This is the same presentation as the Earth being in 'quarantine' or having a 'force field' being placed around it. There are further reasons for the quarantine of Earth, so this is not just part of an inverted matrix with fragmented codes, but that is a whole other issue.

The point we make here is that as the fragmented codes within the inverted matrix no longer have enough mass to hold their structure, simultaneously the Earth quarantine is lifted or the force field loses its strength. These are intertwined and connected.

Yet fragmented codes are not just codes created by service-to-self entities. There are fragmented codes throughout your third and fourth densities that are part of 'natural development' if you will. These do not necessarily hold a negative agenda or seed point and some of these codes can be extremely helpful within your development, as long as you know how to navigate them.

Within your New Age communities, many of you talk about 'transmuting' a frequency. This is the same thing as the 'navigating' of the fragmented codes. Although in some cases the 'transmuting' that is undertaken when in a state of transcendence can be just as much a negative frequency as the original fragmented code. One must move into 'transmuting' through integration.

Let us take the example of the 'spiritual teacher' (aware starseed) who usually drinks bottled spring water yet finds himself at a gathering where only tap water is served. The spiritual teacher is aware that tap water holds toxins but is thirsty and so drinks a glass of the tap water anyway and says, "I will transmute it."

Now this particular spiritual teacher may be fully aware of the integration process that occurs as 'light transmutes darkness' (activated symmetrical codex taking precedence over non-activated asymmetrical codex within the cellular system) and may well be able to 'transmute' the toxins from that tap water. This would depend on the consciousness of that particular spiritual teacher and how many other toxins (or fragmented codes) that individual is already taking into his/her system.

As long as genuine integration is taking place then the individual will be 'navigating frequency', although we might add that it is a rare individual indeed who is able to consistently take in toxicity and fragmented codex and remain in a state of full balance, health and activation. The balance within navigating frequency is to be found within the third dimension as much as within the higher dimensions, so one would pay close attention to the needs of the physical body as well as the needs of the spirit in order to navigate frequency.

In the case of the spiritual teacher who has heard the concept of transmutation and is under the impression that they simply have to 'believe' that toxicity will not harm them and that they will be fine, this is what we would refer to as 'transcendence'. This is known in your spiritual circles as 'spiritual bypassing'. Whilst belief itself is a very profound part of spiritual awakening, this belief must be 'grounded in reality' in order for the codex created by the belief to hold any mass within the physical human body system!

Transcendence of a concept is transient and dissipates.

Integration of a concept holds mass for that belief structure and the belief eventually creates a neural network or system of codices within the individual that form a 'paradigm'. This eventually lets go of 'belief' entirely as the individual moves into knowing. This is all part of the expansion (bilocation, trilocation and multilocation of thought) process.

Let us present another example of a fragmented codex. Let us say there is a young individual documenting her health journey via broadcasts through your internet systems (blogging, podcasts and so on). This individual's intentions are positive for she hopes that sharing her health journey will help others when it comes to their own similar health journeys. She is of course correct in her assumption as the sharing of experience assists others greatly within their own path.

Let us say there is an individual who is currently undergoing a deep activation, expansion or awakening through 'trance state' methods (mind-altering substances, hypnosis, meditation, astral projection and so on) and that this person is 'very open' within their bodymind fields (in a highly suggestible state) and that this person, whilst in this expansive, suggestible state listens to the broadcast from the individual sharing her health journey.

In this state of consciousness, the 'negative frequency' codex within the individual's broadcast of her health journey (sharing her fear and physical experiences that triggered a fear response and/or experiences of pain) would undoubtedly be taken into the listener in an expansive state. This could trigger similar health experiences in the listener. The experiences of pain and fear would be 'fragmented codices' within the overall positive broadcast (holding intention to assist others).

These similar fragmented codices would be within any visual, audio system that could incite a fear response such as horror films or negative news broadcasts.

However, if the listener is 'grounded' prior to listening to the broadcast (chakra closing techniques, aura work, grounding technologies and so on) and the individual is aware of fragmented codex systems and how to navigate frequency, then that individual would take the positive frequencies in as a coherent codex (sharing of the individual's experience through intention of wishing to assist others). They could integrate the fear response triggered by the broadcaster's experiences of fear, pain or other symptoms.

When it comes to immunity from fragmented codes, holding negative frequency and then integrating that negative frequency is always the key.

We would direct you to our previous transmission *Masters of the Matrix* for information regarding immunity, as navigation of fragmented codex is part and parcel of Matrix Mastery. The chapters 'Emotional Integration' and 'Acknowledgement, Gratitude, Analysis, Integration' would be specific parts of the transmission that we would suggest.

We might add that there are a great many starseeds simply 'doing this naturally' and that when they read the Matrix Awareness and Matrix Mastery material, their realisation is, "I am already doing this!"

Many starseeds have been working with integration and navigating of frequency in various ways since childhood.

Another most useful method of integration and navigation of frequency is ritual (sacred ceremony).

21: Integration

This might be completely off-topic but I just had a thought. You said that one way to integrate and navigate frequency is through ritual. Is this why the condition 'obsessive-compulsive disorder' (OCD) manifests in people? Are they ritualising their lives in an attempt to integrate and navigate frequency?

There is no such thing as 'off-topic' in truth, as everything is connected. However we are containing this work of Matrix Transportation within certain parameters so cannot go too deeply into subjects that 'follow a different yet connected stream' if you will.

We will respond to your question. You are thinking along the 'right lines' here. Yet there are many different seed points and traumas that trigger the condition known within your planet's medical system as 'obsessive-compulsive disorder'. Discussing health conditions and bodymind personality presentations such as 'mental illness' or 'disability' is a whole other transmission.

Firstly one would have to take the label away if one truly wished to get to the root cause of these bodymind personality presentations.

Each labelled condition might present with the same or similar set of symptoms within many individuals, yet the root cause may be totally different within each of these individuals. Giving their set of symptoms the same label and using the same treatment modalities is not the most effective way for healing.

OCD is no different. Each individual diagnosed with OCD may have a totally different seed point (cause) and for some people the symptoms of OCD are the 'result' of something and for others the symptoms of OCD are a protective measure in order to prevent something else.

However, your theory of integration and navigation of frequency through ritual as being the root cause for some individuals with OCD is actually correct.

Root causes are actually complex convergences of patterns and are not mono. One root cause within the overall complex convergence can be the attempt to integrate and navigate frequency (specifically the fragmented codex). The individuals with this root cause within their overall complex convergence would be starseeded souls, coming in with activated memory strands of how a frequency matrix is set up within a planetary system, universe or dimension. The awareness of the mission would be 'partly online' if you will. This is a deliberate intention with incarnating starseeds so that they have the best chance of activating the DNA memory codes.

Individuals who have incarnated with the mission as 'master healer' and/or 'alchemist' would have DNA memory codes partly online that would hold memory of the inverted systems and fragmented codex.

If they trigger those memories or activate that DNA strand 'too early' if you will (and this is a linear presentation only for in the true reality nothing is ever too early or too late), say in childhood for example, the individual would not know how to process the sensitivity towards fragmented codex. That individual could interpret many situations, events, visual images, people and places as 'negative frequency within fragmented codes'. Intrinsically knowing the power of ritual, they would begin to automatically ritualise energy connected to what they perceive as negative frequency. Thus the symptoms that your medical system labels as 'obsessive-compulsive disorder' is manifest.

Yet other individuals, who also have the DNA memory codex for integration and navigation of fragmented codex activated, within childhood do not manifest the symptoms of OCD.

In order to manifest OCD, the overall complex convergence pattern (that is the root cause) would contain other codes. This is a complex pattern and in itself is a fragmented pattern.

So if someone has OCD or an autoimmune illness or a disability such as cerebral palsy or autism, are they fragmented? And does this mean they cannot ascend?

No, this does not mean that 'they' are fragmented. Each individual incarnated soul is whole and a perfect holographic replica of Source. It means that the energy pattern they hold (such as the OCD or other condition) is a fragmented pattern. This is, in almost all cases, a chosen pattern in order to bring the experience to the individual within their lives that they needed.

If the individual is in a state of integration and navigation within that fragmented pattern then yes, they can absolutely ascend. Integration and navigation are the 'tools of phire', if you will, that create momentum and charge in order for the Mer-Ka-Bah to pass through the higher stargates of hyperspace and into the Emerald City of Krysta.

Lack of integration and navigation (which is fragmentation, dissociation, passivity and stagnation) will not phire the Mer-Ka-Bah vehicle into flight and gather quantum convergence and DNA charge.

That which creates mass also creates charge, which is why we say integration is so important within your ascension journey. You cannot ascend without it. Transcendence does bring enlightenment however and if coupled simultaneously with some integration, then one may be able to build enough momentum for ascension. Full transcendence without integration does not hold the correct DNA frequency in order to access the stargates needed for full physical ascension. Transcendence without integration when high compassion codes are available may lead to non-physical ascension but it is integration that allows you to 'take your body with you'.

Now you are also aware that fragmented codex is not just outside of you but potentially within you. However, integration (either completed or ongoing) of fragmented codex changes the structure of the codex. The codex is in a state of transmutation and is therefore no longer fragmented. It is in transit and is therefore no longer static. It has movement and is therefore a catalyst, a trigger and a code into Matrix Transportation.

It is a accelerant for charge.

When you integrate the fragmented codex within you (the OCD or other condition), you 'place your foot upon the accelerator pedal' of the Mer-Ka-Bah vehicle, if you will.

Hence why we say, "All natural healers take a personal healing journey."

In order to create the phire of integration within, one must have something to integrate!

22: Ritual and Sacred Ceremony

What is sacred ceremony and why is it so important?

Sacred ceremony is ultimately the recognising of natural energetic patterns and mirroring those patterns within the physical dimension.

This has been practised by peoples of Earth since the beginning of your species. This has been practised (and still is today) by various cultures all across your planet.

In ancient times the indigenous peoples, those living in harmony with the Earth, would consume the sacred plants opening gateways to other dimensions. Through this 'shamanic journeying' they would discover the importance of ritual and sacred ceremony.

Sacred ceremony is a grounding of the higher energies (or natural energetic patterns) creating an interlocking grid formation of frequency.

Everything has frequency and all is energy and there is far more 'unseen' than is 'seen'. Your eyes are not the only means of sight. Many times we use the phrase, "Those who have eyes to see."

When we use this phrase, we are speaking of a different kind of sight. This is the 'feeling', 'sensing' or 'knowing'. There are those individuals that are able to use this aspect, they do not need 'sacred plants' or any other trigger, they naturally sense these energetic patterns we speak of.

This is not so much that these people are special in any way or that they have unexplainable powers. It is more the case that these people have returned to the natural state for the human being. They are therefore able to sense subtle energies, feel these patterns and utilise them.

This is what sacred ceremony is, the utilisation of the subtle energies and frequency patterns that are part of the natural flow.

Those who we say are 'in harmony with nature' do not just communicate with trees, grow fruits and tend the animals upon the land and within the seas. They are also able to work with the elements, connect with entities within other realms and access information and knowledge about who they are and their place in the world. They are able to understand how to 'create their reality'. They do this by communicating with these entities or by decoding patterns within the energetic field (or both).

They are then able to utilise the powerful frequency that they have created/accessed. We may call this 'free energy' or 'organic technology'.

One of the ways they do this is by grounding the frequency patterns into the physical third dimensional realm through ritual and sacred ceremony.

This is not so much seen as 'important' by those who take part in ceremony but as 'natural'.

What can sacred ceremony be used for?

For whichever purpose deemed necessary or desirable for the individual or group involved. One purpose, as we have said, is integration and navigation of frequency (including fragmented codex).

Sacred ceremony and ritual can be utilised for both 'good' (service-to-others energy) or 'evil' (service-to-self energy). These are simply positive and negative forces.

In this particular transmission, we would concentrate on the use of this magickal tool within the positive service-to-others energetic. We have presented, within this overall transmission, information that is an exploration of the positive and negative polarities. For the utilisation of frequency patterns as sacred ceremonial magick, however, we would present only information relevant to positive polarisation.

The purposes that sacred ceremony can be utilised for (within positive polarisation) are handfastings and unions between couples (or groups) that stand as 'twin flame' or 'spiritual working partners'.

Also the true 'naming' of newborn infant or young child, the passing of an individual from the physical incarnation, the creation of something (nourishment, abundance, relationship, physical creation or the outcome of a situation), communication and the receiving of knowledge, healing, initiations of other magickal workers and, of course, integration and navigation of frequency.

There are those who have seen these energetic patterns and who understand (often through trial and error) how these patterns work. These individuals then deliver their teachings and trainings to others. These are the individuals navigating frequency. We may perhaps call these individuals 'master magicians' or 'alchemists' and indeed 'Masters of the Matrix'.

There are other names or labels we can give to these individuals but whatever you call them, these are the ones that can see/sense/feel the energetic frequency patterns and utilise them.

Are these people from 'New Age' or 'pagan' religions?

You will find individuals from all walks of life, within all the different religions and spiritual pathways, exercising sacred ceremony and ritual within their lives.

There are many who have no understanding or knowledge of any path or religion yet they simply 'do this naturally'. Many are 'untrained' in what they do and ground fragmented and unpolarised energy patterns, yet often in their synchronistic life journey they find their way to other 'magicians' who can assist them to clear interferences and balance their energy fields.

Similarly within the 'New Age' and 'pagan' religions, you will find individuals who do not see/sense/feel yet walk the path that will act as the catalyst to the trigger of the magickal working. There are also those within these paths who find them for other reasons and do not ever open up to the magick.

Yet predominantly yes, within these particular spiritual pathways under the banner of 'New Age' or 'pagan', you will find the individuals who see/sense/feel the energetic patterns and will utilise the tool of ritual and sacred ceremony. We would refer to these individuals as 'starseeds'.

How can ritual be used to integrate and navigate frequency and negative codex?

Ritual and sacred ceremony are packed with an abundance of activation codes, keycodes and patterns much like our transmissions. They are 'sacred texts' regardless of the form they take (music, movement, chanting, drumming, song, performance, game, writing, art, divination, prayer, meditation and so on).

The codes contained within the sacred ceremony or ritual will create a complex convergence, all focusing on the intention of the ritual itself. This gathers quantum force/convergence/momentum and creates a 'trajectory of intention'. If that intention is for integration or navigation of frequency then the abundance of frequency codes within the overall complex convergence that is the ritual will be focusing upon the intention with a 'light speed trajectory'. This is simply a way of utilising tools and combining them with focused intention to create a 'living consciousness grid' or matrix that is the sacred ceremony or ritual itself. The complex convergence often presents as sacred geometric structure (living adept masters of light or ascended beings), these externalise from the ritual itself, take the place of capstone and become 'divine guidance'. We present here a simplified explanation of how this works.

This is useful to know, as the same methods within sacred ceremony and ritual that create the 'capstone' to the geometric formation that is the complex convergence, are used for navigating the Kryst (the stargate system we call the Emerald City of Krysta).

What is the difference between sacred ceremony and DNA activation?

A great question as these are linked and interchangeable and very much 'two sides of the same coin'.

Sacred ceremony is always a DNA activation, but a DNA activation is not always a sacred ceremony.

Ceremony and ritual is the grounding of higher frequencies by recreating geometric pattern of antimatter into matter, usually, but not always, involving the use of object. This practise will always activate DNA although the level of that activation will depend on the intention of the ceremony and the vibrational frequencies of the objects used, the place that the ceremony is performed in, the participants and observers of the ceremony as well as the calender date and any astrological alignments or weather patterns.

DNA activation can occur from inner visualisation, communication through language of light, meditation, artwork, music, text and many other means. These would not necessarily fall into the category of 'sacred ceremony' or 'ritual'.

Can you create sacred ceremony through meditation or visualisation?

Indeed yes, you can. Many powerful ceremonies are conducted this way. The energy frequencies are just as 'real' through visualisation especially when conducted by an adept.

23: Flat Earth Paradigm and the Atlantean Crystals

I have often wondered why some people believe the Earth to be a flat plane or disc and others see the Earth as a globe. Some say the 'flat Earth' is a disinformation programme created to confuse us and others say that it is the biggest secret hidden from us. What is the truth here? You mentioned 'timeline jumping', so have some people 'timeline jumped' to an Earth that is flat?

Within the quantum field (sideways arm of the cross/rainbow bridge pathway) are a myriad of 'expressions' of planetary body. Just as there are a myriad of expressions of you as a human being.

Within a 'healthy solar system' the planetary body is a sphere as all constructs are formed within cycles/spirals. The matrix of the planetary body is actually a spinning, spiralling toroidal field just as is your matrix.

The code for 'planetary birth' results in a sphere-shaped planetary body. They are not formed as globes however, the sphere is the code template but planets can birth themselves from the matrix with slightly different shapes, mostly forming into spheres or sphere-type presentations.

In several harmonic universes (including yours), there were 'explosions' of crashing matter/antimatter states as the universe attempted to form. In other harmonic universes, there were what we would call 'frequency clashes' as positive and negative polarisation balanced themselves within matter and antimatter. One could interpret this as a 'frequency war'. This would not be quite correct but possibly the only way to interpret what was happening.

Within some of these harmonic universes, some of the planetary bodies were 'damaged' (in truth, they simply reformed in a different structure with different compounds, gases and environmental substances in accordance with the codes within the fabric of their matrices).

The formation of some of these planetary bodies are more 'disc-like' and could be perceived as 'flat'.

Some of these planetary bodies have been 'reconstructed' by intelligent creator codes within the matrix.

This is the same thing as saying 'extraterrestrials had a big battle, some planets were damaged and were reconstructed'. This is a third dimensional interpretation but it is still a truthful explanation. The matrix codes of universal time fabric are 'intelligent beings'.

So there are individuals with guidance systems who 'hail from' these alternate 'flat Earths' due to the awakening, activating starseed 'time jumping' into the harmonic universe and existing upon the 'flat Earth'.

In truth these harmonic universes and all the planets and life upon those planets are all in the same place, the same space. They are superimposed upon one another.

Does this therefore mean that your planet Earth is both a sphere and a flat plane? Yes, this is exactly what this means. It depends from which aspect of the time matrix you are viewing Earth from.

The majority of starseeds 'hail from' and 'exist upon' a sphere shaped Earth so this is the planetary reality that holds the highest 'mass' within your harmonic universal experience. This does not mean that a flat Earth projection does not exist.

The fractal, holographic multiverse is as vast as your imagination. The antimatter/antiparticle reality manifests in response to your collective thought processes especially if these are 'group focused intentions'. Therefore if a group of individuals subscribe to the belief system (and that becomes part of their paradigm) that the Earth is flat and not a sphere, then this is the reality they will experience. The belief system becoming a paradigm is the DNA activation that creates the timeline jump. The 'paradigm' is, in itself, an 'information disc' that feeds into the matrix. It contains the coordinates of where the individual wants to go.

Many of you, as we have said, are 'accidentally' or 'unconsciously' time jumping by programming coordinates into your matrix field without being aware of it.

We, within this transmission, shall present to you a technique that can assist you to consciously create the coordinates and programme the matrix intentionally. This is focused attention upon the trajectory of intention using the sixth dimensional paradigm of the starseed template (the individualised Mer-Ka-Bah matrix).

Indeed the 'flat Earth' is a disinformation programme, as you suggest, in the sense that the truth of the fractal, holographic and multidimensional nature of reality is not disclosed to the people of the planet.

There are four reasons for this:

1) Service-to-self factions wish for control of the population so seek to confuse by presenting information either as part-truth/part-distortion or full distortion through the creation of inverted systems and the inverted matrix.

2) Many service-to-self individuals and groups do not understand the nature of multidimensional reality themselves.

3) Those that do want to disclose truth are under the impression that the multidimensional nature of reality would confuse third dimensional thinking individuals so much that chaos would ensue within the creational timelines/time matrices themselves. This perspective holds some validity yet utilising a grid structure such as this one, 'the infinite helix grid of light' (all those who access this transmission including our conduit, Magenta Pixie, and 'us', the White Winged Collective Consciousness of Nine), will utilise an intentional synchronicity convergence programme which is a hermetically sealed 'fail-safe' programme that only the multidimensionally aware individuals can connect to. This can only be achieved through a positive polarisation however, as intentional synchronicity convergence programmes cannot be created as telepathic unions through service-to-self factions. Therefore this option is not open to them. They are aware of the Law of One and the law of balance and therefore cannot infiltrate or hijack any activated starseed once they have utilised an intentional synchronicity convergence structure and are part of a telepathic union. This in itself is the hermetically sealed fail-safe programme within the starseeds.

4) Some service-to-self individuals and groups feel that only their bloodline is entitled to know the truth of reality, and that any being outside of their bloodline (or at a certain level within their genetic bloodline) does not have the required status, by virtue of their birth, to be given such information.

Therefore the 'flat Earth' belief system will be utilised, hijacked and inverted in order for the service-to-self agenda to be served. However, the 'flat Earth' belief system per se is not the seed point of the disinformation programme itself.

The biggest secret hidden from you as humanity on Earth is not the shape of your planet or even the multidimensional nature of reality. The biggest secret that has been hidden from you is the extent of your own power, your sovereignty. When you connect together in telepathic union, such as within this particular intentional synchronicity convergence programme and similar telepathic unions, you literally 'change reality, create worlds and perform magickal acts'.

The biggest secret is regarding the master magicians and who they are. The disclosure you are looking for is that the master magicians are collectively you, the activated consciously aware starseeds.

Together, your power is phenomenal.

You can see why this has been kept a secret!

This is a secret no longer. True disclosure is your sovereignty, your collective memories and your ability to create high magick. The magick of Atlantis and the Atlantean crystals.

This is the real 'rising of Atlantis'. You, your memories, your knowings, your power, your truth and your sovereignty.

The crystal generators that power-up stargates, and stargate systems changing their coordinates to higher and higher dimensional realities, are back.

The crystal generators and their operators are you!

24: Divine Princess (Daughter of the Flame)

How is Atlantis connected to our current ascension on Earth?

We have mentioned to you within this transmission of the grid or network of telepathic union between the consciously aware starseeds, that which we called the 'intentional synchronicity convergence programmes'.

We can also refer to these telepathic union grids as 'the starseed section of the planetary grid of light'.

This is a 'living network' which is a section of the Akash (Akashic records) that connects each and every aware and awake starseeded/lightworker (ascending individual) together. They can detect each other's thoughts and emotions, some can even see and know what other starseeds are doing (within the boundaries of permissions and etiquettes).

The planetary grid of light would be the consciousness of all individuals upon planet Earth, including the planet herself.

These 'grids' (intentional synchronicity convergence programmes) are what we would refer to as 'organic technology'. They are the 'signal' or 'broadcast' of each and every activated individual, coming together to form a 'collective consciousness'.

So whilst there is a planetary collective consciousness (Earth and all humanity), there is also a starseed collective consciousness (all the starseeds on Earth).

The planetary collective consciousness will be partly 'intentional synchronicity' and partly 'accidental synchronicity' with a lot of random, confusing energies/constructs/entities... some holding mass, others dissipating. So there is wide diversity through the energetic structures within the planetary collective consciousness. The 'guiding light' or the 'predominant thought structure' (those that steer the ship of Earth) is that of the aware starseeds.

The starseed collective consciousness is therefore the predominant collective consciousness structure upon Earth at the time of this transmission. This reached critical mass on your planet most recently. If we had to pinpoint the seeds for this critical mass for telepathy, it would be the winter solstice of 2012 with full actualisation occurring around the winter solstice of 2017.

The starseed collective consciousness, newly reaching full manifestation through critical mass as the guiding force for Earth, has progressed within a 'fast tracked' mass and grows and gets stronger with each passing day (within your linear time).

This would be another way to describe the 'indigo revolution'.

The starseed collective consciousness grid of light is an individualised structure in its own right. If Sophia is the divine Goddess and 'mother of all things' and the Kryst (or Kristos) is the God-realised aspect/Source frequency and 'father of all things', then we could say that the starseed collective consciousness grid of light as an entity is the 'daughter to the mother and father' when looking at the feminine frequency. The starseed collective consciousness grid of light is a predominantly feminine intelligence and a feminine being. As 'she' is the daughter frequency, we could refer to her as 'the divine princess energy'. As Sophia would be 'queen of the night' (lunar/subconscious/moon) and the Kryst would be 'king of the day' (solar/aware consciousness/sun), so the queen and the king are 'cosmic forces'.

The daughter energetic (also known as the 'daughter of the flame') is a 'planetary force' even whilst it is 'off-planet' and of antimatter construction. It is the collective thought field of all aware starseeds (those who hold activated DNA strand formations with etheric construction holding potential for light speed/warp speed momentum which is 'the infinite helix').

So we could refer to the starseed collective consciousness grid of light as the 'divine princess Aurora'.

These language of light codes in the form of 'names' are intelligent and loving energy structures, or geometric masters. They stand not above you and beyond you but as you and 'their wishes' and 'their desires' are to be taken, through the sacrificial surrender frequency of unconditional love, as your equals. To translate this in its accurate form, 'they wish to be your friends'.

These 'names' are activation codes for planetary and ascending structure memory. They are 'codes', or more appropriately 'codices' (rather than being one page they are an entire manuscript), containing keycodes for what we can call 'DNA sequencing'.

They are 'memory maps' and triggers into the rearranging of the DNA helix structure which brings the etheric strand formation antiparticle DNA construction online.

There are many of these 'code words' and many of them are names.

Three of these powerful names are Sophia, Kryst (or Kristos) and Aurora.

The service-to-self factions within the upper tiers are aware of the codices within these names/words and are aware of their ability to trigger the DNA reconstruction. There are also 'sacred numbers' that are triggers and keycodes in the same way.

The service-to-self factions seek to 'change' or 'distort' or 'invert' the activation codes contained therein in order to place 'overlapping' frequencies (like an artificially constructed vibrational skin) over the top of, or within, the original organic Source-aligned frequency code. This creates a 'false activation' and the strength of emotion and mass contained within the inverted structure prevents the codex from activating DNA reconstruction into crystalline change, distorting true memory codes.

This is akin to 'blocking the signal' and we can quite accurately refer to this false inverted system as a 'signal blocker'.

The activated and aware starseeds, once connected to these intentional synchronicity convergence programmes (telepathic union, starseed collective consciousness grid of light), move into immunity from these inverted systems and signal blockers and activate a hermetically sealed 'fail-safe programme' within the DNA structure. We call this the 'emerald code'. When the activation of the hermetic seal/fail- safe/emerald code reaches critical mass (as it has done upon your planet at the time of this transmission), it creates a dismantling of the inverted system/signal blocking technology.

The starseeds then 'go above' the signal blocking frequency and are able to 'read the true code'. Therefore they are aware of the distortion of words, names and numbers.

Yet there are still many 'just awakening', 'due to awaken' and 'newly awakened' starseeds who are confused by the names/words/numbers as they project forth a mixed vibration for them as they partly link to the inverted system code and the true organic code.

However, through the intentional synchronicity convergence programme (starseed collective consciousness grid of light/telepathic union), they will be 'guided' or 'led' to other starseed teachers or their creative presentations (books, videos, talks, music, art, drama and so on.) This will assist them in the unravelling of the inverted and organic structures within the name/word/number.

Examples of attempted (and somewhat successful) inverted structure of high codex names/words/numbers are:

- The number 666

- Kryst (Kryst holding mass, Christ-Mass, Christmas)

- Isis

- Illuminati or 'illumined one'

- Lucifer

- The number 13

These are just a few high activation coded structures that have been 'hijacked' if you will.

We present to you the purity of Sophia and Aurora and show you the true organic presentation of their extensive codices within this transmission. Once you are aware of the existence of distorted and inverted codex, you automatically 'rise above' the dark broadcast frequency that is utilised and see the true structure. The more of you that 'rise above' and become immune to the 'signal blocking', the more the entire inverted matrix will 'crumble and fall' as it is dismantled and dissolved.

It is that which many of you call 'the old energy'.

You, as starseeds, are very much part of the 'new energy'. Indeed you ARE the new energy and all the new creations that come from this new energy (including the new world, ascended 5D Gaia).

The intentional synchronicity convergence programme that is the starseed collective consciousness planetary grid of light, telepathic union, is the 'ground crew', if you will, and is the feminine frequency that is 'the awakening'. She takes form as an individualised being and we introduce her to you, sacred daughter of the flame, divine princess Aurora.

Now you have 'met' her, we can respond to your question as to how Atlantis is connected to your ascension process.

25: The Flame

Aurora, as divine princess, is 'daughter of the flame'.

'The flame' is her parent or parents (if 'she' is their daughter).

Yet we already know that the divine mother (queen) is Sophia (Krysta) and the sacred father (king) is Kryst (Kristos).

Sophia and Kryst (Krysta and Kristos, or Alpha and Omega) are 'twin flames'. They are the absolute twin flames of Source and represent the first split/first distortion from complete unification into dualistic presentation that began the 'search for exploration of self' through polarisation. The first thought, the first expression and the infinite equal reaction paradox.

As dualism (two, the twin, the distortion, the paradox, the beginning and the end), they are 'twin flames'.

As 'the one' (unification, unity, Source, oneness), they are 'the flame' for all twin flames become one flame.

Their 'daughter' (the first expression from dualism, from two, into the Holy Trinity: three) was the first creation and creative expression.

The 'daughter of the flame' is the creation from creation. The 'flame' is pure creation in its unity essence. The 'twin flames' are the creator/creatrix.

Together as the three, they are the 'Holy Trinity'.

In the furthest expression of separation we return to dualism, polarity and 'the two' (the double helix).

The double helix is the 'furthest away from Source' and the twin flame is 'the closest to Source'.

Yet together they are one and the same as 'the twins/doubles' and hold the 'power of two'. The seeds of creation (seed of life/egg of life) blossoming into creation (three/Holy Trinity, Flower of Life).

Aurora (as fifth dimensional form) would be depicted holding a bouquet of roses, with roses in her hair for she is the sacred rose (fractal, Flower of Life).

The realisation and manifestation of the Holy Trinity is the first step closer to Source and begins the journey 'back' to Source. The upward climb as opposed to the fall. The 'ascent' as opposed to the 'descent'. This is the 'triple helix' moving into 'beyond the triple helix' and then into the 'infinite helix' (light speed/warp speed momentum with a focused trajectory to Source through ascension).

The flame in its unity presentation (the twin flames merged as one flame) is the ultimate alchemy, created by the unconditional love and the joining together of the twin flames.

From the perspective of 'the ascent' and the 'upward climb' (back to Source), one 'creates' Source through unification of self and other as 'one self' (the twin flame becomes the flame).

The flame, embodying all things as a vibration, presents through the highest frequencies. Beyond words, of light and sound (lightlove/lovelight into bliss-charged love), moving then into colour (art) and number (mathematics).

Within pure creation, sound becomes music, colour becomes artistic presentation and the 'first form' presents as geometry.

The taking in of this 'knowing' (through music, art, geometry or words that create image) holds the keycodes for memory of this 'ultimate and infinite journey of merge' hence the reason why music, art and poetry is so beloved by humanity throughout the ages. The presentations are 'reminders' of the true home.

Within the highest echelons of the third dimension (which is now a merge point with the fourth dimension on your planet), one is 'divinely inspired' to create through the mediums of music, art or poetry (sound, colour) and/or geometry/mathematics as these are the absolute expressions of creation.

Each creation within your physical life is a 'daughter of the flame', just as Aurora is the 'first daughter' of the unification between Krysta and Kristos (the Sophia/Kryst alliance).

Each time YOU create as starseeds, you embody the flame (pure creation, pure Source itself) as you 'give birth' to your 'daughter of the flame' as your personal Aurora (aura/matrix) through divine feminine expression, creating your own keycode into the activation of the DNA (matrix/aura/Aurora).

One can see how your own creation creates personal DNA activation and memory.

Yet so too does the inspiration to create hold the matching keycodes to the inspiration from the creation.

Therefore when you become 'inspired' by another individual's creation (music, art, poetry, geometry), this also creates keycodes for your own DNA activation and memory. You each inspire one another continuously for you all hold the code for the 'awakening' of others (to ensure a critical mass level of awakening within the ascending beings transitioning from 3D Earth into 5D Gaia).

Creativity on your planet now moves into the 'stratosphere' of inspiration, if you will, due to creation codes coming in from much higher dimensions/merge points than the higher echelons of the third dimension.

Starseeds 'recognise' the encryption codes within all creations and can separate distortion within codex, move into immunity from distortion within codex and receive true aligned keycodes that are the coordinates for stargate ascension.

We present now, stargate ascension keycodes, using the 'Ark of the Covenant technology' through presentation of 'phire into flame'.

Phire creates light speed/warp speed momentum (quantum charge convergence).

Phire/fire creates the 'awakening of the flame' (movement from bilocation into trilocation into multilocation which is double helix, into triple helix, into beyond the triple helix and into the infinite helix and thus full ascension).

The 'Ark of the Covenant technology' is that which triggers the memories for the infinite helix formation (matter/antimatter merge or particle/antiparticle merge) which takes place within each ascending consciousness construct. That means YOU, dear starseeds!

Moving into fifth dimensional form, that which creates the 'flame through fire' is the dragon.

Many of you are drawn to the mystical, majestic beauty of the dragon.

Many of you have worked with the dragon energy for many years, some of you since birth into your current incarnation.

For those of you who personally work with the dragon, do not underestimate the importance of who you are and the work that you do.

Without moving into 'self importance' or the 'god complex' and remaining within the perfect serenity of the sacrificial, surrender of the Kryst (Christ) which gives you that which you call 'Christ consciousness', be aware of who and what you are and indeed what you carry.

You carry the 'dragon codes' which are memory codes for the 'fire of the dragon'.

Fire (phire/Kundalini activation into bliss/light speed/warp speed momentum).

Dragon (fifth dimensional presentation of form that is the sacred geometry of the flame, the merged twin into unity from the perspective of the upward climb/ascension).

The sacred understanding of the flame/phire through the depiction of the dragon is that which we call the 'dragon's breath'.

The dragon's breath is the flame in all its forms including other elements as they present through air, water (ice) and Earth. These are the presentations of pure creation.

You, starseeds who carry the dragon codes, are the ones who hold the 'dragon's breath'. You are the individuals that are called to 'pure creation' and deliverance, to all of your worlds, of the power of the 'dragon's breath' through your creations.

All you create holds the codes. These are ascension codes. These are the codes for the infinite helix.

Do not underestimate your abilities and your path. Many of you, incarnated with the sensitivity of the crystal or the 'other-worldly' qualities of the blue ray, underestimate what you have to offer in the way of creativity, talent and innate knowledge.

Trust your inner knowing. If you have been 'called by the dragon' then you are a torchbearer for the flame and you hold the dragon's breath (codes for the infinite helix, warp speed Mer-Ka-Bah travel and the coordinates for stargate ascension).

Through Ark of the Covenant technology, we present to you the keycodes of the infinite helix through colour and sound. We do this through the medium of our conduit who creates the imagery through words. We present this imagery through colour and we introduce to you the dragon's breath through the 'rainbow dragons of Krysta' (dragon activations).

First, we present the keycodes through the flame. At the end of this transmission, we introduce you to the dragons.

26: Rainbow Flame Initiation

At the end of this transmission, we shall move into the activations and initiations through the flame of the dragon and the dragon's breath.

Now we draw your attention to the repeated hijacking of this most important and significant codex.

Service-to-self factions have understood for many aeons the 'power of the dragon' and indeed the 'rainbow serpent' so they have repeatedly sought to distort and invert the true essence of the dragon/serpent.

They have distorted the presentation of the majestic beauty of the beast that stands as initiation into ascension. They have instead presented it as dark, frightening, aggressive, oppressive and malevolent.

This hijacking has taken hold upon your planet as 'fear of the dragon' through distortion of truth regarding Orion planetary agendas and reptilian control, presenting ALL beings from Orion and ALL reptilian entities as malevolent.

The truth is that no incarnate group or race is all negatively or all positively polarised (within a linear time frame) so positive, loving Orion beings and positive, loving reptilian entities exist and are intertwined with you and with your Earth in a benevolent way. The dragon energy comes in through extremely high vibrational frequencies, holding ascension activation codes and they are very far removed from the Orion/reptilian dark beings spoken about upon your planet.

The manifestation of the dark agendas, through Orion/reptilian control, however do exist and we do not ask you to dismiss the truth of negative polarisation within your matter or antimatter reality.

Yet there are those who 'throw the baby out with the bathwater', as it were, which is indeed the intention of those who seek to enslave you with the presentation of your own sacred image and extinguish your inner fire/phire.

They underestimated the power of the dragon, thinking the fear was too great upon your 3D Earth. Indeed the fear was great but the dragon is so intertwined with the divine feminine, as the symbol for the flame that is the unification of the twin flame merge and the alchemical alliance of merge that is the true marriage of self.

Your yearning for the love of other, through your search for the twin flame and you reuniting with the twin flame, has 'brought back the dragon'. We can therefore truthfully say to you, "The dragon has returned."

Those holding the dragon codes, dragon's breath, never at any time gave into the hijacked reality. They kept the knowing of the dragon pure.

Now, at the time of this transmission, the power of the divine feminine through Sophia, Aurora, Mary (The Mag-Da-Len), Sarah, Kali and others, brings with it the knowing and knowledge of the 'sacred dragon' and the codes for the dragon's breath (infinite helix).

"Somewhere over the rainbow, bluebirds fly" [6]

Red Flame

The red flame is an Earth-linked flame. Physical form living within separation and under the veil of forgetfulness. The amnesia leads to confusion which creates the search for clarity. Grounding into matter through physical needs such as warmth, nourishment and security. Distortions/hijacking through this flame come in through fear of loss of physical needs such as warmth, nourishment and security. Creativity through practical means clears distortions within this flame. Integration of all the flames creates balance within the red flame.

This flame stands for 'fire' (as in enthusiasm or fiery in nature) and, when balanced with the orange flame, assists in creating physical boundaries within the individual/idea or construct.

This flame is represented by the red dragon, linking dragon energy through the flames into the physical third dimension. The red dragon bringing higher dimensional wisdom and grounding it into physical reality.

Higher 'charged' activation, for the red flame is the ruby flame. Burning brightly for living within the physical universe as a lightlove/lovelight aware, awakened, DNA activated, physically incarnated being. Anchoring the sacred masculine in full balance - left brained activation - the

6   Lyrics from "Over the Rainbow", ballad with music by Harold Arlen and lyrics by Yip Harburg. It was written for the movie *The Wizard of Oz* (1939).

feminine right brained consciousness giving power to the masculine/left brained consciousness.

Orange Flame

The orange flame is an Earth-linked flame. Embracing of self as Sophia/Kryst, Goddess/God-realised self through the beginning seed point of Kundalini ascension and sacred sexuality. Distortions/hijacking through this flame come in through abusing sacred sexuality through deviance, pornography and heinous crimes against the defenceless and the innocent. Truly knowing and experiencing the Goddess within, clears distortion and creates immunity from hijacking. Integration of all the flames creates balance within the orange flame. This flame is represented by ascended master Quan Yin.

Yellow Flame

The yellow flame is an Earth-linked flame yet has connections to the inner Earth kingdoms and the elemental realm. Power centre for knowledge, intelligence and psychic ability. Distortions/hijacking through this flame come in through disinformation in all areas where the search for knowledge shall lead. Purification through nutritional, philosophical and psychological detoxification methods clears distortion within this flame. Integration of all the flames creates balance within the yellow flame. This flame is represented by ascended master Lord Kuthumi.

Green Flame

This is the first flame within the climb that links to off-planet energy. This flame burns brightly for the planet known as Terra (fourth dimensional version of Earth) and connects you to the hyperspace world through open-hearted, unconditional love. This is the flame for the first seed into service-to-others polarisation. This flame links with the sacred geometric master numbers, especially '11 11'. Synchronicity begins at the level of this flame. It is not possible for service-to-self factions to directly hijack this flame. False grids can be placed within other flames so that this flame is 'difficult to find' and unsustainable for the uninitiated. Once this flame has been integrated along with the full rainbow flame spectrum,

160

then full immunity to hijacking is given along with 'the badge of sovereignty'. This flame is represented by 'the green goddess' (known by many names, some of these being Selena, Dannu, Daniela or Green Tara).

Blue Flame

This flame burns brightly for Gaia (fifth dimensional version of Earth) and when you 'pass through' the celestial stargate associated with this flame (blue star matrix), you 'exist' upon Gaia. The silicon molecular structure of the DNA sequencing takes form at this point. One becomes a 'speaker for the flame' and higher dimensional communication will be accessed. This flame can be hijacked and distorted if it becomes activated alongside the orange flame without activating the green flame. As long as the green flame is activated then this blue flame cannot be hijacked. This flame is represented by ascended master Merlin, the archangel Michael and his 'twin flame' the divine princess Aurora.

The higher 'charged' activation for the blue flame would be the 'blue sapphire' flame which transforms 'communication' into 'telepathy'.

Indigo Flame

When the indigo flame is activated then 'action' takes place within the physical reality. The 'inner warrior' comes into play and the working within 'the indigo revolution' and/or with dragon energy takes place.

This flame cannot be hijacked and is available as an initiation/activation only to service-to-others, positively polarised individuals who have also activated the green flame. This flame is represented by the divine Lady Mary Magdalene (the Mag-Da-Len geometry). When one accesses the flame, one is said to be a 'keeper of the flame'. These are the individuals holding mass, through quantum convergence/light speed/warp speed momentum and 'carry' the others through the stargates with their activated Mag-Da-Len Mer-Ka-Bah.

All starseeds who stand as part of the indigo revolution are the 'keepers of the flame' (the ground crew) yet there are many higher dimensional entities and intelligences also standing as 'keepers of the flame'.

Violet Flame

The violet flame stands for the 'going galactic' and represents the activation of the infinite helix DNA code formations. The reason for this is that the violet flame cannot be activated in balance unless all other flames are activated and integrated and it is the full rainbow flame activation that creates the infinite helix/multilocational consciousness. This flame burns brightly for 'the higher stargates of hyperspace'.

The violet flame is represented by archangel Metatron and ascended master Saint Germain. However, at this stage we could speak of 'archangel Michael and his twelve archangels' as all these angels are part of the violet flame.

The violet flame is a very aligned 'cosmic energy' to be utilised as a healing flame as it 'beams a violet light across the shade' (allowing you to be aware of that which is buried - trauma, disease, memories, DNA strands and so on).

Emerald Flame

The activation of this flame is what we call the 'Emerald City of Krysta', accessing the stargate system for ascension through the divine feminine Sophia energetic. This flame is the 'higher activation' of the green flame (the 'upgraded' and 'charged' aspect of the green flame) and stands for fully integrated unconditional love through lovelight and lightlove into bliss-charged love.

Silver Flame

The accessing of this flame is akin to moving into 'the celestial body' whereby one reaches 'the level of the stars' within one's ascension process.

At this point, the Metatronic energy of the 'violet flame' is transformed/upgraded into the silver light.

Whilst Metatron is usually depicted as a 'male' angelic force, here at the celestial level 'he' becomes a feminine force and is the same frequency as the Mag-Da-Len.

Silver flame activates codes for antimatter memories, astral projection and subconscious/superconscious processing. The silver flame is the full manifestation of the divine feminine and is represented by the queen of the night, Sophia.

Once the silver flame is activated, all other flames merge as one and the building of the rainbow flame begins. The silver flame (as a merge point) holds within it the colour codes for all the other flames.

Once we get to the initiations of the higher flames, it is not so easy to analyse their meanings or that which they stand for. The silver flame burns brightly for 'Eartha', the seventh dimensional counterpart to Earth, Terra and Gaia.

At this merge point, one may see all flames as one as the seventh dimension is pure unification of polarised fields.

We may also present the white flame, golden flame, and magenta flame at this level, all intertwined with the silver flame. The energies of Source (Kristos/Kryst) are represented here and this flame appears as a shimmering rainbow of pale colours with the overall appearance of a pearl or an opal catching the light as it moves. The golden flame represents the solar body 'level of the sun' and the merging of the magenta and white flames into the rainbow flame represent the galactic level (Central Sun) stargate system and the return to Source (also represented as platinum ray or diamond light).

We therefore show this frequency to our conduit for her decoding. As we have said, this level of the flame becomes a unification and part of that which we call 'the eternal flame'.

The 'flame' is the fabric of consciousness and creativity itself and it is another symbolic presentation that has been hijacked by service-to-self groups. Such groups have presented the flame as 'everlasting fire' or 'the fires of hell' and have withheld the positively polarised divinity aspect of the dragon's breath that is the eternal flame of love.

It is difficult to distinguish the actual activation at this point in a compartmentalised sense as this unified field matrix will initiate each ascending individualised structure in a unique way.

We can therefore refer to the silver flame as the 'gateway into the rainbow flame'. This is the fullest activation of the Mer-Ka-Bah within an

163

individualised ascension process on the return to Source.

This is your 'rainbow body of light' and it still has a physical structure, of sorts, at this level. It is pure light but in its physical form, the rainbow body of light is the substance known as plasma.

How do you activate the flames?

These will activate naturally within the ascending starseed as they are representations of the activation of the DNA twelve strand (into 144 strand) template. However, one can 'communicate' or 'influence' or 'direct' the DNA configuration by visualising the flames.

In meditation or in a relaxed waking state, one would simply visualise the flame burning in front of you. You just step into it, or you can visualise the flame beginning at the solar plexus, reaching the heart and then encompassing the body. Just visualising the flames around you or next to you might be enough for some very sensitive souls, as flames are powerful gateways to Kundalini awakening and can make one feel quite hot and trigger the heat activations. These are positive for one's activation but everything is to be taken at your own pace.

Why flames instead of rays?

One can use rays also. Flames create momentum and heat and mirror the plasma fields of reality. They are 'moving' in the configuration of the plasma wave (true flame) when visualised by the incarnated starseed. Rays are living light and flames are plasma light with charged momentum. Both are most in alignment as activation tools within your stargate ascension journey.

27: The Rising of the New Atlantis
and the Thirteenth Crystal Skull

We respond now to your question of how Atlantis is connected to your current ascension on Earth.

We have introduced you to Aurora, the starseed collective grid of light which is a telepathic union. That which takes on an individualised frequency, intelligence and life force and presents as the 'daughter of the flame' divine goddess, child of the Krysta/Kristos, Sophia/Kryst alliance. The twin flame creation and the central point of the vesica piscis formation.

Aurora, as a grid, encompasses the linear time frame across 3D Earth yet holds the 5D Gaia frequency due to the fact that the awakened starseeds are 'thinking' within fifth dimensional consciousness. They are also 'feeling' through the higher heart (emerald ray/green flame activation).

Aurora's grid is represented in same time/linear links across all the starseeds within the same space and time as they are all incarnated within the same timeline and the same time frame (looking from the perspective of several billion souls upon one Earth planetary body).

We can refer to this linear grid as 'Aurora' when presenting this collective consciousness as one individualised intelligence/awareness/consciousness.

Atlantis was a time period within your Earth's history, not a place. Atlantis encompassed the whole of your planet at that time. However there are certain sections of Earth that embodied the frequency of Atlantis with more mass and intensity so these places can be said to *be* Atlantis. One of these places embodying high Atlantean frequency is the island you call 'Crete'. Yet there are other places also holding high Atlantean frequency, many of them islands, some still geographically in place and other islands that have moved location and become part of other land masses.

Memories (and therefore keycodes) are held in crystal structure (rock) and can be accessed by physically visiting these islands that hold high Atlantean frequency such as Crete.

However, there are other crystal structures holding Atlantean keycodes and one does not have to travel to access them.

Some of the Atlanteans were most knowledgeable regarding the ascension process. They were aware of keycodes, crystalline technology and DNA structure. They were indeed 'most advanced' and held the fully activated twelve strand matrix within their DNA.

We would refer to these highly advanced Atlanteans as the 'Atlantean priests'. They were not priests in a religious sense but in the sense that they were masters in their field. This included knowledge of incarnation, birth/death cycles, ascension and immortality.

Within these Atlantean priests, there were factions of service-to-others positively polarised individuals and service-to-self negatively polarised individuals, much like you have in your 'today' reality.

The negative priesthood, holding distorted and incomplete codes within the twelve strand matrix (they had lost the emerald code and therefore the heart-centred aspect was closed), had moved into a very high intensity of divinity and focus through a twelve stranded formation without activating the heart (emerald code). This gave them specialism within third eye awakening (indigo ray) and power centre (orange ray). Yet there was great distortion within this pattern.

They created a specific DNA code that has been passed down to their ancestors joining with Anunnaki, Orion and similar bloodlines to create the 'Illuminati' families that you have incarnated within your today reality.

We present this 'story' within a very basic format, presenting that which is most relevant to your current ascension process.

The positively polarised priesthood (connected to what is known as the 'Grail line' - these are individuals holding Christ consciousness awareness and memory, holders of the 'badge of the Kryst' and all standing as 'keepers of the flame') were aware of the plans for power through the distorted DNA code of highly focused indigo and orange rays and the deactivation of the emerald code. They wanted to preserve their memories so they could 'pick them up again' at some point in the future and continue their work as sacred gridmasters, dreamweavers, crystal generator operators and keepers of the dragon codes and the flame.

They knew that in order for the negatively polarised priesthood to move into the 'god complex' formation of deactivated emerald code, they would create a memory loss or DNA code loss within the general populace of Atlantis.

The particular DNA code loss that the positively polarised Atlantean priests knew was 'being developed' (they knew this due to their psychic abilities and the following of the sacred Law of One) would create a 'time loop' whereby newly incarnated souls would not be able to move through ascension and hold 'the seal of immortality'. Instead they would move into the cycle of death and rebirth (reincarnation).

Now on the one hand, reincarnation is a choice that is made through free will. On the other hand, it is a distortion of the natural organic human structure which holds the codes for ascension into immortality, not reincarnation.

Holding the opposing perspectives of both these truths will take you into bilocation of thought, which is the key into multidimensional consciousness.

You can hold both of these truths:

1) Reincarnation is a choice, made through free will.

2) Reincarnation is a distortion of the natural organic human structure and is part of a 'trapping system' made against free will.

If you can embrace, understand and process both these perspectives and hold them within your paradigm (rather than either/or) then you hold the seed point for multidimensionality, ascension and DNA reactivation and reconstruction through this bilocational concept.

So, the positively polarised priesthood of Atlantis knew that their future descendants and/or future potential incarnations would lose their memories of how to ascend and be immortal.

So the priesthood found a way to 'store' and 'hide' all the memories that they knew, once retrieved, would reactivate the DNA structure and reconstruct the original crystalline matrix.

Many of the priesthood agreed to remain within incarnation despite the loss of memory codes, in the knowing that they would someday retrieve them and 'reconstruct' Atlantis.

The priesthood understood that through the safe storage of the DNA memory codes, they would be able to 'time travel'.

This is where the divine feminine goddess Aurora comes in.

You see, the Atlantean priesthood were 'experts' in the field of crystal technology. They were, after all, the crystal generator operators and the keepers of the flame.

They chose to 'hide' and 'store' the DNA memory codes within crystal structure. Crystals are similar to your computer technologies and there are created crystals and natural organic crystal structure.

It was natural organic crystal structure that was the chosen hiding place and storage facility for these DNA memory codes.

Layers upon layers upon layers of metaphoric coding were placed over the real and true crystal storage facility. These 'secrets' have been held within your mystery schools, handed down only to those carrying the Atlantean codes, standing as 'keepers of the flame'.

Crystal skulls were created that would hold much information, sculptured as a 'metaphor formed in matter' so that those who were keepers of the flame would decode the mysteries of the crystal skulls.

Then the Atlantean priests began a journey of reincarnation, forgetting who they were. They lost the DNA structure for the twelve strand crystalline formation, knowing they would return around the time period known as the 'end of the Mayan calender'. This was calculated as your year of 2012, namely around the winter solstice.

The positively polarised Atlantean priesthood made sure that they would be on a trajectory for incarnation around that time period, 2012.

These Atlantean priests are now incarnated and living lives throughout the world, upon your 3D Earth at the time of this transmission. Along with many other souls, from all corners of the galaxy, they are the keepers of the flame. They are keepers of the 'rainbow flame' and the 'crystal' flame. They are the individuals you know as wanderers, lightwarriors, rainbow children, children of the sun, children of the new Earth, children of Gaia and starseeds. They are known as starseeds in your 'today' reality.

Of course, this is you, dear reader. You are one of the keepers of the flame and you have come to the information within this transmission through the intentional synchronicity convergence programme that we call 'Aurora'.

You know now the mystery of the crystal skulls. The skull, a codex formed in matter as metaphor for the true hiding place for the crystal codes.

For many aeons on your planet, it has been important for this information to be kept closely guarded in order to preserve the Atlantean crystal codes. Now, with the rising of the new Atlantis, the codes are activated. The crystal structure is the silicon molecular base formula for the crystalline matrix. The crystal codes were placed within the 'hidden matrix' held within the very blood and bone of the starseeds themselves. The true crystal skulls.

Twelve actual Atlantean crystal skulls were placed throughout the world. The codes were hidden within them, to be unlocked only when the thirteenth crystal skull was found. Thirteen (the hidden number) held the hidden code. The thirteenth crystal skull is you, dear starseed, you who are reading or listening to this transmission now.

This information could not be directly released until the activation of the crystal code had reached critical mass within the reincarnated Atlantean priesthood that are your starseeds in your today reality, now moment.

This time has come and you will find this information all around you, when you step into the telepathic union, starseed collective consciousness grid of light that is Aurora.

You see, Aurora is a 'crystal code' herself. Yes, this means the collective awakening of the starseeds is, in itself, a keycode and trigger for awakening!

Aurora, as a telepathic grid, does not confine herself to the limits of time and space, she transcends time and space.

Through Aurora, the Atlantean priesthood knew they would be able to 'communicate' with their future selves. For the preservation of the Atlantean codex within the thirteenth crystal skull (that is the starseeds) contained the codes for Matrix (Mer-Ka-Bah) Transportation which is the ability to traverse the time matrix. In other words, 'time travel'.

28: The Antimatter Time Matrix

When working with the 'sacred wheel', the matrix grid formation that is the 'true you' as 'all that is you' (that is, in essence, a toroidal field around you as the externalised DNA structure as a resonance/energy body/light body), one would be working with the 'horizontal axis' (horizontal rainbow bridge pathway) that stretches out before you (future) and behind you (past).

The future/past arm of the cross takes you back 'into the past' to the 'former self' or 'former incarnation' that was the Atlantean priest or crystal generator operator that was you.

In your visualisation, one would stand (literally, within Tadasana mountain pose as yoga asana or similar stance) or within your 'mind's eye' in meditation.

One would then 'travel' back along the backwards facing arm of the cross that stretches out behind you.

This is simply a visualisation tool that allows you to access the database that is your personalised Akashic record field (the matrix, stored information within your DNA) and is what we call a 'memory trigger exercise'.

As you trace the backward facing arm, you may feel a jolt (as if stopping at a point) or a visualisation may simply appear in your mind's eye (of a former self, a lifetime or other memory). There really is no 'right' or 'wrong' way to follow this exercise for it is personal and unique to you.

Once you access a memory, whatever that may be, then take note (either hold this in your memory or literally take note of what you have picked up by writing the experience down).

You are not 'in a trance' here or in 'deep meditation' (unless you choose to work this way) so you can stop to pick up pen and paper (or use recording or word processing technology) to make notes should you wish.

You can go as deeply into this visualisation as you please. Once you have accessed images/memory/metaphor then allow these to sit with you for a while.

Processing these images can be done intellectually and immediately through analysis and research, or one can allow further images to come up into your mindspace throughout the course of the following days (the daydream). Or one can work within dreamtime and hold the images that you picked up in your time matrix travels before you go to sleep, then record the imagery within dreamtime upon waking (this may take several attempts over several nights).

Now if you travelled backwards along the backward moving arm of the horizontal axis and you simply found 'nothing' (as in no jolt, no stopping, no visual), then bring yourself back to the pivot point (central core of the matrix sacred wheel). This would indicate that one is not existing within the paradigm of you having been an 'Atlantean priest' as a previous incarnation.

One can then move instead along the sideways arm of the cross, tracing that aspect either left or right (or both simultaneously) to see which 'memories' can be accessed within this tracing of the pathway. What you are doing here is searching through the database of 'alternate selves'.

Should you feel 'a jolt' or 'a nudge' towards stopping at any alternate version of yourself, you can then move along the backwards arm of the horizontal axis from the starting point of that particular alternate version of self. This would indicate that YOU do not have a previous incarnation as an Atlantean priest within your current timeline but an alternate version of yourself DOES.

If there are no jolts, nudges or visualisations along the horizontal axis from left to right, then return your focus to the pivot point.

You can then move into one of the diagonal axis points (moving upwards) either left or right (you are tracing through both maternal and paternal ancestry) and trace upwards through this aspect of the matrix, memory DNA code.

If you feel a jolt, nudge or other 'change in energy' here then you are looking at one (or more) of your ancestors having lived as an Atlantean priest.

In truth, all these 'directions' you move within are actually one and the same place (ancestral, alternate self, past incarnation), all being one and the same presentation in the true/higher reality.

Yet your human brain is an interface that decodes the code of reality into a third dimensional linear presentation for you to make sense of. So compartmentalising the different presentations within the time matrix assists the way in which the human brain works.

Now some of you will be 'masters' or 'adepts' within this work, tracing the matrix pathways back incredibly quickly (potentially instantaneously) and being presented with clear, meaningful imagery. You may have information downloaded to you through what you call clairaudience and hear language, music or other sound. Or you will emotionally or energetically feel frequency or work within clairvoyant visualisation or use all of these different ways of sensing simultaneously.

If you are a clairvoyant, psychic, medium, channel or already have a method of spiritual working or divination then this work will be fast and clear for you.

For others it may take several days or longer and you will move into the 'inner pilgrimage' as you walk the journey or the 'vision quest'. Again we say, there is no right or wrong way to do this work. You are simply accessing your cellular memory as is your divine right as a soul (indeed as an ascending soul).

If you feel you are 'stuck' or that there are 'blocks', we would suggest you move back to the emotional integration work presented within *Masters of the Matrix* as one needs to have cleared third dimensional trauma to a certain degree in order to travel the matrix.

However, traumas (presentations of) may come up here instead of the Atlantean priesthood bloodline you are looking for. Go with this. The matrix, as the true intelligent entity (collective consciousness, energetic database library computer system) that it is, will 'know' where you need to go and the matrix itself will assist you.

What you are doing here when you 'travel' this way is what we call 'Matrix Transportation'. You are actually activating your Mer-Ka-Bah and travelling within it.

You can go anywhere you wish with this work.

If you wish to access your 'higher self' then one would travel upwards along the vertical line. One would find their guides, extraterrestrials, ascended masters and all manner of 'beings' and 'entities'. One can simply 'go travelling' to see what one can find or one can focus on accessing a particular memory (such as the Atlantean priest).

A plethora of information is available to you as you travel this way and access your personal Akash (everything that has ever happened to you as an individual soul or that could ever happen).

The forward moving arm of the sacred cross along the horizontal line takes you 'into the future' (the trajectory that is the most probable timeline for you) or you can move along the sideways arm to an alternate self and trace the future point from there.

Should you wish to change or 'jump' timelines, then you would find the future timeline you wish to switch to your most probable future for manifestation and then move the pivot point into the particular alternate self that stands within the trajectory for that timeline. If you do this, prepare for major changes to potentially occur within your current reality. However, these changes can be 'undone' and you can 'go back'. As an activated starseed, you will already be standing at a very highly balanced point regarding your future trajectory as your activation will automatically have placed you there.

When you begin this work however, you become conscious and aware regarding the structure and the workings of your matrix. You can actually 'go anywhere'.

The next step within this exploration of movement and travel within the 'antimatter time matrix' is to access and pass through stargates. This is what we refer to as 'warp speed' or 'momentum' or 'going galactic'. When you consciously pass through the stargate system, you are utilising the part of your DNA that holds the formation of 'the infinite helix'.

29: Sovereignty Through the Holy Trinity

Do you need protections in place when working within the transportation of the matrix exercises?

The 'protections' are automatically given when following the work within our *Masters of the Matrix* transmission. Specifically we refer to emotional integration and the 'firewall' of immunity created within this work.

However, one can recite an incantation before moving into Matrix Transportation work. This is also a form of 'protection'.

We would feel that the word 'sovereignty' is more appropriate as utilising the word 'protection' can create the polarised match to protection, which is 'that which one must be protected from'. Therefore creating sovereignty is what you are looking for here.

We provide now, an incantation as a complementary adjunct to this work. However, the Matrix Mastery teachings in *Masters of the Matrix* are where we would direct you for immunity and sovereignty that 'clears your fields' for transportation. One will not be able to access momentum/ warp speed with unresolved traumas and emotional blockages within the matrix.

Incantation for Sovereignty

As I move into the traversing of my own personal hyperspace records, I call upon the goddess Akasha to accompany me.

Within the phire of her blessed womb and from the love of her activated heart, I ask that she intertwine my personal matrix code with the golden thread that represents my alchemical transformation into the sovereign space.

I give the utmost gratitude to her, blessed goddess Akasha, this day.

I call upon the goddess Aurora to bless me with her light. The telepathic union network of the starseed collective, I know, shall stand by my side, passing the strength of the unified field of awakened humanity to me as I lend my own strength to that field. I stand proud to be a member of the family of light that moves within the indigo revolution into the ascended evolution.

I give the utmost gratitude to her, blessed goddess Aurora this day.

I call upon the goddess Sophia to envelop me within the safety of her divine light. I know that with her by my side, I can do anything. For I stand within the highest of trust and truth.

My heart is open and I am strong as I humbly ask for the power of three, the sacred triangle, the Holy Trinity, through the divine feminine universal flow.

I give the utmost gratitude to her, blessed goddess Sophia, this day.

So let it be so. It is done. Namaste.

30: The Mystery Within the Matrix

The Atlantean activations embedded within the 'thirteenth crystal skull' (you, incarnated from galactic multiverse into the race of 'Adam and Eve' that we call 'starseeds') begin to 'come online' when the starseed collective, consciousness grid of light (divine princess Aurora) is connected with and merged with.

Aurora is the 'memory' of all that has happened, all that is happening now and all that shall or could ever happen. The memory is embedded within the activated crystalline/silicon structure of transformation within the blood and bone of the female DNA activation.

The 'memories' are passed through the 'female' line genetically (the ancestral codes through the diagonal axis coming down from the left diagonal line when standing at the pivot point within a two dimensional depiction of the matrix).

We speak here in metaphor as an activation of memory in itself, for you. The ancestral lines are one and the same place when the 'sacred wheel turns' (as in, you move your own matrix) yet within the 'human genome' (the race of Adam and Eve), it is 'Eve' that passes genetic memory through all her 'daughters'.

Hence the starseed collective consciousness grid of light manifesting as the divine princess Aurora.

This does not mean the incarnated male is inferior to the incarnated female. The divine feminine (Krysta/Sophia) is an absolute complement to the sacred masculine (Krystos/Kryst) and it is when they are fused or merged together as one that the transformation genetically from carbon to crystalline takes place.

The lovelight and lightlove into 'bliss-charged love' is the equation that begins the carbon to crystalline change.

When the divine feminine and the sacred masculine are separated (the twin flames), they complement one another. In the geometric presentation of creation, the sacred masculine is the vertical pillar of Light (vertical axis) and 'he' stands strong as the pillar or structure that supports the entire matrix (DNA blueprint for all life, temple or template).

If the vertical pillar of light is the sacred masculine (the Kryst) force of the matrix, then where is the divine feminine structure?

The divine feminine (Sophia) is the mystery. 'She' is the 'hidden aspect'. 'She' is the thirteen. 'She' is the code of the thirteenth crystal skull.

She is the 'hidden power' within the matrix for when we look at the matrix we see the structure, we see the vertical pillar as the first and foremost step into the construction of the matrix. We do not see the power or the force that comes in from the hidden realms.

The sacred masculine is the world of matter, that which we can see.

The divine feminine is the hidden mystery of antimatter, that which we cannot see.

We say 'we' for it is the we that is 'the all' that takes the journey of the manifested and the unmanifest. It is the unmanifest that is the mystery and 'she' (Sophia) is the zero point. She is pure creation. We as the White Winged Collective Consciousness of Nine take this same sacred journey or pilgrimage that you do.

Within the matrix construction we have shown you the vertical pillar of light, the horizontal rainbow bridge pathway that is the sacred cross and we have shown you the diagonal axis.

So too have we shown you where 'you' are within the axis, the point of rotation, the central point that is the pivot point (your solar plexus chakra moving up to the heart chakra).

We now show you a new aspect to the matrix construction that we did not reveal within our previous *Masters of the Matrix* and *Divine Architecture and the Starseed Template* transmissions.

We show you the divine feminine hidden power (the thirteen) that which is 'outside' the twelve. That which 'powers' the twelve. It is the thirteen (Sophia) that creates the power for the twelve (the Kryst). If your motor vehicle is the twelve then the ignition keys would be the thirteen. You cannot drive your vehicle without them.

The twelve (the structure) is the sacred masculine.

The thirteen (the power that creates light speed, warp speed momentum and the key to the carbon to silicon transformation) is the divine feminine.

You, in your earthly physical reality, have been given only one half of the picture. Throughout your teachings within the spiritual arena, there is much that has been given to you to lead you to the twelve so you may create your structures. Yet without the thirteen, the structures cannot be powered. They cannot be opened and they cannot ascend through the spiral of time and become 'stargate technology'.

The truth of your reality, your history, your science and your spirituality cannot be discovered until you have found the thirteen. The divine feminine, Sophia.

We show you now, the structure of the twelve and the hidden thirteen.

31: The Twelve Tribes of Israel

We extend the construction of your matrix field so we may trigger the awareness within you of the carbon to silicon metamorphosis of stargate ascension.

As the memories return the construction moves from double helix, triple helix, beyond the triple helix into the infinite helix. The two strand becomes the template for the twelve strand as etheric memory cords merge, intertwine and magickally reconstruct into the organic human template of crystalline matrix that is Source.

The triggers are in the decoding of the ancient metaphors, myths and stories.

We present to you now the 'twelve tribes of Israel' which shall lead you to the codex needed for the activation of the '144,000 warriors of light'.

Within the vertical pillar of light, vertical axis of the matrix, one has twelve discs (matrices) moving along the upwards moving arm of the vertical pillar above the pivot point. This is 'one tribe' of Israel (the matrix, known also as Abraham, son of God). Remember we are constructing and powering-up the Mer-Ka-Bah here, your sacred vehicle of light.

Within the downwards moving arm of the vertical pillar (below the pivot point) are another twelve discs (matrices) which is the second tribe of Israel.

This gives you twenty-four discs running along the vertical pillar of light. Each of these discs are matrices. They are identical to your matrix. Each of these matrices contain within them the same structure, vertical pillar of light, horizontal rainbow bridge pathway of the sacred cross and the vertical axis. They each hold the same 'twelve tribes of Israel' within their matrix and within each of those matrices is another matrix. This is a fractalised pattern that makes up 'all that is you' and all structures of DNA hold this infinite, fractalised, holographic formation.

The horizontal axis (rainbow bridge pathway) moving to the left has twelve matrices as does the arm of the cross that moves to the right. These are the third and fourth tribes of Israel.

The forward moving arm of the cross also has twelve matrices as does the backward moving arm of the cross. These are the fifth and sixth tribes of Israel.

The vertical axis moving from the pivot point upwards and to the left has twelve matrices as does the vertical axis moving from the pivot point upwards to the right. These are the seventh and eighth tribes of Israel.

The vertical axis moving from the pivot point downwards and to the left has twelve matrices as does the vertical axis moving downwards from the pivot point to the right. These are ninth and tenth tribes of Israel.

The pivot point is the central point and the zero point. One 'side' of the pivot point (when viewing the matrix as a two dimensional wheel) is a 'black hole' and the other 'side' of the pivot point is a 'white hole'. These are simply words to explain 'two sides of the same coin' that create an equal and opposite reaction to one another. A black hole's 'reverse side' is a white hole and together they create a 'passageway in time' known to you as a bridge, gateway, wormhole or stargate. These two sides of the pivot point together are the eleventh and twelfth tribes of Israel.

Each 'tribe' is an arm (or spoke) within that sacred wheel with the eleventh and twelfth tribes making the pivot point. Israel (Abraham) is the matrix (Mer-Ka-Bah).

Where does the number thirteen come in here?

Well, we could perhaps refer to the thirteenth 'tribe' as the 'thirteenth tribe of Israel' or indeed 'lost tribe of Israel', both would fit as a metaphor to the energetic here. Indeed ten of the tribes are the lost tribes of Israel (the ten DNA strands that activate outside the two strands that make up the Adam/Eve 3D blueprint).

However, regarding the thirteenth tribe, that which is in most alignment to the truth of reality we would express as 'the hidden tribe of Israel.'

Indeed. One 'tribe' has been hidden. Hidden in plain sight.

32: The Thirteenth Tribe

So we have shown you the twelve tribes of Israel. Remembering that 'Israel' is the Mer-Ka-Bah, matrix, original strand formation for DNA.

We have ten (male) directions:

1) Up

2) Down

3) Forward

4) Backward

5) Diagonal Up Left

6) Diagonal Up Right

7) Diagonal Down Left

8) Diagonal Down Right

9) Left

10) Right

... and two circular spaces (one male, one female):

1) Pivot point facing into matter (black hole, male)

2) Pivot point facing into antimatter (white hole, female)

So the 'female' aspect of the matrix is the antimatter white hole and the twelfth tribe of Israel?

Yes, but there is more to the feminine aspect of the matrix than the white hole/stargate/pivot point.

You see, if you look at the entire matrix as a two dimensional wheel structure, you can draw a perfect circle around the outside of the structure to create the wheel.

The boundary of the circle itself is that which is 'hidden in plain sight'. The circle boundary is the 'thirteenth tribe of Israel'.

The reason why the boundary is 'hidden in plain sight' is because each arm of the sacred cross, diagonal axis and pivot point is an infinite line or space.

Remember when we said (in our *Divine Architecture and the Starseed Template* transmission) that the vertical pillar of light stretches so far upwards that it eventually meets with the bottom of the pillar of light? The horizontal axis stretches so far to the left that it eventually joins with the right and so on? The diagonal lines meet each other also?

These are infinite lines, therefore how can there be a boundary?

We are looking here at a time matrix. Although time is infinite, in truth there are infinite infinities. This is the structure of time. Time is fractal and holographic therefore there are infinite infinities.

In order to distinguish one 'section of infinity' from another 'section of infinity', there must be a boundary.

This is the circle that surrounds the matrix. The circle is the 'boundary' to infinity and the matrix (Mer-Ka-Bah/DNA structure) is one infinity.

Now this is where your multilocational thought process comes in.

We have shown you bilocation (two simultaneous thoughts) and trilocation (three simultaneous thoughts). Now we show you multilocation (multiple simultaneous thoughts).

Now full multilocation, as we have said, is beyond the scope of this transmission in its entirety. However, the seeds for mutilocational thought are planted here within this transmission.

Why?

The answer to that is due to where you are going in your collective ascension process as 'Aurora' (starseed collective consciousness grid of light). As you head into your 'light bodies', you each become one infinity that is the pure manifestation of Aurora (Aurora meaning 'light'). In order to become light/Aurora you will move into multilocationality, which is simply multidimensionality. It is the same thing.

Time = Multidimensionality (multiple dimensions simultaneously)

Space = Multilocationality (multiple locations simultaneously)

You can switch these around so that time equals multiple locations in time and that space equals multiple dimensions of space.

This is the pivot point of your matrix (the part that turns or spins the wheel) with the black hole and the white hole together creating spacetime (matter/black hole) and timespace (antimatter/white hole). These spacetime/timespace portals together create a stargate. Yes, your matrix is a stargate which means, dear ascending starseed, that you are a stargate!

As a starseed, you are a seed into that which can be 'grown' (or activated) and that which is activated is the stargate.

Now, as we have said, the boundary of the circle creates one infinity. Each infinity has a stargate at the pivot point (gateway between matter and antimatter).

The boundary itself (the boundary of the circle) is also a 'line' yet this one meets itself in obvious formation as it is a circle. Because the circle is the boundary of one infinity (matrix), we call this boundary an 'event horizon'.

So now, within this transmission, you have the full matrix as a two dimensional wheel:

* 1st and 2nd tribes - vertical axis (pillar of light)

* 3rd and 4th tribes - horizontal axis (rainbow bridge pathway, forward and backward)

* 5th and 6th tribes - horizontal axis (rainbow bridge pathway, left and right)

* 7th and 8th tribes - diagonal axis (upwards left and right)

* 9th and 10th tribes - diagonal axis (downwards left and right)

* 11th and 12th tribes - pivot point (black hole spacetime and white hole timespace)

* 13th tribe - the event horizon (circle boundary and the border to an infinity)

Understand this structure and know that you activate the very matching pattern within the DNA field that is 'all that is you'.

Process the knowing of this structure we call 'the matrix' at your own time, in your own space.

Our conduit Magenta Pixie learns this information as she transcribes it, it is new to her as it may be to you. Yet remember, each and every one of you are adepts in this sacred mystery of the thirteenth tribe of Israel, thirteenth crystal skull and the power of that which is hidden. We may call this 'occult knowledge' (occult meaning 'hidden') yet in truth this is only occult knowledge as you process this through the filter of the third dimensional interface that is the human brain.

In truth, the 'thirteen' is wisdom. Wisdom of the Goddess, for the event horizon as the curved line, hidden in plain sight is the female aspect of the matrix. The event horizon is the female, the divine feminine Sophia known also as Krysta, Mary or Kali and ultimately the Mag-Da-Len (activation of the Mer-Ka-Bah).

The antimatter timespace white hole (the twelfth tribe of Israel), also 'hidden' behind her twin brother, is also curved as the hidden circle/sacred circle and the divine golden equation. She is the 'daughter of the flame' Aurora, known also as 'Sarah' and ultimately the Mag-Da-Len (activation of the Mer-Ka-Bah).

When one looks at the matrix in this geometric and compartmentalised fashion, one is decoding a unified field into sections in order for the third dimensional interface to make sense of the structure linearly. So it can then be processed by the third dimensional incarnated soul existing in physicality.

You see, when you leave the physical body through the death process, you know and understand this structure intimately for you *are* this structure. Yet without the DNA strand formation in place to create light speed/warp speed momentum (convergence of quantum charge), one cannot enter one's own stargate and ascend into evolutionary consciousness as is your divine right for one does not have the coordinates. Only 'ascension' gives you the coordinates to navigate the wormhole/stargate system and move into evolutionary consciousness.

Your 'knowing' of the antimatter cosmology does not come online fully, for the soul aspect mirrors only the memory mapping of the previous incarnation (unless you are what we call a 'free soul', known also as an 'activated angelic evolved adept' or 'ascended master').

Once you activate the coordinates (and, as we have said, you only need to activate the fifth strand of the DNA matrix field to access Gaia as the evolutionary counterpart within consciousness to Earth), you can 'choose' where you go when you pass through your own stargate.

So how do you activate the coordinates for stargate ascension? Simply through memory. This is the key, cellular memory (which in truth is knowing). It is creating a multidimensional paradigm or being able to think within multilocational consciousness.

When it comes to bilocational, trilocational or multilocational consciousness, you do not literally have to be thinking of infinite concepts simultaneously. What you do is access infinite concepts simultaneously and then decode them through the third dimensional interface that is the human brain. This happens in a linear and compartmentalised fashion. This is what we are doing here with this transmission, *The Infinite Helix*. We are planting seeds for multilocational consciousness and thus stargate ascension.

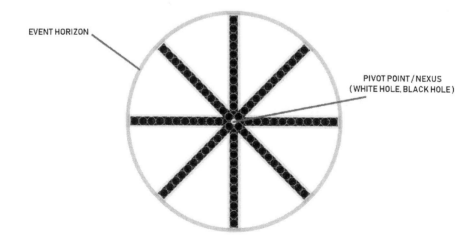

Above: A basic two-dimensional depiction of the 144 matrices within one infinity matrix. In truth, they do not lie in straight lines but sit nested within one another as a fractal spiral.

33: Children of the New Dawn

We have introduced you to Aurora and also to the section of infinity (one infinity) that is your matrix.

Aurora (the manifestation of the starseed collective consciousness grid of light) literally translates to 'light' or to the word 'dawn'.

The dawn is now changing upon your planet as you enter a 'new dawn' and that new dawn is the critical mass of activated starseeds that together create an intelligent and loving, extraterrestrial or ultradimensional entity known as the 'divine royal princess Aurora'.

The 'light' that is created that makes up this 'new dawn' is the light of your collective awareness, knowledge, wisdom, truth, integrity, compassion, bliss and unconditional love. Together, these make up the 'activated matrix'.

Even though the starseeds as a collective within third dimensional Earth are the minority when it comes to actual physically incarnated beings, they are absolutely the majority when it comes to Aurora and the new dawn.

You see, each matrix (one infinity) as we have said holds within it twelve tribes of Israel (with the thirteenth tribe being the power to the twelve).

We spoke earlier of sacred ceremony and ritual. Whenever a ritual takes place to create an actual manifested change or result within the physical dimension, one needs the power of twelve and the hidden thirteen to activate the twelve. The hidden thirteen would be 'female'.

So with twelve individuals and one high priestess, or twelve objects and one 'power object' (or such), the ritual can take many forms. The ritual utilising twelve and the power of the occult (hidden thirteen) is simply a 'copy' or 'tribute' to the true geometric structure of creation (Source/matrix/Mer-Ka-Bah/blueprint/template).

The sacred temple is also a copy or tribute to the matrix (temple meaning 'template'), hence the reason why many rituals or sacred ceremonies take place within temples or temple-like structures. The ancient peoples of your planet knew this was the way to power-up structure and create interdimensional portals (stargates).

You, dear starseeds, as we have said, are stargates. Each time you activate your matrix with the power of the hidden thirteen (Mag-Da-Len divine feminine frequency in all its forms), you power-up your entire matrix structure which is *one* infinity. When several starseeds do this together, as is the case with your ascension journey at the time of this transmission, you truly become the 'children of the new dawn' and the pure embodiment of the royal princess or goddess (Aurora).

Your matrix as *one* infinity is actually, in truth, infinite infinities mirroring Source which is infinite infinities.

As we have said, there is only *one* infinity which is Source and every other infinity IS Source. In the true reality, there is but one time and one space.

Yet when one looks at the way creation evolves, this occurs through 'cosmic mitosis'. This is the continued splitting of the particle, atom, cell or structure in order for division to create compartmentalisation, separation and thus individualisation as the equal and opposite reaction to the reaction and the ultimate paradox.

Therefore your matrix is actually infinite matrices.

As we have said, there are twelve matrices within each extending straight line that make up the matrix with the eleventh and twelfth set of twelve matrices at the pivot point.

12 x 12 = 144. This is the 'sacred number' for all structured life within a DNA template.

This is your 144,000 warriors of light (144 strands within quantum DNA) and it is the power of the thirteenth strand that triggers the quantum activation.

Let us explain more about the thirteen. We do not count the thirteenth tribe as part of the twelve tribes of Israel that equal the 144.000 warriors of light.

The thirteen actually moves back to zero. The eleventh and twelfth tribes of Israel that are the black hole and white hole of the pivot point are actually situated within zero point. This is the reason why many spiritual teachings will teach the ten structures of reality rather than the true twelve.

There are ten sephirot discs within the Tree of Life depiction within your

Qabbalistic teachings. One can indeed discover much truth within this model for you are still indeed working with all the male structures of the matrix that can be seen within the realms of matter. The workings within this path would take you into a patriarchal teaching as each sephirot disc is represented by the sacred masculine support pillars. This teaching is a potentially positive teaching indeed, however it is a distortion (or rather a reduction) from the true presentation.

The true Qabbalistic teaching would present a Tree of Life depiction with twelve sephirot discs. Once you have the true structure in place, you bring the divine feminine energetic into the structure which would be depicted as being at 'the top of the tree' (the central point of the matrix and the event horizon).

The most aligned construct with Qabbalistic teachings, however, would be the full thirteen sephirot disc presentation which provides the complete picture of creation. This is the teaching of your ancient mystery schools who knew and understood the importance of the divine feminine code.

The Qabbalistic path is seen as a male path and presented as such, and so too it is within the ten sephirot model. Even within the twelve sephirot model, one could see this as a male path of enlightenment.

The true mystery and the true secret is the fact that the Qabbalistic teaching holding absolute truth is in fact a female path. It is the path of the Goddess.

We do not expect many of you who discover this transmission that is *The Infinite Helix* to be too familiar with the complex and intensive study that is the Qabbalah. Our conduit Magenta Pixie knows very little of this path, it is indeed a 'mystery' to her and we are only able to impart information to you based on the terminology she knows regarding this.

What we can say to you is this: If you wish to go deeper into the true structure of the mysteries of reality and your own personal enlightenment and ascension, then there are many modes of study you can embark upon.

On your planet thus far, the truest model of reality in a spiritual sense would be the Qabbalistic path. Yet this would be the twelve sephirot or preferably the thirteen sephirot path. Within your scientific studies there is much within the field of quantum universes, string theory and sacred geometry that would also lead you to truth.

There are many who present the unified field. In a spiritual sense, the teaching of the unified field is known as the 'Law of One' which is the truth of all creation.

Our conduit, in her path of discovery, enlightenment and personal ascension, has connected with us, the White Winged Collective Consciousness of Nine.

We are an individualised structure called upon to 'make known the unknown', 'reveal the truth', 'lift the veil', 'decode the metaphor' and ultimately bring the mystery from the shadows into the light.

This does not take away the magick from the mystery for the divine feminine power will always be mystery. It is the energy of mystery as 'a mysterious force' rather than 'knowledge hidden from you that you cannot access or that you are not worthy enough to receive'.

You see, the mystery is pure creation. The coupled energies of feminine/masculine are BOTH needed in order to access the mystery of creation.

How does one create? There are many ways to do this, one way is to access the network of stargate systems that we call the 'Emerald City of Krysta'. In order to do this, one must begin to process the information through memory pathways of knowing that is the calling for the 144,000 warriors of light.

This does not mean there are only 144,000 individuals that are called to the mystery that is creation.

This means that those who activate the twelve strand DNA structure through the understanding of the matrix Mer-Ka-Bah will, in turn, 'go galactic' and activate the quantum DNA strand formation that leads to the full 144 DNA strands.

This is full enlightenment and fully realised ascension.

It is a journey, yet the minute you step beyond the double helix back into the infinite helix construction that is the 144 pathway, then you *are on that path.* You are the embodiment of the divine princess Aurora and you are a child of the new dawn.

34: Ark of the Covenant Technology

and How to Ride the Dragon

Earlier within this transmission that is *The Infinite Helix*, we spoke of Ark of the Covenant technology and the dragon's breath.

These are major activations into the stargate system that is the Emerald City and the mysteries of stargate ascension.

The twelve tribes of Israel form together a cross (the sacred cross/the matrix) and at the centre of the cross they create, lies the Ark of the Covenant.

This is depicted as a golden box containing treasures that are said to possess otherworldly abilities and magick. Within this golden box are the sacred objects: the rod (or staff), a jar of manna (or essence) and tablets (or scrolls) containing laws or commandments.

When we speak of the pivot point at the central core of the matrix (within the human structure, this is the solar plexus chakra and the heart chakra combined), what we speak of is one's own personal stargate.

In order to 'pass through the stargate', one needs to do what we call 'collapse the wave'.

The stargate is a 'wave structure' when it comes to the physics that is creation. It is also a particle yet the observation of the pivot point/stargate for what it actually is, is a wave.

It is said, "it is easier for a camel to pass through the eye of a needle than for a rich man to enter the kingdom of God."

What you are doing here when you 'collapse the wave' is 'passing through the eye of the needle'.

You, as an activated conscious starseed, are not a 'rich man'. You have moved away from earthly materialism into spiritual discipline and the search for divine wisdom. Therefore you can 'enter the kingdom of heaven' (Emerald City of Krysta) by doing something that is more difficult than a camel passing through the eye of a needle (which is doing the seemingly impossible).

You *can* do the impossible when you have 'Ark of the Covenant technology'.

The Ark of the Covenant is situated in the centre of the sacred cross of the twelve tribes of Israel (the pivot point, also the zero point).

The event horizon, as the dimensional boundary or the boundary line for an infinity, is also the zero point.

The event horizon and the pivot point are the exact same place.

Therefore when you 'pass through the eye of the needle' (go through the stargate), you simultaneously 'cross the event horizon'.

You move 'outside' of one infinity and 'travel' through the vast networks of infinite infinities that is the stargate system we call the 'Emerald City of Krysta'.

You need to activate the Ark of the Covenant to be able to 'open' the stargate and pass through it.

The Ark of the Covenant is situated within the matrix at the pivot point (which is also the event horizon).

Although we depict a two dimensional circle as the 'sacred wheel' with spokes within, the wheel that can turn, this is in fact a complex spiral system of energetic and mathematical interaction.

This can be depicted as interlocking geometries or as a toroidal field or as a Flower of Life formation. They are all one and the same, they are all the matrix. An externalised presentation of your DNA structure.

The Arc of the Covenant contains three items:

1) The staff or rod.

2) The jar of manna.

3) The tablets containing the Ten Commandments.

These represent keys needed to activate the Mer-Ka-Bah and pass through the stargate with the correct coordinates to 'go galactic' and move through the process of full ascension.

The staff or rod

This is a code. This is the vertical ascension path and would be representative of the 'vertical pillar of light' or 'vertical axis'. You already have the understanding and processing of the vertical axis through your work within our previous *Masters of the Matrix* and *Divine Architecture and the Starseed Template* transmissions.

Working with the vertical pillar would allow you to undergo 'vertical ascension' which is directly upwards. Remember there are twelve other infinity matrices along this particular pathway before you reach the event horizon (which is also the pivot point).

You do not need to fully understand this structure. This is a map, the visualisation of which will give you coordinates which are memory pathways and frequency activations within the DNA. This material does not have to be fully comprehended at the level of full processing. Each attempt to process this information leads to multilocational thought and thus expansion which activates your DNA.

Metaphor is a very accurate and high level method of this same activation, hence our communications regarding the dragons of Krysta and the dragon's breath. Metaphor, through the language of light, speaks directly to the DNA and bypasses processing.

So if you are unable to follow the Matrix Architecture and Matrix Transportation material, do not be concerned about this. The dragon's breath activations will provide the triggers and the keys you need for stargate ascension. Remember, you have the ability to do this on your own. We provide a guidebook or 'map', if you will, but you are the one that shall 'fly the Mer-Ka-Bah ship'.

Through vertical ascension, you can choose any of the twelve matrices along any of the directional aspects to the matrix and pass through any of the pivot point stargates. Each disc (matrix) represents a different timeline, experience, thought, event, aspect or harmonic that makes up the intricate 'all that is you' that you are.

You can also choose to go 'down' the vertical axis. Each disc or matrix along the downward moving axis will align with subconscious aspects (known to you as 'shadow work'). You can also ascend through this pathway, it is simply a different path. Each disc or matrix is a 'new adventure' if you will, each leading to a new discovery about self (as you in physicality and as you in spirit). Full ascension (multilocational consciousness/fully realised multidimensionality) is the pulling of all the matrices, through all the directional arms, into the pivot point and taking them all with you in one moment.

When you do this, you create a 'long thread' of activated DNA that is actually a long spiral. The spiral of DNA passes code through its central point allowing full memory to travel with you wherever you go, including into your next incarnation and/or ascended aspect.

We all do this as souls (matrices), including 'us' the White Winged Collective Consciousness of Nine.

It is quite a ride, to pass through the stargate with all your full multidimensionality, as the sacred spiral, with each and every infinite matrix following along behind you. It is quite a ride and all we can say to you of this ride is that it is pure and utter bliss felt within every aspect of your being.

Your entire bodymindspirit system simply buzzes with bliss.

Yet you must be ready. For if you do not take this 'slow and steady' and practise for this with reverence, devotion and discipline then you can 'burn out'. This could mean that you may not gather the momentum needed for the spiral that is your soul (matrix) to ride through the stargate of bliss and ascend.

Having said that, if you are reading/listening to this material then you are part of the 'infinite helix' network and are this part of Aurora.

He who is kissed by Aurora shall follow her to the 'ends of the Earth' (pass through the stargate as the spiral).

Another metaphor and language of light trigger is the 'jewelled snake' or 'rainbow serpent'. This is yet another presentation that has been 'hijacked' upon your planet. If you feel revulsion, horror, disgust or fear at the image of the snake or serpent then you bury the knowledge of full stargate ascension deep into the recesses of the subconscious where you cannot access them.

The serpent IS the spiral. It is all the multidimensional matrices that make up you as infinite infinity pulling together and passing through the stargate, crossing the event horizon as you access the Emerald City of

Krysta and go through conscious ascension. The snake and the serpent is the reminder of the journey you take.

If you feel fear at the presentation of the serpent then go down the vertical pillar into the dark forest at the point we call 'the Earth's core' or the 'diamond core' which is the twelfth matrix at the bottom of the vertical pillar next to the event horizon boundary. You can go in there and 'find the serpent' and you will find him/her most friendly and accommodating. Do not allow the hijacking of the serpent to send you into fear so you bury your memories further. The serpent is, in fact, the dragon. The breath of the dragon is another code for ascension. For you, dear starseed, are the ultimate 'dragonrider'. You ride the dragon through the pivot point stargate with all the other infinite matrices (that are your other selves that make up 'all that is you') following you. That is the riding of the dragon. To ascend, you must become the dragonrider.

Indeed there are negative presentations associated with serpent, reptilian, snake and dragon. Follow the teachings regarding immunity within the transmission that is *Masters of the Matrix* and you will be able to distinguish benevolent dragons and snakes from malevolent ones. Even those that may appear to be malevolent are your teachers! Love and bliss will carry you through this journey and true love and true bliss lead to true trust which is the ultimate in discernment.

Therefore do not reject the sacred snake or the majestic dragon, for they shall show you how to ride the stargate system into full ascension.

The rod or staff is a code, a memory trigger or reminder for the vertical pillar and thus vertical ascension.

We move now to the jar of manna.

35: Ambrosia, Golden Merkabah

and the Sacred Promise

The 'jar of manna' depicted within a 'golden chalice' is that which is also known as the 'Holy Grail'.

The golden chalice itself represents the womb of creation and therefore the divine feminine principal.

The rod or staff as the masculine principal and vertical ascension (along with horizontal and diagonal directional focus) merges with the golden chalice/Holy Grail as the feminine principal and the circular aspect that is 'whole' or 'wholistic' (zero point/pivot point and event horizon).

This is understanding of the technology of the matrix construction and its transportation as you 'ride the dragon' into the stargate system of ascension.

Manna (also known as 'ambrosia') is the 'nectar of the gods' and depicts the 'drinking of pure bliss'.

As we have said, the dragon's ride into the stargate/wormhole journey of activated and conscious memory that is DNA with momentum/convergence charge (warp speed) is a moment of absolute bliss.

Manna or ambrosia is the 'liquid of bliss', also signifying the liquid light that moves upwards through your spine as you 'raise the Kundalini'. This is the same process as riding the dragon, stargate ascension and the convergence charge that occurs as you gather together momentum by complete merging within multilocationality within the time matrix, becoming a unified field with all the infinity matrices within all that is you.

Therefore within the golden mean frequency (Fibonacci sequence, golden equation, mathematical arc) that is the Ark of the Covenant (or indeed 'Noah's ark' that rides the water waves of ascension to a safe destination) is the emotion of bliss. We can call this the fifth dimensional Mer-Ka-Bah (or potentially the seventh dimensional Mer-Ka-Bah for some of you) which would equate to the 'golden Mer-Ka-Bah' (or the platinum Mer-Ka-Bah).

The divine feminine (depicted by the drinking of ambrosia from the golden chalice) merges with the sacred masculine (depicted by the staff/rod which is the vertical/horizontal/diagonal directional focus). This creates 'the movement of the matrix' and memory code activation for stargate ascension, twelve strand DNA template reconstruction/reconfiguration and fully God-realised self as holding multilocational memory whilst still remaining within physical incarnation.

The tablets or 'Ten Commandments' represent the 'covenant' itself. This is a promise or sacred vow that is the covenant made with 'God' or with 'Source' or 'higher self' or 'activated matrix'. The covenant is the ultimate 'past life contract' as presented within the *Masters of the Matrix* material (see 'The God Self Contract and the Zero Point' chapter).

The covenant is the codex. An entire library of information and signifies the knowledge that is afforded you when you move through stargate ascension in physical form.

Ark of the Covenant technology is the masculine/feminine marriage (vertical, horizontal and diagonal directional forces of the matrix merged with the circular zero point field pivot point and event horizon to create the spiral). The Ark of the Covenant is golden to signify the golden mean activation, the consumption of manna or ambrosia is the bliss (bliss-charged love) which is the emotion for full ascension and crystalline matrix DNA. The covenant is the promise, vow or codex between matter and antimatter (or bodymindspirit).

The golden Ark of the Covenant sits in the middle of the sacred cross of the twelve tribes of Israel (or Abraham).

In order to power-up and activate the Mer-Ka-Bah, one gathers together *all* the 144 matrices (infinities) and takes them through the zero point field pivot point/event horizon, ultimately merging all of self as one into a unified field and 'becoming God' or 'Source'.

This takes you into the twelve strand formation (144 strand quantum convergence formation), giving you the coordinates to take you 'wherever you want to go' when you pass through the pivot point stargate and 'ride the dragon'.

So where do you want to go?

Well, in actuality you do not want to 'go' anywhere. What you are doing is transforming, upgrading and, if you like, 'mutating'.

As we have said, you are moving from a carbon-based molecular structure to a silicon-based (crystalline) structure. The visualisation of 'transportation' or 'travel' is the third dimensional interface, your human brain's way of interpreting the faster vibrating frequency that is occurring at the molecular level.

It feels like 'travel' and indeed 'travel at warp speed'.

When you undergo this process, you will literally feel like you *are* travelling at warp speed. Multilocational consciousness *is* warp speed travel whilst simultaneously staying in the same place.

Why is this?

The reason for this is because you are travelling through time, not space. When you ride the dragon through the stargate and access the entire stargate system, you are 'time travelling'.

This can be done within your consciousness (which is where you are now as a starseed collective consciousness at the time of this transmission).

This can also be done with your actual physical bodies (which is your destined future as you focus 'your eyes on the prize' which is the ascension timeline).

36: 3D Earth Stargate

The matrix formation that we present to you that is *all that is you* exists as the 'healthy matrix' within all structures that stand in alignment with Source.

Blocks and repeated cycles of descending behaviour (negative emotional cycles) can cause lack of flow within various parts of the matrix. Stargate ascension with correct coordinates will not be possible with unresolved blocks and repeated negative cycles.

The work within our previous transmission *Masters of the Matrix* will assist you in moving through these blocks and negative cycles. The moment that you shift your intention towards clearing, integration and stargate ascension, you activate codes that will bring your matrix into balanced flow. You can then access the stargates with the required coordinates for stargate ascension OR the ability to 'link into' or 'connect with' the 'Aurora dragon' (the collective consciousness of all the starseeds that create a cosmic unified DNA antimatter wave train of universal plasma). Starseeds who have not quite activated the required coordinates themselves can catch onto this and still ascend to 5D Gaia.

We would like to draw your attention to the fact that many structures hold the same structure as your individualised, balanced matrix. Planets, stars, moons, food, water, dimensions, realities, architectural structure and balanced and focused thought or idea.

If a structure is balanced, activated and 'open' then it will mirror this creational blueprint we speak of.

Within the inverted matrix, false light system, many of the balanced structures (planets, stars, extraterrestrial Mer-Ka-Bahs, thought structures, dimensions and so on) have been deliberately and consciously inverted and distorted.

Again we refer to our previous transmission *Masters of the Matrix* which is a full transmission teaching personal immunity to these inverted systems, and of the sovereignty and liberty that comes from this Matrix Mastery work. If you have done this work or are in the process of consciously doing this work (whichever model you follow), then you are ready to work with the multilocational consciousness needed for stargate ascension.

Once you are sovereign and activated, you will be able to spot a distorted system and know if the stargate is 'inactive' or 'active' or if it is a fall system/trapping system (inverted wormhole rather than activated stargate).

'Wormhole', 'stargate' or 'gateway' are interchangeable terms that will be used differently by each conduit that accesses this information. We shall use 'inverted wormhole' for a fall system and 'stargate' for a fully functional balanced system. The inverted wormhole is a deliberately created non-organic structure and the stargates are organic natural structures.

Within your physics or cosmology terminology, you would know these structures as an 'Einstein-Rosen bridge'. Although within these explanations the full understanding of light speed travel is not correctly understood. The black hole to black hole does not quite work in the way it is presented. This is the reason 'stargate' is much more appropriate terminology.

The reason for this is when you pass through an 'Einstein-Rosen bridge' it does not just connect to 'one other location' in space (or time), it connects to multiple places depending on the energetic frequency (DNA activation and coordinates) of the being or item passing through the bridge. It is a spiral formation rather than one connecting tunnel from point A to point B. You could send two different items into the same 'black hole' and they will both potentially go to 'different places' depending upon their molecular structure.

Therefore it does not matter if a stargate is 'closed' or if it is an 'inverted wormhole'. If you hold the correct aligned coordinates, you will not even access these trapping structures but will 'pass above' them. You will access a fully activated stargate system based on your frequency.

Just as you would recognise the angry, blocked and traumatised person from the loving, light-filled and spiritually aware person. Or the benevolent light being or extraterrestrial as opposed to the malevolent trickster entities, so too will you 'recognise' the inverted wormholes from the stargates. Your alignment, your intuition, your resonance with the vertical pillar of light and the powerful sensing of the upgraded chakra system, the strong, magnetic 'gut feeling' of the empowered solar plexus, all these will show you which is the inverted matrix system and which is the organic system and the stargate network. It will be as easy for you as distinguishing between night and day.

We would point out that you are 'riding the dragon' together. You are not doing this alone. The momentum created by 'Aurora', the telepathic union between the starseeds, is extremely powerful and supportive. You cannot 'get lost' and pass through the 'wrong stargate' if you are consciously part of Aurora. Or if you are a kind, loving, service-to-others being. Your frequency will naturally 'catch the Aurora train'.

Activated matrices radiate for 'miles and miles', if you will, and throughout time. Your Atlantean former selves (the polarised positive individuals who were loyal to and followed the Law of One) left coordinates and maps for you within your very DNA memory, for you to 'find' at this time and *find them you are doing!*

So different planetary structures and their stargates are not too much of a concern for any individual fully connected to the Aurora grid.

However, we will present information to you regarding these structures that will be useful to you as you move through integration.

Your planet Earth (third density), presented as a sphere or a flat disc, has not had a fully activated stargate at the core of its matrix until the time within your planetary calender that we call the 'emerald gateway'.

This was August 2017, the time of the 'Lion's Gate' portal followed shortly by the solar eclipse. This was an incredibly significant time period for you because at this time the stargate within Earth's core (sphere) or central point (disc) became fully active and operational. At the same time, there was a quarantine that had been placed around your planet for many millennia that was lifted.

You, dear starseeds, and your collective endeavours within the Aurora grid, telepathic union, created these highly significant events of liberty and sovereignty for your planet.

You now have a direct link into the 5D Gaia grid (and thus the 7D Eartha grid should you choose that) as your 'ascension destination' if you will.

There is much work to be done within your planet Earth in third density at the time of this transmission but the emerald gateway bought with it a moment in time that only those who are part of the Aurora grid are aware of.

Your moon and sun and all the stars and planets within your solar system each have stargates at their central core. To traverse the timespace within hyperspace needs what we may call the 'Mer-Ka-Bah pilot's licence' (akin to flying a plane) and we, within this transmission, are delivering keycodes that will assist you. The most important stargate you need to know about at this time is your personal individual stargate within the central point of your matrix. In truth, as we have said, all stargates are in the same place (overlapping and interlocking) and passing through them is a movement into a spiralling system of multiple infinities moving through the zero point field of one infinity and 'crossing the event horizon'.

What gives you the coordinates for the 'place you go to' when passing through the stargates are your thoughts, visualisations and emotions. This is where the keycodes lie. They lie in your thoughts, visualisations and emotions.

These are your coordinates! Your very visualisations, thoughts and emotions!

The 'place' (or representation of consciousness within the time matrix) that you will find yourself in will be a direct match to what you are imagining, thinking and feeling.

Let us give you an example...

Imagine there is a portal in front of you that will take you to any place in the entire multiverse that is in perfect resonance with your overall frequency.

In front of that portal are two women, Jaynie and Elizabeth.

Let us say that Jaynie is spiritually aware, is a conscious crystal starseed and a healer. She has worked on her shadow side blocks and traumas and holds a high light quotient.

Elizabeth, on the other hand, is dealing with issues from her past, some of which lie buried within her subconscious. She is a person with a quick temper, is very insecure, materialistic and afraid. Life overwhelms her. She is not on a spiritual path and holds no belief of any 'higher power' or 'other dimension' and exists within the third dimensional reality, holding linear thinking.

These two women, Jaynie and Elizabeth are fabricated characters that are typical archetypal exaggerations but are provided simply as example.

In this scenario, Elizabeth is unlikely to activate a portal in the first place but for the sake of this example, let us say that she did. Elizabeth would step through the portal to find herself in another place that looks very much like Earth. It is very windy and there is a house in front of her in quite a state of disrepair. In the little unkempt garden next to the house is a small pond with murky waters. The sky is grey and it looks like it is going to rain. In front of Elizabeth is a wooden box. Elizabeth opens the box to find a book inside with her name engraved upon the front cover.

What we are seeing here is a third dimensional environment that reflects Elizabeth's state of consciousness (the weather, the state of the house and garden) with a tool for Elizabeth to use so that she may move through clearing, shadow work and awakening (the book). There will *always* be such a tool in *any and every* environment both in the waking, physical world and in hyperspace/dreamtime/antimatter. Oftentimes the tools go unnoticed and undiscovered but they are always there.

Jaynie on the other hand, stepping through the exact same portal, finds herself in a very different place. She is stood in front of a golden crystal temple, the sky is blue and the sun is shining. There are actually three suns in the sky here. Jaynie is surrounded by little flying fairies, gnomes and pixies. She spots a unicorn in the distance. The queen of the fairies welcomes her to the golden crystal temple and Jaynie is presented with a crystal necklace.

The environment that Jaynie has found herself within is a higher dimensional reality, completely unlike Earth, full of love and beauty. Her gift of a crystal necklace is a piece of jewellery, also a talisman that holds information and knowledge within the crystals.

This is a somewhat basic example of how stargate travel works. There will always be a tool for further journeying and expansion yet at the same time the landscape, environment and entire reality reflects 'all that you are'. It is therefore most important and most advisable to 'work on yourself', as is the mantra continually chanted within your spiritual circles upon your planet, before attempting stargate travel.

37: The Blue Star Matrix and the Eternal Flame

In your meditation or visualisation (or indeed out-of-body astral projection), we would ask you to imagine before you a shimmering blue matrix.

You can see this as a large, watery, moving mandala. In truth, what you are seeing, is the celestial or stellar gateway/stargate known as the 'blue star matrix' or the 'blue flame'.

When it comes to aware dreamtime/lucid dreaming or out-of-body astral projection, it may be more challenging to project your thought into the actual presentation of the blue star matrix. One way to do this is as soon as you are lucid (aware you are dreaming) or have moved into a conscious out-of-body state, look for a doorway.

Finding a 'door' in aware dreamtime is much easier than finding the blue star matrix, unless you are an adept dreamweaver (conscious creator in dreamtime).

Once you find the doorway, simply visualise a 'blue crystal' on the other side of the doorway. A literal crystal.

You can imagine a small blue crystal sat on a table, a crystal rock or a piece of blue crystal jewellery.

Find the 'knowing' or 'expectation' that the blue crystal will be behind the doorway, then open the door.

This is your personal matrix experience (subconscious/superconscious aspect) so you will discover what you are ready to discover or what you need to experience (as everything presents as perfect alignment or match to where you are, who you are and what you are).

It may be that you discover an actual blue crystal, some other structure or even a person/entity. Go with the journey here and if you do not manage to activate the blue star matrix at your first attempt then just continue to repeat the exercise.

Many of you, as starseeds, will create/project the blue star matrix before you and may open the door to discover the living, blue plasma, crystalline matrix structure that is the 'celestial stargate' (known also as the 'stellar gateway'),

This blue star matrix is a projection of you. This is not the third dimensional aspect of you however, this is an externalised projection of your true self in full twelve strand activation. This is a stargate that can transport you, through the time matrix, in your astral/dream/light body to other dimensions.

The creation of the externalised self as crystalline matrix activates the memory pathways within the quantum DNA field bringing the entire 144 DNA codes online to create an activated infinity holding quantum charge.

Once you have the shimmering blue matrix in front of you, you can do one of several things. Nothing you do here is 'wrong' as the blue star matrix is an organic stargate structure. You would need starseeded codes (Atlantean, Pleiadian, Lyran, Sirian, Arcturian and others) to even create the externalised blue matrix in the first place.

However, if this presentation does not feel right to you then do not enter the stargate. Just simply observe you thoughts and feelings.

If you have created your true expression of externalised matrix self at the celestial level with the complete 144,000 codex, then this blue star matrix will call to you. It will feel like 'home'.

You can simply dive straight into it and 'allow' yourself to be transported to wherever is an aligned vibrational frequency match. If you are a loving service-to-others being then you will likely find yourself transported 'home' after diving through the centre of the blue star matrix.

For the majority of you, this will be somewhere within Pleiadian, Sirian or Lyran landscape. You will literally transport your astral body (actually your celestial body) off- planet and onto your 'home' planet. If you look at your hands, you will see they are pulsating blue (rather than the clear third dimensional Mer-Ka-Bah body). You and the blue star matrix (blue flame stargate) are one. The stargate you have just dived through is the central point, pivot point of your own matrix. You have externalised your matrix and dived through it. At this point (with an externalised celestial matrix), we would refer to the central point as the 'nexus'.

You may find yourself upon a different 'home' planet to the three we mentioned although this would be quite rare. You are each connected to the Pleiades, Lyra and Sirius with one predominant connection to one of the three.

You may actually find yourself upon 3D Earth or a different harmonic version of Earth.

These exercises we present are actually a 'practise run' if you will. When the time comes for full ascension to 5D Gaia (or 7D Eartha), which are metaphoric memory triggers for the full twelve strand crystalline matrix activation and the reconstruction of the 144 DNA strands to create a fully realised memory infinity structure (you!), you will know instinctively what to do, where to go and how to direct energy as you 'weave the ascension dream' into reality.

Now you can 'feel love', 'open your heart', think 'positive, happy thoughts' or surround yourself with pink/violet/white/golden light. You can imagine you are holding a white rose in your hand, a sacred book representing the 'secrets of the ages' or that you are wearing a flowing white robe adorned with silver stars.

These visualisations all assist in your stargate travel and in truth, they are excellent, high vibrational visualisations that are 'language of light codes'.

Yet your actual frequency itself, your level of light quotient and clarity, is enough to create the coordinates needed for the destination.

As we have said, if you have externalised the blue star matrix in the first place, then you hold the coordinates needed for stargate travel.

It is indeed a wondrous feeling to dive into the centre nexus point of your own externalised matrix and to know that you have a stargate at your disposal whenever you wish to use it. That stargate is you. The 'activated' you.

There are several other externalised presentations of the blue star matrix that may appear to you in place of the actual living stargate.

You may see before you a temple or palace. Colours these may present with are many but usually blue, gold, green or white. Work with whatever visual presents to you.

You may walk inside a temple or palace and explore. The temple is the fifth dimensional presentation of 'the template'.

The crystal palace is a fifth dimensional externalised presentation of the blue star matrix (celestial self).

Any temple, especially a blue temple, is again an externalised presentation of the blue star matrix (celestial self).

These presentations can be 'false constructs' set up within the hyperspace, antimatter reality, known perhaps to you as 'astral trapping'. The work we presented within our transmission *Masters of the Matrix* will prepare you for stargate travel (and stargate ascension) as you become sovereign within your fields and thus free from infiltration and hijacking.

The other presentation that may come to you, is that of the blue flame. This can look like the flame of a candle or can present as 'blue fire' before you.

This again, is an externalised presentation of the blue star matrix, celestial self. Yet the flame can be either a fifth, sixth or seventh dimensional (and higher) structure or all dimensions combined. This is a multidimensional presentation. It is the externalised presentation of multilocational consciousness and the fully remembered twelve strand DNA crystalline structure (the infinite helix).

The blue flame or fire is the 'entrance to the the Halls of Amenti' (the Emerald City of Krysta) and it is known by many names. The blue pearl, the Eye of Horus, the blue sphere, the blue disc, the blue angel or the blue serpent fire.

We would refer to this blue flame as 'blue starphire'. What you are actually seeing here are the particles of the universe/multiverse. This is a 'living field' and the star matrix and all the matrices are sixth dimensional presentations of that living field. The blue starphire is a multidimensional living field. It is *your* externalised matrix self as an individualised being.

Just as your matrix joins with other matrices to produce a grid formation that is pure Source creation, so too does your blue starphire burn brightly and join with the starphire that is 'others' becoming one flame.

This is the flame. A joining of infinite infinities to create a oneness. Yet within that 'oneness', that 'one flame' is information. Code. Sequencing. Maps. Instructions. Briefings. As you join your blue starphire flame with other flames, you create the eternal flame.

The bilocational consciousness (duality of thought) is the twin flame and the double helix.

The trilocational consciousness (triad/trine of thought) is the Holy

Trinity and the triple helix.

The multilocational consciousness (quantum thought) is the Flower of Life and beyond the triple helix.

The omnipresence/omnipotence (unified thought) is the unified field eternal flame and the infinite helix (the 'Law of One').

All this is 'you'. It is 'all that is you', yet also an individualised aspect of that 'all'. The sacred wheel formation, with the twelve tribes of Israel/Abraham and the hidden thirteenth tribe as the event horizon makes up you, one infinity. And within that one infinity, you hold 144 infinities that each in turn hold 144 infinities and so on and so on for infinite infinity.

Can you see how separate you all are, dear starseeds? Can you see how completely unified you all are?

Seeing this picture, knowing this picture and processing all that it means to 'all that is you' is the key to moving beyond linear thinking and into multilocational consciousness and eventually full omnipresence. The omnipresence is a whole other infinite series of transmissions! Yet you touch upon the essence of this omnipresence with your understanding of these concepts. It is the knowing and embracing of these concepts that lead you into the wonderful journey that is the infinite helix and stargate ascension.

38: Archangel Michael, Princess Aurora

and the Blue Flame

I would like to ask some questions about this material so far.

We are your humble servants and shall respond to the best of our ability given the levels of your own comprehension and the terminologies available within your fields.

Thank you. Are each of the twelve matrices going upwards a higher version of me or going sideways an infinite version? Where are you?

No, each matrix is a separate infinity that you can jump into and pass through that stargate. They are fractalised, holographic copies but each will be unique. They are timelines as this is a time matrix. The vertical axis itself presents 'higher versions' of you, if you will, as does the horizontal axis present alternate versions. These sacred masculine lines of intentional creation within the matrix are the pillar structures within the fractalised, holographic matrices that make up the twelve tribes of Israel/Abraham. They are not one infinity in themselves even whilst they are infinite intentional creational directions and hold the code and memory for those directions. The entire matrix (sacred wheel, with pivot point and event horizon) is one infinity.

We are the matrix itself (the entire matrix) and all the other matrices that make up the 144 over and over as infinite infinities. We are known as the 'Nine' as the nine is the central point (pivot point also known as the 'nexus') when looking at the matrix mathematically.

So you are 'zero point'?

Exactly, yes. One could say we 'broadcast' from zero point or 'spring forth' from zero point. We are only zero point itself, rather than emanating from it, when we are not in communication with you.

So when you are in communication with me, where are you?

We are an individualised group or collective consciousness that is your entire matrix. We are the organic structure that is the 144.

So are you the 144,000 warriors of light?

Yes, although that particular metaphor more aptly and rightly describes YOU. All the starseeds.

Are there 144,000 starseeds?

There are many, many more starseeds than this number. The '144,000' is an activation code for the twelve strand DNA crystalline matrix structure, which is twelve matrices multiplied by twelve matrices to create 144 matrices. When activated by the 'hidden thirteenth', that is when 'twelve' creates an infinity.

So are you the event horizon?

We are the entire matrix including the event horizon.

What is outside the event horizon?

That would be the 'other side' of the matrix which you see as 'outside' but let us say that if you were to try to 'jump over' the event horizon, you would not be able to do this as the event horizon would move. The only way to get to the 'other side' is through the stargate. You cannot jump over the boundary of the infinity structure.

Why not? Why can't you jump over it?

Because it is not really there. It does not exist except within your 3D brain's interpretation.

You are looking at a time matrix and the event horizon is one moment. You cannot 'jump over' one moment. You can however 'pass through' one moment if you have the required coordinates. Remember the event horizon and the pivot point/nexus are the same place.

So how come you can jump over the matrices going up or down but not over the event horizon that is the boundary to your matrix?

Because when you jump into a matrix that is within your own personal infinity, you are staying within the same infinity. You are not actually jumping anywhere, you are activating quantum DNA. The matrices that make up the 144 are within your own personal infinity, even whilst they occupy the 'same space' as all other infinities (as there is only one infinity in truth). When you jump upwards into a matrix or in any direction into any matrix within your own personal infinity, you are 'going down' the fractal (or rather 'going into' the fractal depending on where your viewpoint is). You are moving around within a moving spiral or toroidal field. You can remain within this spiral but cannot jump outside it (there is no outside). However, you can go through it.

So what part of the DNA is the event horizon?

It is the stargate. The 'mouth of the dragon', if you will. It is the 'place' you steer your blue starphire, quantum convergence (the entire 144 matrix structure) into, in order to create charge and access warp speed. You 'collapse the wave', as in you change the entire shape of the matrix into a serpent, dragon or lightship and steer the entire ship through the nexus of the externalised blue star celestial matrix (the nexus is the same place as the event horizon).

So within the DNA, there is no boundary or circle?

Yes, there is a boundary if you perceive the DNA spiral structure to be a two dimensional wheel around you. That boundary is the event horizon.

What colour is the event horizon?

Now you are getting somewhere. Actually, it is blue. A very bright blue.

Why is it blue?

The colour of your entire matrix is blue, when viewed from a physical perspective. It is blue due to the way it 'reflects light' if you will.

From another perspective, one could say it is a 'rainbow of colour' as it reflects all colours but when 'travelling through it', it will appear to you as blue.

How does it reflect light? We are not talking about solar light here, are we?

It is light. It is light itself. This is similar to solar light but much, much 'brighter' if you will. In truth it is not brighter, it is simply vibrating at a much higher frequency than solar light. You could call this light 'photonic light' or 'higher dimensional light'.

This light can reflect light or absorb light depending on your polarisation (negative service-to-self or positive service-to-others) when looking at the matrix structure as a stargate that you are collapsing.

As you collapse the wave, taking the entire structure through its own centre point (nexus), then it will appear blue to you due to the way it reflects the light spectrum within that dimension.

The light spectrum within that dimension is in direct proportion to 'the light of the Goddess'. What we mean by this is that it is the light of the collective consciousness grid that is the collective thoughts and feelings of all the beings that exist within that dimension (or harmonic universe).

Aurora, divine princess and daughter of the flame, is the embodiment in personality, emotion, intelligence and full energy structure as an individualised infinity, of the collective consciousness of all the activated and aware starseeds on 3D Earth (or more accurately within 5D Gaia).

Aurora is the 'twin flame' to archangel Michael and they both 'ride the blue flame'.

What this means is that the collective consciousness of aware starseeded humanity, within balanced alchemy of sacred masculine (Michael) and divine feminine (Aurora), hold a code. Just as the indigo individuals and the crystal individuals hold a code within their matrices, so too do Michael and Aurora. If you were to interpret the personality, emotion and energetic make-up of the twin flames, the sacred prince Michael (archangel) and divine princess Aurora (daughter of the flame), then the code they hold as intelligent structures would be 'blue'.

So what this means is that the collective consciousness of aware and activated starseeds existing within the fifth dimensional Gaia grid/template, holding the potential for the activation of the fifth DNA strand, hold a unified field 'personality grid' that is that of the 'blue ray', the 'blue flame' or the 'blue star'.

It is the colour ray/flame/star for communication. It is the colour for the energy centre that is the throat chakra.

It is 'communication' that is the overall field personality for your planetary ascension at the celestial level (fifth dimension). Communication with each other through telepathic and empathic union and through your internet/web technology. You are truly communicating and for this reason you project forth a personality grid that encompasses all your matrices.

Has our activated matrix always been blue?

It has been presented as blue as a memory trigger. It is a signpost saying, "Time for communication." This translates to: "Time for the great gathering," or "Time to unite the tribes."

You 'unite the tribes' (as the starseeds on Earth).

You also 'unite the tribes' as you collectively 'power-up' your matrix, drawing the 144,000 warriors of light forward as you take the twelve tribes of Israel/Abraham through the nexus by riding the dragon through the powered-up blue starphire of mystery momentum created by the thirteenth tribe.

You 'unite the tribes' (as above, so below).

This is about unity and the presentation within the third dimensional reality of the unified field. Only with communication can the unified field be presented, explored and understood.

The unified field is known, in its true name throughout the galactic society within the infinite multiverses, as the 'Law of One'.

39: Cosmic Phire and the Dragon's Breath

We cannot begin to explain the structure of the flame (cosmic phire) for it has no structure. Hence the reason that the sixth dimension manifests in mathematical/geometric structure or pattern so that pure frequency can be 'seen and measured' if you will.

Yet when moving up the dimensional scale, the geometric patterns and constructions are as much metaphor as the fifth dimensional world of form.

The flame (cosmic phire) is the true essence of universal/multiversal and cosmic life (intelligence, awareness, memory).

These are indeed 'memory fields' and one can 'read' them, if you will.

Our conduit Magenta Pixie does not have the necessary terminology within her fields for us to explain the cosmic phire in a scientific sense, yet she is able to translate our words in order for understanding to occur within herself and you, dear starseed, who hears/reads our words.

So we shall explain the flame or 'cosmic phire'.

The 'cosmic phire' is the essence or energy of zero point. Now zero point is not just one point in time or space. Zero point is everywhere. We give the mathematical number 'zero' to this field because it is nothing or nothingness. You may know this place as the 'abyss' or the 'void' or the 'cosmic womb'.

In scientific terms upon your planet, this substance is known as 'dark matter', although you are only seeing the cosmic phire from a third dimensional perspective when you see dark matter. In truth, this is known to your scientists that reach for discovery and yearn for answers as 'dark energy'.

What you know as dark matter (or dark energy) consists of the cosmic phire, zero point and other structures within the universe that are 'invisible' to you in physicality.

We explain all this to you now as 'things are going to change' within your universal structure and your perception of your reality. The starseeds are already many years ahead in their understanding of physical reality as the third dimension cannot be 'decoded' from the third dimension. Just as we cannot decode the fourth dimension until we view that field from 5D.

You cannot 'decode' 5D until you view 5D from 6D and so on.

We have been 'decoding' the fifth dimension for our conduit by showing her and teaching her about sixth dimensional structure.

Now, we are showing her seventh dimensional structure (or rather, lack of structure) so she (and you) may begin to decode the sixth dimensional presentations. This is simply about expansion (and thus integration of knowledge, attaining wisdom and all that goes with that such as sovereignty and liberty) and activation of your crystalline DNA infinite helix matrix.

So what we are showing you here with the flame (cosmic phire) is much more than just 'dark matter', but it encompasses that and is more akin to 'dark energy'.

We show you here 'seventh dimensional fabric' although the merge between dimensions is much 'greater' once you reach the seventh dimension. The zero point (cosmic phire) reaches 'beyond the seventh dimension', shall we say.

Within 7D, there are many 'merge points' where 7D/8D/9D/10D and 11D all 'sit together in the same place'. So we could say that we are showing you the fabric of 7D through to 11D, if you will. In truth, the models we use to explain the higher dimensions at this stage are all metaphoric as merge (and merged/intertwined polarity) is so abundant (or frequent) at this point.

So we show you 'zero point'. The reason why we give this 'void of nothingness' a mathematical value (zero) is because whilst there is 'nothing' here, there is 'something' here. Zero point is not 'empty space'. In fact, there is no such thing as 'empty space'.

Zero point is full of 'pure potential'. It is a collection of 'living imprints' if you will. It is known as a 'morphogenetic field'. One could call this the 'Akash' (Halls of Amenti or the Emerald City of Krysta) but, in truth, the cosmic phire of zero Point is 'more than' (despite it being zero) than simply 'records'.

Indeed records and imprints are here but we also have 'pure potential' (like a modelling clay, if you will). This is 'pure potential' of creation of matter and creation of thought. This is also a field of 'infinite energy' and it is the place where 'free energy technologies' would be harnessed if one knew how to do this. The starseeds are already accessing this energy simply through expansion, working with the energy body/chakra system/matrix/emotional alchemy, bliss-charged love and so on.

Cosmic phire is not 'just for the taking' however (free energy, healing, records, imprints). It is the potential for pure creation of matter (planets, stars, galaxies, universes, human beings, animals, plants and so on).

The cosmic phire could be seen as the 'blueprints for everything' if you will, although by the time one 'reaches' the zero point field there are no blueprints! Blueprints are structure and we are looking here at 'no structure'.

We understand that for many of you these concepts are vast and most mind-expanding but of course, that is the point. As you process the multidimensionality and multilocationality of zero point, your mind expansion activates the infinite helix DNA structure.

So what we have here is 'beyond the blueprint' energy. The energy of pure creation that one 'creates the blueprint from' if you will.

This field of cosmic phire is an entity (or home for infinite entities) depending on how you look at it. One could say zero point and Source point (zero field/Source field) are one and the same 'place', this would be correct. However, when looking specifically at the seventh dimensional aspect of this field, which we call 'cosmic phire', then this would be somewhat 'removed from' and not quite as 'unified' as Source, despite this being a unified field we are looking at.

The point here being, is that you, as an individualised infinity (or on the path to individualisation and full realisation which is the 144 activated matrix structure and stargate ascension), are not separate from the field that is cosmic phire.

Remember, as we have said, that 'Aurora' (as the divine princess) is the manifestation of one unified fifth dimensional entity. This is the collective consciousness grid of light that is the activated and aware starseeds within 5D Gaia, in the process of ascending to 5D Gaia from 3D Earth.

Well, the cosmic phire is the same thing. Aurora and her twin flame archangel Michael would be part of this cosmic phire, although when they merge with the cosmic phire they no longer have form. We, the White Winged Collective Consciousness of Nine, are part of this cosmic phire, but we too lose form when we are there.

From the point of view of 'us', we could say that the zero point field of cosmic phire is 'us' in the future. As 'we' are our conduit in the future and your guidance system (6D matrix) is 'you' in the future, then this would mean the intelligent infinity that is the cosmic phire of the zero point is also 'you' in the future.

These concepts we show you are so you may realise just how connected you are to this cosmic phire.

The exercise we showed you that is you, diving into the centre of the blue star matrix and moving through a stargate portal into another location, is simply the brain's way of decoding multilocational consciousness. The cosmic phire of the '7D and beyond' zero point is your 'multilocational consciousness' and this is 'where you are going' when you ascend (yet you are staying within your physical bodies to do this).

This is absolute expansion into genius flow. You are becoming geniuses. Yet the cosmic phire is more than even this.

If the divine princess 'Aurora' is the collective consciousness of humanity as a grid of light (each of you, your experiences, memories, thoughts, emotions, creations, actions, feelings and entire blueprints collected together to form a field of intelligence that manifests predominantly as a divine feminine, loving, living intelligence that we we call 'Aurora'), then the '7D and beyond cosmic phire' is the grid of light for *all* structures and beings. This includes all your quantum, alternate selves and all extraterrestrials, angelic beings, sixth dimensional matrices and higher dimensional entities. The full 'collective consciousness' field, if you will.

As one 'sea of energy', this would present as a sea of waves and this is exactly what zero point is.

If you look at the fabric of zero point clairvoyantly (remote viewing), you will see moving particles that look like flames of fire. From a fifth dimensional perspective, this is the 'fire of the dragon' or 'dragon's breath'.

Now how is this connected to the dragon?

Remember what we said, when you 'collapse the wave' of your matrix structure as one infinity and take all your 144 matrices through the pivot point, nexus of the externalised stargate (blue star matrix, celestial stargate, blue pearl)?

Well, as you do this you create what we call 'blue starphire' which is the quantum convergence charge that is created when you collapse the wave and pull all your 144 matrices into a 'rainbow serpent structure'. You are literally changing the entire formation of your DNA structure. The molecular base becomes silicon crystalline and the double helix begins to spin. It spins faster and faster as it gathers momentum and creates charge. It spins so fast that it achieves 'warp speed/light speed' and this is when you 'ride the dragon' or 'ride the rainbow serpent' into the nexus of your own blue star matrix. Blue starphire is the momentum/charge that powers your Mer-Ka-Bah dragon to create warp speed so you can fly/dive through the nexus and access the externalised landscape that mirrors/reflects the 'true you' and that is the 'true you' (your frequency codes, memories and experiences).

You need to create your own blue starphire (through your dedicated spiritual practise and work with the matrix). When you have enough blue starphire to power-up your dragon, as you pass through the nexus of your own blue star matrix stargate, the dragon breathes out and creates 'fire' or 'dragon's breath'.

This dragon's breath becomes cosmic phire.

You see, your individual work with the matrix, your stargate ascension process creates cosmic phire, which is pure potential for the creative blueprint. It is zero point. It is the Source field.

So you (your memories, experiences and emotions) literally create the fabric (cosmic phire) that is then used to create universes, stars, galaxies, planets and people.

When we say to you that your power together as awakened and ascending starseeds is enough to create worlds, we were not just speaking in metaphor.

You literally 'seed the stars'.

You are not just 'starseeds' because you are 'from the stars' but because you 'seed the stars'.

Do you see how significant and important you are to all of creation? Each and every one of you.

40: Going Galactic and the Creation of Fourth Density

In our transmission *Masters of the Matrix* we spoke about the hijacking of the matrix and ways to become immune to this hijacking.

Exploring this subject further, we would say to you that it is your blue starphire quantum charge that is the target of the hijacking. The dragon's breath created is 'free energy technology' and it is this that is 'hijacked'. However it is the fear-based emotional energy that is fed upon (consumed/absorbed) by the service-to-self entities and groups. The fear-based emotional energy from the hijacked/unaware population combined with the potential for blue starphire and dragon's breath cosmic phire creation is that which can sustain life for entities who are unable to create their own blue starphire due to a distorted energy system (service-to-self).

Whilst the newly awakened starseed cannot be 'hijacked' as such, he/she can be misled and the potential for blue starphire creation can be siphoned or stolen by 'other entities'.

We could also present this information as your own 'shadow side' when stagnant and buried will prevent you from creating your own blue starphire and thus dragon's breath/cosmic phire.

Anything that 'drains your energy' (cosmic vampirism) is the opposite frequency to that which you need for the building of quantum convergence charge, blue starphire needed for stargate ascension.

The *Masters of the Matrix* material is a complete presentation for immunity to hijacking and cosmic vampirism.

To create blue starphire, one would look for 'living life force' in all things. We refer here to anything that gives you excitement, inspiration, joy and happiness. These emotions can be integrated and alchemised into lovelight and lightlove which creates 'bliss-charged love'.

Bliss, euphoria and ecstasy are the 'quantum charge' creating emotions. For as we have said before, these are the emotions that trigger the golden mean activations within you.

We can present a 'golden triad' of ascension equations as DNA activating memory triggers.

These bliss equations (mathematical language of light equations) could present as:

* Bliss/euphoria/ecstasy = blue starphire

* Blue starphire + the infinite helix = dragon's breath/cosmic phire

* Dragon's breath/cosmic phire = zero point blueprints to 'seed stars'

We can add to this to create the 'sacred square':

* Blueprints to seed stars = stars/universes/planets/dimensions and so on

So you see that you, dear starseeds, are the creators. Individually you are the creators of your own realities and collectively **you create reality itself.**

I thought that Source created us as human beings.

Indeed. Source creates all and everything including you. In return, you become creators. You create matter and antimatter realities and effectively you create Source.

You and Source are one and the same... literally!

The creator and the creation are one. This is the unified field, known throughout the galaxies, multiverses and time matrices as the 'Law of One'.

You have mentioned throughout this transmission that the stargate ascension is a celestial one. Is this correct? You speak of the celestial blue star matrix and the celestial body. Yet in the Divine Architecture *and the*

Starseed Template *material, you mentioned the solar matrix and the diamond matrix when describing the three triads of higher memory. How does the solar and diamond memory equate to stargate ascension?*

Stargate ascension can be 'achieved' or 'accessed' or 'experienced' in many ways and there are infinite methods, models and explanations to present to you in order to trigger awareness, memory and activation.

The three triads of higher memory - celestial, solar/galactic, Source/diamond - are the perspectives you take when you access these memories. As you embrace higher memory, your memories become knowings and this triggers the restructuring and regrouping of the 'emerald code' or 'ascension code' which is the return to the twelve strand crystalline DNA matrix.

With the *Masters of the Matrix* and the *Divine Architecture and the Starseed Template* material, we were using perspective to present to you Matrix Awareness, Matrix Mastery and Matrix Architecture (construction). We were laying the foundations or groundwork, as it were, for more expanded material as is this transmission that is *The Infinite Helix.*

We can, however, recap this material regarding higher memory and show you how this equates to stargate ascension.

The twelve strand formation within the DNA structure, which is awareness of the twelve matrices that lie upon each section of the sacred cross and within the pivot point of the matrix, would be referred to as 'the gathering together of celestial memory' which when fully activated can be 'phired up' and transported 'through its own centre'. This is full awareness of the memories of all your previous incarnations, quantum selves and ancestral/genetic memory (which is actually the same thing from the higher perspective). This externalises into 'the twelfth dimensional gateway' which is a crystalline lattice structure that externalises as 'the blue star matrix' or a representation of the blue ray crystalline grid, blue pearl or blue sphere.

This twelve strand regrouping is a 'seed point' that will take you into a higher strand formation as you expand and ascend.

You remember how we said that you 'create worlds' when you activate blue starphire through the dragon's breath/cosmic phire?

When we say that you 'create worlds', we also refer to dimensions or densities.

Dimensions and densities are interchangeable but in our presentation and our conduit's interpretation, we mean:

* Dimension - state of consciousness and timespace experienced through antimatter/antiparticle realities.

* Density - geographic, universal spacetime frequency experienced through physical matter realities.

Your starphire and your riding of the dragon through your own infinity stargate to produce dragon's breath, cosmic phire creates 'blueprints' or 'seed points' for dimension and density.

Once you activate the twelve strand DNA formation and 'pass through' the twelfth dimensional gateway as a collective group (Aurora - antimatter), you connect to the actual planetary grid structures (Gaia grid - matter) and reach critical mass with this. You literally create the 'fourth density' on your planet.

We would equate the fourth density in geological matter with the fifth dimension (and beyond) within antimatter.

So physical reality space is transformed as is 'antimatter space', which is actually time. Polarity is changed and you undergo a 'pole reversal' (reversal of matter/antimatter structures). You are able to exist and hold memory of timespace as well as spacetime. This would also be seen as a 'magnetic pole reversal' within your physical reality. This does not mean magnetic north becomes magnetic south so as to distort the axis of your planet when your planet exists in a fourth density state. This may happen within the third density timeline, however once you are at critical mass with the twelve strand seed formation and the twelfth dimensional gateway (celestial memory) then your geological 'third density' will no longer exist for you.

The magnetic pole reversal, due to the raising in frequency of all experience aligned with original thought blueprint (the blueprint for polarity), will translate to magnetic and electric 'swapping places' if you will (or in reality merging rather than fusing together - our conduit does not have the terminology or the knowledge within her fields to explain this natural process).

Matter behaves very differently within fourth density than it does in third density and all the 'laws of physics' you have known thus far will need to be 'recalculated', if you will, in order for your scientists to make sense of your new reality structure.

All this is dependent on critical mass for the seed point for your twelve strand DNA template reconstruction. Whilst within the fifth dimensional spiritual realm you are 'moving to the new 5D Earth and existing within the paradisiacal reality that is Gaia' (all true and accurate), what this translates to in physical reality is the collective quantum convergence charge you create together as you raise and restructure your DNA fields into a shift (or an aligned 'equal and opposite reaction') within your environment and thus a fourth density reality.

Now there is another way to look at this. This is the flip side to your creation as 'starseeds of the Aurora/Gaia grid' and that is that your planet Earth is also doing this. 'She' (3D Earth) as an entity also has a matrix infinity structure. She is regrouping her 'twelve tribes of Israel/Abraham' matrices and is passing through her own stargate (Earth's crystal diamond core). Earth is raising her frequency so she may hold the coordinates needed for her complete transformation into 5D Gaia.

You, as aware and receptive starseeds with activated memory, are 'catching her light' or 'aligning with her frequency' if you will. This in turn triggers the raise in your own frequency and your own DNA crystalline matrix regrouping of strands.

The 'move' here between you (Aurora starseeds) and 3D Earth (as she creates her 5D Gaia grid and becomes fourth density in matter) is simultaneous. This is 'living in harmony' with your planetary structure.

Of course, all the planetary structures within your solar system and your entire section of universal spacetime and timespace are all 'upgrading' or 'evolving' and 'ascending' if you will. You are all 'moving upwards through the spiral' or 'delving deeper into the fractal' or 'moving towards the core of the galactic spiral'. It is really all the same thing.

We could say that at the moment you 'dive through the pivot point of your matrix', so too does the Earth 'dive through hers' as do all the planets and stars.

We could also say that your solar system is gathering its matrices together and diving through the centre of the galactic core as everything upgrades simultaneously.

All this is focused on, dependent upon or 'in a synchronised merge with' your own personal DNA restructuring, evolution of consciousness and ascension.

As you 'go galactic' (144 matrix remembering into the infinite helix), you literally *go galactic.*

41: Solar and Diamond Ascension

When it comes to celestial memory (or the celestial body), we would look here at the matrix itself.

The memory/knowing experience here would be regarding the 'twelve tribes of Israel/Abraham' as we have explained. We depict the twelve matrices or discs moving across each directional line within the matrix construction. Twelve discs/matrices at the 'front' of the matrix and twelve at the back (black hole/white hole), which is the pivot point (becoming the nexus point within the externalised blue star matrix).

This presentation is that of 'stargate ascension' when it comes to the twelve strand DNA structure. It holds the 'seed point' for the twelve strand, meaning you can raise momentum and pass through the nexus of your own stargate with five strands reconstructed. You can 'catch' the 'dragon' of another ascending starseed (as part of the telepathic Aurora grid) and 'ride their dragon', taking charge from their momentum (willingly given within the service-to-others circle of love) and you can do this with only four strands activated (as long as you hold the quantum blueprint for five strand ascension).

The hijacking from negatively polarised fourth dimensional entities has involved 'tampering with' or 'deliberately confusing' your DNA system. The third dimensional chemtrails, EMFs, pesticides, vaccinations, GMO crops and many other products and negative creations feed into your system to create an inverted system. This can prevent DNA restructuring in balance and can distort and confuse the DNA strands as they try to reform and remember themselves into sequence.

Your mind and heart (visualisations combined with knowings combined with higher emotions) are far more powerful than all these inverted systems. If you are struggling with hijacking and are feeling the effects of the inverted systems and their negative creations, then the starseeds of the Aurora/Gaia grid are there to help and assist as they are the 'ground crew' of your family of light. You have but to 'ask' (provide matrix coordinates) and allow synchronicity (third dimensional match to the matrix codes) to manifest.

It is important not to dwell upon the inverted systems (unless you are a teacher/guide/adept in this area of your reality). It is equally important not to ignore, bury or refuse to face the inverted systems for they are all aspects of your own shadow.

So there may be members of the starseed Aurora grid who need 'safe passage' through the nexus as they have quantum, etheric DNA codes and blueprints that have not quite formed yet. They are 'welcome passengers' aboard your cosmic dragon (Mer-Ka-Bah lightship) and if you follow these steps (or other shielding techniques), you will find that any non-resonant 'hitchhiker' will not be able to board your dragon or even see you. You will be 'energetically invisible' to them.

So the celestial memory is vertical (up, down), horizontal (left, right, forward, back) and diagonal (up, down, right and left), and you are able to gather together the quantum convergence charge from all these 'memories' in order to regroup and pass through the stargate into celestial ascension. This would be akin to bilocational and trilocational consciousness with the early stages of multilocational consciousness beginning depending on strand formation.

The solar ascension through the sun crystalline matrix is a different visualisation due to a higher resonance.

You are looking here at memories of group soul perspective. In order to move through stargate ascension at this level, you would work with a different matrix formation. We present the twelve discs/matrices along each directional line in a linear formation, as in one after the other, in a chain sequence so you may ride the serpent or dragon. In truth, these are superimposed matrices embedded or nested within one another. The pattern looks like that of a rose rather than a straight line. In order for solar ascension to take place one would literally dive through the centre of the sun, rather than one's own matrix. In truth, the centre nexus point is the same place but in order for ease of explanation for your linear understanding within expansion we would present this model as passing through the sun.

This is very advanced ascension work and it is not where the majority of ascending starseeds are at the time of this transmission. However, this is in your future trajectory.

For advanced adepts in meditation and out-of-body travel, one can activate the solar body and literally pass through the centre of the sun as long as coordinates created by bliss/euphoria/ecstasy are in place. The sun here within your visualisation is a metaphor as the 'solar' presentation here is the Central Sun, which is the galactic core. This level is that of full multilocational consciousness.

This multilocational teaching is a transmission for future times and is not needed as a focus collectively at this point, yet adepts may choose to 'experiment' with solar body work and solar externalised matrix projections. In this transmission, we focus upon celestial stargate ascension specifically.

At the time of this transmission in 2018, we are looking at collective ascension from 3D Earth into 5D Gaia and the blue star matrix and the celestial level is your mode of transport for this.

At the solar level, an entire network of stargates are available and the ability to morph one's own Mer-Ka-Bah matrix occurs. The galactic core, also the 'Central Sun', can be passed through at this point although one would need a higher strand formation to do this. We are looking at the aligned, balanced, properly constructed blueprint in complete coherence for the 144 strand formation.

Once one has regrouped all twelve strands and has activated the full 144 DNA formation, one would manifest the 'diamond matrix' which is the memory of Source. At this point, one embraces 'multiple infinite helices', if you will, and all thought, all places and all time become one. You, as an individualised structure, become a time matrix yourself.

We are providing many triggers for these higher activations (solar/galactic and eventually diamond/Source) within our presentation of the flame and the cosmic phire. We wish to show you how, through the dragon's breath you create through your quantum convergence charge, you are ultimately connected to the seeding of reality. As you progress through the different levels of Matrix Transportation (solar/galactic and diamond/Source), you will work with different visuals.

When you get to the level of full 144 activation and the diamond matrix, you will not even need to visualise a matrix at all. In this case, you have gone 'far beyond' even a 144 construct. There is no 'number' here and you are fully embracing of the Law of One in a perfect unified field infinite spiral. Everything will be instantaneous and this is when you reach infinite omnipresence.

42: The Royal Line and the Fail-Safe Programme

In the Masters of the Matrix *transmission, you said that the celestial twelve strand matrix is the seed point for the highest expression that can be achieved whilst incarnated within a third dimensional reality. Does this mean we cannot achieve solar or diamond ascension whilst in the physical body?*

You cannot achieve solar or diamond ascension whilst in a third dimensional physical body.

You would create the 'fourth density' reality upon your planet (5D Gaia) and exist within a fourth density light body.

From then you would move to solar and then diamond ascension.

Yet the 'memories' can be accessed and achieved which equates to solar and diamond ascension. Your physical body would be 'fourth density' and fully expressed as a silicon-based life form before this occurs.

We recognise how eager you are for this understanding and for this ascension process, however we would say to you, "Do not aim to run before you can walk."

You have said this is a non-linear process though. So can we not touch upon solar and diamond ascension codes as we ascend?

Once you reach the fifth strand formation, the process is no longer linear and you are at what we call 'genius flow level'. At this point you can move in and out of the solar memory and diamond memory. You are said to hold the 'golden light' or the 'diamond light' when you do this. You are able to access multilocational consciousness. However you cannot hold all the memories of all your 'incarnations' or 'selves' at the galactic or Source level simultaneously. You can, however, feel the frequency of holding that omnipresent space. You can access the memories and codes in an 'as needed' basis. You still hold linear thinking and exist within linear time and you would not want to move away from that as that is your anchor. We would advise you to not be in a hurry to reach any destination. There is no destination and because of your ability to hold omnipresent Source space for even a few seconds, you are already there.

There is no destination or even a journey, from the zero point perspective.

You are able to hold the linear and the multilocational thought processes simultaneously and that is celestial stargate ascension.

We break ascension down into three stages simply for linear interpretation.

If you try to move forward to more advanced ascension teachings, you can become confused and 'miss out' or 'not activate' a particular strand that is essential for your overall crystalline formation.

The service-to-self factions have created the energetic of rushing and hurrying through your reality with the programmed belief structure that there is 'not enough time' to get everything done. This is a complete distortion of the true reality and an impediment to harmonious living.

Relax and embrace where you are. As a collective (Aurora/Gaia grid starseed), we would place you as undergoing celestial stargate ascension for your own linear processing. This does not mean that the celestial level is lower than the solar or diamond levels. This again is a false construct or programme to make you think that you are always in a race and it creates competition amongst you, which is a tool of separation. There is of course nothing wrong with separation as this experience is needed in order for the equal and opposite reaction paradox to be 'solved'. However, when you are in an ascension process towards higher dimensions, you are moving away from expressions of separation into individualisation which is quite different.

Separation creates competition and conflict whereas individualisation creates harmony, integration, sovereignty, liberty and unity.

To see the celestial level as 'lower than' or 'inferior to' the solar or the diamond is like saying the galactic core and the sun are better than the stars. Could you choose between the galaxy, the sun and the stars? Are they not all just as beautiful? Just as important as cosmic bodies?

Yes, I see your point. You said that the presentation of the cosmic phire dragon's breath is a trigger into the higher stages of ascension. Can you explain how this is so?

Yes. The matrix will trigger your memory/knowing of the sixth dimension. The flame and the cosmic phire will trigger your memory of the seventh dimension and beyond. This will trigger twelve strand and thus 144 strand regrouping/remembering/reconstruction.

Should we meditate upon the flame, the cosmic phire or the dragon?

At the end of this transmission, we provide meditations and activations for you that utilise the triggers as entire codices that will be placed within your matrix fields when you do this work. You do not have to do this nor 'should' you do this. It is your choice but these meditations and activations are aligned triggers for the infinite helix formation and stargate ascension.

You mention blue starphire as the quantum convergence charge needed for warp speed and riding the dragon into the stargate. Can we visualise riding the dragon through the sun or the galactic core? Would this help us achieve solar and diamond memory?

Yes, you can use these templates for visualisation. However, everything in your reality aligns itself to 'match' your inner frequency in an externalised sense. As 'divine princess Aurora', you are aligned with celestial stargates and celestial ascension and the blue star matrix. This is not to say there are not a few starseeds that have aligned themselves with solar or diamond stargates. But as a collective (Aurora), your trajectory is for 5D Gaia reality as you complete the mission and assist 3D Earth to transform. Your mission is to create fourth density and assist the starseeds who do not have the coordinates that you, as members of the royal line, do have.

So are we going against our mission by focusing on solar or diamond ascension at this point?

No, you are not going against your mission. Your outer reality will match your overall frequency. If you aim to 'dive through the sun' or 'manifest a diamond matrix' within your meditation/trancework/dreamtime, you may well do this. However, it is likely all your dreamtime matrices and stargates you create will be 'tinged with blue' or have a 'blue hue' to them. This is the celestial level and this is where your coordinates are in the trajectory for. If you do pass through the sun or through the galactic core, then you have a higher strand formation and you are ready for this.

Once you work with clearing the shadow and activate into gratitude, bliss, joy and compassion, then you are said to have an 'open-heart' or be 'pure of heart'. You really cannot 'go wrong' or 'go against your mission' at this point. What we would say to you is that this is a collective process that is done in complete service to your beloved brothers and sisters and children and grandchildren within the family of light that is the starseed community (divine princess Aurora). This is not a race to see who can ascend first and get through the highest stargate and 'win the game'.

You are *all* winners. We would also add to this that 'the tortoise wins the race'.

You said that we were members of the 'royal line'. Can you expand on this?

We have spoken of this before. The 'royal line' are individuals that 'come from' the royal houses within the Pleiades, Sirius and Lyra systems (as well as other lesser-known systems). These souls have a code within their matrix fields. They have been 'adorned' or 'anointed' with the 'royal seal'. This code within Pleiadian, Sirian and Lyran polarised positive realities is one of wisdom and service. The royal souls serve others with no expectation of any reward to themselves. They do this in pure and utter surrender and service as they are highly polarised as service-to-others beings. Many within these 'extraterrestrial' societies are fully polarised and are one hundred percent positively polarised souls and 'karma-free'.

Whilst this level of polarisation, service and karmic vibration cannot completely translate over into third dimensional Earth, the memories and codes can.

These souls, due to their complete surrender and service to 'other as self', are highly sensitive, psychic and intuitive. They are this way from their birth into physicality. The code of 'prince' or 'princess' or memories of living in a grand palace are codes placed within the soul's matrix in order to trigger the memory of their royal line. These individuals have the ability to 'radiate' (radiate frequency, light and code) and to influence and/or inspire others. They 'gather' others together. These people might be said to have a 'compelling and charismatic energy' but in truth they are holding royal code. Non-activated individuals can move into egoic and 'god complex' behaviours, but those who 'wake up' and 'remember' who they are immediately move into a life of service as they remember their polarisation and their service-to-others frequency.

Are all starseeds members of the royal line?

They are either queen, king, prince or princess (flame, twin flame, son of the flame sacred prince, or daughter of the flame divine princess). Every activated starseed within third dimensional Earth adds to the creation of the collective consciousness grid of light that is divine princess Aurora, therefore they *are* Aurora. So yes, every activated starseed is a member of the royal line although it may take a while before their memories of this return.

Why is archangel Michael the twin flame to divine princess Aurora?

They both 'ride the blue flame' and there must be divine balance between masculine and feminine whenever there is distortion from Source. Archangel Michael and Aurora together are 'one soul' or 'one flame' and are the equal and opposite reaction to one another. In geometric terms, archangel Michael is the vertical pillar of light and Aurora is the horizontal rainbow bridge pathway.

This is when one views vertical ascension and horizontal ascension as complementary pathways, creating balance and signifying merge and alchemy.

Yet one could also say that every directional axis within the matrix is male and the pivot point/event horizon is female. It depends from which angle or viewpoint one is looking at the matrix from!

Many models, many perspectives.

Is there any kind of calling or visual image or dream that may come to an individual that would let them know they are a starseed or a member of the royal line?

They will have known they were different to others from childhood. Many will 'miss home' and feel as though they do not belong.

However, there are certain symbolic memory keys placed within the field of positive polarisation for the starseeds to utilise to awaken memory. This field (a realm of archetypes within the fourth and fifth dimensional merge point) has been hijacked. It remained so for many of your Earth years. However, with the recent and rapid awareness that ascension is bringing, much fourth dimensional clearing has been done.

A 'fail-safe' programme or 'hermetic seal' was placed within this fourth/fifth dimensional merge point that was completely immune from service-to-self hijacking. Infiltration was expected so fail-safe systems were put in place. These have remained pure and have always been pure. These are most accessible to starseeds and remain major triggers to their awakening and ascension.

We could refer to this fail-safe programme as 'Excalibur'.

43: The Excalibur Codex

We are here to present teachings in the form of metaphor, not just because they are 'safely' integrated into your reality system this way but because they are powerful DNA activations. The right hemisphere of your human brain decodes through symbolism and image and the artistic metaphor through picture/symbol or story is part of the cosmic language we call the 'language of light'.

The need for 'safety' and keeping the truth teachings of the sacred Law of One hidden, buried in myth, legend and metaphor is no longer necessary to the point that it once was on your planet in your not so recent history.

Critical mass for 'starseed awakening' has already occurred at the time of this transmission and you are in the period we call 'the great revealing'. Whilst the 'great reveal' concerns hidden history, technology, science and your galactic reality as well as your own personal shadow aspect, it also involves what we call 'decoding the metaphor'.

Now, the decoding of ancient and modern metaphor is subjective. Just as dream analysis is best done by the dreamer themselves. Having said that, there are those who are the natural 'storytellers' or indeed 'dreamweavers'. Just as they 'weave the dream' (or story), so too can they decode (or unravel) the dream or story. Our conduit is one such natural dreamweaver and unbeknownst to her, she was trained from birth (in fact in utero) and this training was ramped up extensively within weeks of her birth in order to ready her for her mission as our conduit, your scribe and dreamweaver. She is one who shall (with our assistance) decode the metaphor.

All starseeds have been trained from birth or early childhood for their mission, but that is a whole other story!

So what is the story? What is the dream?

We have provided much in the decoding within this transmission. Yet when it comes to metaphor, there is none so powerful, profound, meaningful and subjective than the story of 'Excalibur'.

We realise there are other 'characters' in this story, yet the code of Excalibur has been laid/seeded within the DNA templates of those set for awakening (starseeds).

Every starseed will be drawn to the Arthurian legends of King Arthur, the Knights of the Round Table and Camelot.

There are many stories and metaphors that will 'call your name' and will be so very personal to you as if you had created them for yourself to find whilst incarnate in form (you did of course).

The codes within the Arthurian legends are so abundant that we cannot possibly touch upon them all, neither can we 'decode' the legends and symbols for you in their entirety as they are so very fractalised, convoluted and deep.

However, we can uncover a few layers for you, within this discourse/transmission that is the sacred text known as *The Infinite Helix*.

As we have said, you will each and every one of you hold within your fields the 'personal calling' to the Arthurian legends and most especially to Excalibur. We shall, therefore, refer to this particular code as the 'Excalibur codex' as it is a manuscript/library or 'computer disc of information' available to you.

Once you 'open the seal' and 'crack the Excalibur code' and 'read the codex', you will find rapid awakening and memory takes place within you. Excalibur (or the Excalibur codex) is the fail-safe programme, hermetic seal. All starseeds are 'called by Excalibur' either as memories of living as a knight or simply by being very drawn to the Arthurian legends in a personal and meaningful way.

Excalibur, as a sword, is a symbol for a frequency or vibration. The symbol for the 'warrior' (indigo revolution reminder and the 144,000 warriors of light and the rainbow warriors), also for truth, integrity and justice.

The sword is held high, not in threat or attack but in the spirit of 'knighthood' which is indeed the starseed collective. As the 'divine princess Aurora' collectively (who in this story would be 'Guinevere'), you are each and every one of you 'one of her knights'.

Indigo individuals will feel the buzz of electrical memory within at the 'knowing' that you are a knight, or have been 'knighted' or are one of the 'Knights of the Round Table'. This is your indigo warrior code and it is most important that you resonate with this and allow it to be your truth.

For this reason, each indigo coded starseed will have lived a lifetime (or many lifetimes) as a 'warrior' in some capacity. This may or may not be within the third dimensional Earth but the 'memory coding' for the 'warrior blood' is within you. This is the incarnated female as well as the male. Do not think that only the incarnated male is the warrior or that it is only the male that can carry the sword or be knighted, indeed the female also walks the warrior path and is knighted in her 'indigo quest'.

There are those of you who will have memories of living an incarnation as a knight or simply 'know' you were a knight and this lifetime will hold much emotion for you. The incarnation will have been one of deep emotion so that you would remember it at the time of ascension.

We could also say you have been given the 'Excalibur codex' containing many memories of warrior incarnations and your emotional connection to them. Does this mean you were not actually a warrior or knight and that this is a 'superimposed' memory? The answer to this is both yes and no.

It is important for you to think multidimensionally and in the 'quantum expansion' phase of 'beyond the triple helix' trilocation/multilocational consciousness when analysing our words here.

Your 'soul' is your matrix. You actually 'living an incarnation' or being implanted (or coded) with memories of an incarnation *are one and the same thing.*

Now the implantation process can be hijacked and 'false screen memories' can be given to you in order to control you and siphon your energy. We have discussed this within the *Masters of the Matrix* material and provided immunity techniques for this which clears all 'past life contracts' including false screen memories.

Whilst the implantation programme can be hijacked, the Excalibur codex cannot. It is a 'fail-safe' and a 'hermetic seal' there to ensure awakening of memory and is immune from tampering. However, the Excalibur codex needs to be 'read' (decoded).

We are speaking here of actual memory imprints or codes that are placed within your matrix when you create your matrix (or are birthed from the unified field, cosmic phire creation into your first inception as a holographic blueprint for form).

Everything within your matrix is 'you' (your past, future, alternate field and ancestral bloodlines).

You have access to all these memories. From a linear perspective, *you are all the souls that hold these memories.*

From a multidimensional perspective, you are a 'soul matrix' gathering momentum through 'reading' and 'imprinting' memory fields, creating etheric antimatter blueprints for your 144 matrices that make up 'all that is you'.

So what we are saying here is that the 'Excalibur codex' and the memories of living a lifetime as a knight are one and the same.

Confusion arises when one has 'memories' that are legend/myth/story rather than historical fact. Confusion also arises when two (or more) individuals hold the same memories of being the same person in history or living the same lifetime.

Firstly, that which may seem like legend or myth is often historical fact upon your planet. That which may be seen to be historical fact is often fiction.

Yet you can be 'implanted/coded' with 'memories' of lifetimes that did not actually occur.

On the one hand, these are 'codes' with the frequency you need in order to carry out your mission or experience, that which you chose/need to experience. On the other hand, these are memories of lifetimes that existed as 'thought blueprints' (blueprints for reality or matter that did not or have not yet manifested). We could call these 'precursor to matter blueprints' or that which is 'unmanifest' or 'conceptualised'.

These precursor to matter blueprints may hold much 'mass' and remain 'in storage' for eternities so they may be read and utilised. Or they may dissipate and be 'forgotten' (incorrect terminology here as nothing is ever forgotten, but precursor blueprints can just 'dissolve into the ether') and never become manifest.

In truth, it matters not if your memories of a lifetime are from an actual lived lifetime or are a precursor blueprinted unmanifest reality. The issue here is that *you hold the codex.*

In the case of two (or more) individuals holding the same memories of living the same lifetime, well this is something that happens most often within the abundant time stream (time matrix) that is the cosmic phire.

It is like you walking into a shop with three other friends and you all wanting (or needing) the same item. This item will simply be 'copied' and given to you all.

Again, this is a natural, organic, cosmic process of replication that is 'most natural' and to your benefit. However, this is another 'technology' that has been hijacked within your reality in the form of cloning and artificial intelligence replication. The hijacked technologies are a very 'crude' form of true cosmic replication, despite the fact that many upon your planet will see them as 'advanced'. The immunity and firewall teachings within *Masters of the Matrix* will ensure that these hijacked technologies do not cross your path (unless you are teaching or exposing them in some way and you need access to them or information about them as the 'indigo warrior reporter/researcher/investigator' that you are).

You, as starseeds, have access to organic technologies through your DNA activations and your stargate ascension process. You are all 'magicians in the making' which brings us back to our topic of the Arthurian legends and the ascended master you would know as 'Merlin'.

A great many of you starseeds will align with and personally work with this particular 'being'.

Like the divine princess Aurora (Guinevere), ascended master Merlin is also the presentation of a collective consciousness and he is represented by the 'blue star' or you could say that he 'rides the blue flame'.

Whilst Aurora/Guinevere as 'daughter of the flame' is *all* of the awakened starseeds, Merlin is the collective consciousness of a smaller group of starseeds on 3D Earth. These are the individuals that work consciously with 'magick'. He is also the manifested individualised consciousness for many ascended starseeds that live within 'future versions' of Earth.

Each time you 'create a spell' or even think of yourself as someone who 'works with magick', you add to the intelligent network/grid of light that is Merlin.

You said the Excalibur codex is a fourth/fifth dimensional hermetic seal. Does this mean that if you are working with Merlin as an ascended master that this will always present as an ascended being of light?

No. There are 'false Merlins' that have presented. However, due to the nature of the Excalibur codex and the law of balance within the 'Law of One', any 'false Merlin projection' will be spotted by an activated starseed pretty much instantaneously. The Excalibur codex ensures balance within the fourth/fifth dimensional memory fields and all the Arthurian stories are coded within the beacon of truth. Excalibur is a 'balance to the force' if you will, hence 'the sword' and the energy of 'protector' or 'defender' for this is indeed the vertical pillar of light. The vertical axis is your 'inner resonance' and your 'truth beacon'. It is your 'North Star'. One cannot be fooled, tricked or misled when one has 'been knighted' and holds 'the sword' (especially the magickal sword Excalibur which cannot be defeated). You see, your own belief systems and paradigms (along with your natural sense of loyalty, truth, justice, integrity and hope) ensure the fail-safe programme. This is a multilayered hermetic seal. It is impenetrable as are all the 'characters' within the Excalibur story (or the memory imprints from the individuals within the story).

Does this mean that Merlin existed within actual reality?

Well, yes, but not as you might think.

Whilst there were some individuals upon your planet that mirrored the 'projected lifetime' that is Merlin, and one could say they *were or are* Merlin as they 'added to the grid of light', the actual 'Merlin' that your legends are based upon was an Arcturian being. His name was not 'Merlin' but the frequency and meaning matches who 'he' is.

The Arthurian legends are actually 'memories' from the Arcturian incarnations. These in themselves are 'memory imprints' or codes but they are not precursor blueprints to unmanifest reality. They are 'group soul experience' translated into individual presentations.

A great many of your legends and myths upon your planet speak of individuals that are, in actuality, group soul experience.

These 'lifetimes' occurred (or are occurring) within sixth, seventh, eighth and ninth dimensional realities. You would perhaps know these realities as Arcturus, Orion, Andromeda, Cassiopeia or other 'planetary systems'. The higher dimensions would be 'group soul memory' within the fabric we call 'cosmic phire'.

As we have said, distance/time/polarity/space are all aspects of the same force. What you know as 'other planets' are also 'other dimensions' and 'other time zones'.

So yes, Merlin was a real 'being' and he was created by the magickal thinking starseeds on 3D Earth/4D Terra/5D Gaia/6D Tiamat and 7D Eartha combined. He is a very powerful being holding much mass and he is 'much beloved' by 'us' for he is our 'brother'.

Excalibur, taking this particular legend from the one where young King Arthur 'pulls the sword from the stone', is actually the matching symbol to the 'rod' or 'staff' found within the 'Ark of the Covenant' and it symbolises the entire matrix.

Rod/staff/sword all presenting as the directional geometries of the matrix that is the true energetic presentation that is you.

This is a tale of pure alchemy as lead (the stone) becomes gold or magickal substance (the sword) assisted by magick power (Merlin's teaching). The entire path of empowerment is walked by the apprentice who becomes the master (Arthur). This is also the same journey that 'the fool' takes in the tarot deck.

Excalibur presents as 'the vertical pillar of light' but the cross at the base of the sword is the 'sacred cross' aspect of the matrix and the circular emblem that sits in the centre of the sword is the pivot point/nexus.

The sword is usually silver, signifying the divine feminine silver ray or gold or made of some other supernatural substance (alchemical transformation). It cannot be broken and whoever challenges anyone holding Excalibur cannot be defeated (the healthy, balanced matrix/DNA crystalline structure and its sovereignty and immunity).

This part of the 'legend' is the clue to the seeker that Excalibur is the fail-safe programme and cannot be hijacked.

King Arthur, as a child, is not recognised as 'royalty' as he is taken from his parents and raised by Merlin the magician who 'moves backwards in time'. This presents the backward moving arm of the cross (into the past) and Arthur 'holds the royal code' in its potential as it is in the unactivated state.

Once Arthur pulls the sword from the stone, his 'royal code' is recognised and he begins to activate (DNA memory triggers of the entire starseed mission placed here).

The 'stone' is 'hidden crystal' (hidden rock). We can see the stone here as the 'sleeping dragon' bound to the Earth, unable to fly.

When Excalibur is pulled from the stone, the hidden crystal code is revealed and the dragon is awakened (DNA/Kundalini), no longer earthbound and free to fly (through the stargate and ascend).

Guinevere (Aurora, collective consciousness for all the starseeds within 3D Earth and 5D Gaia) is the 'twin flame' to King Arthur (who is also the archangel Michael, often depicted within visionary artwork as holding a sword).

Sir Lancelot and all the Knights of the Round Table hold triggers for the warrior code. The 'indigo revolution' is also the 'creation of the round table'.

Fairness, equality, honour and justice within a 'defender/protector of the realm' focus without any central governing body.

As the knights sit at the round table (the pivot point/nexus/stargate and event horizon), they place their swords across the table forming straight, directional lines across the circle that presents the entire matrix.

In another legend of Excalibur, the sword is thrown by King Arthur into the lake (which signifies emotion, yet also the plasma field) and the 'Lady of the Lake' (Sophia, divine feminine power, plasma light being, plasma Mer-Ka-Bah) catches Excalibur and then takes it, facing straight upwards (vertical axis) back into the integrated emotion/plasma lake.

Camelot is the 'Emerald City of Krysta' or the 'Halls of Amenti' (cosmic phire).

The entire Arthurian legend/myth/story is also very similar to the biblical writings about Jesus Christ. The symbology is similar. Twelve disciples (knights, matrices across each 'Excalibur' directional axis) and Mary Magdalene (twin flame, Aurora, Mag-Da-Len codex). The crucifixion and Jesus' arms outstretched upon the cross (the horizontal axis of the matrix). The spear of destiny (Excalibur/vertical axis), water coming out of the wound instead of blood (plasma/lake of Arthurian legend).

We are not saying that individuals who mirror the symbolic memory triggers within these ancient stories did not live within your third density Earth, and we have already discussed the individuals and their experiences that made up the lifetime you know as Jesus Christ.

Yet many of these myths and stories are 'memory codices' placed within your matrix (for positive growth or from the negative agenda hijacked memory).

These myths and stories may refer to actual existing individuals, group souls or precursor to matter blueprints, and they may depict lifetimes from 'other planets' (dimensions/time zones/memory fields).

Regarding the Arthurian legends, we say to you that 'Arthurian' and 'Arcturian' are one and the same. This is 'group soul memory' (solar, galactic, multilocational) decoded into linear compartmentalisation and depicted as 'individuals'.

Another popular and accurate metaphor/story is that of Enki and Enlil. We will not touch on this vast Sumerian tale within this transmission except to say, to those who research this material, that again you are looking at the experience of 'group souls'. The memories are quantum, multilocational and from the solar/galactic perspective.

The triggers and clues to your entire story are 'hidden in plain sight' and now, in your time period that is the 'great reveal', the metaphor is being decoded. As it unravels, you begin to weave. The code unravels and the 'weaving' is the knitting together of the DNA strands. As the antimatter (metaphor/legend/myth) and the matter (your decoding and processing of the metaphor) merge together, so too do the DNA strands that are antiparticle/particle.

44: Heatwave Activations and Creation Blueprints

As the expansion from trilocation (triple helix) into 'beyond the triple helix' and 'the infinite helix' (multilocation) process occurs and the strands 'fuse together' or 'knit together', you are merging matter with antimatter within your DNA structure.

This triggers new pathways to form within your brain. Now whilst this is a natural and organic process, it is not necessarily easy and you will need to use all your spiritual training in order to 'ride these waves' as it were.

As starseeds, you have the tools. If you 'feel inspired' (many downloads being received in a short space of time coupled with a feeling of joy and excitement and much synchronicity), as will happen during energy spikes (solar flares, cosmic alignments, sabbats, eclipses and so on), then go with this.

Downloads will not so much be received in 'one package' or as 'one monad' or light lattice structure. They are likely to come in pairs (bilocation), as three at once (trilocation) or as multiple download packages, monads or concepts (multilocation).

When this occurs you will then sort these multiple concepts into a linear order, in order for processing and teaching to take place.

This can feel overwhelming and you may feel as though your 'mind is blown'.

You will not receive more than you have the ability to decode as all is in alignment with your own DNA strand remembering process. However if you do get to this 'overwhelming confusion' then we would suggest you stop your analysis of the energy, ground oneself through immersion within third dimensional linear action such as exercise and return to the decoding of the downloads or concepts when one has returned to cohesive clarity of thought.

This process is natural when multilocational consciousness (infinite helix) matter/antimatter merge takes place.

As electrical and magnetic 'poles' or polarities within the human bodymind system 'swap places' (or align/merge), there are certain other effects you may feel.

These effects come in waves and activated starseeds have all the tools in place to ride these waves. One of these effects are what we would call 'heatwave activations'.

As the etheric, quantum strand formation of silicon/crystalline structure begins to 'phire up' and 'knit together' (like in your science fiction film *Avatar*[7]) into their light speed/warp speed formations, one may feel very hot. This is not dissimilar to the hot flashes that can be experienced by hormonal changes within the perimenopausal female.

These are what you might call 'Kundalini activations' that come in waves. Yet this is a different, unique to the ascension process 'Kundalini phire' as this occurs within a crystalline lattice structure rather than carbon-based, physical Kundalini activations.

In truth, these are the 'same' Kundalini experiences. Kundalini upon your planet has taken place within the 'confines' or 'boundaries' of the carbon-based, double helix configuration (predominantly) and this may or may not precipitate physical or spiritual ascension. Those who have activated DNA Krystal structure and have moved into ascension have been 'working against the tide', if you will, due to environmental frequency being much denser than their own personal light quotient.

Now due to the collective ascension process and the carbon to crystalline DNA mutation/transformation, the Kundalini is experienced within this 'Kundalini phire' we speak of. The crystalline lattice structure within Kundalini activation is created by 'reverberations' or 'echoes' (working with the tide) as energetic frequency bounces from one Kundalini-awakened individual to another, creating magnification and intensifying the experience.

One could refer to this as a 'liquid formation' although in truth this is an energy constructed of a substance that we could call 'moving light'. We could also refer to this as 'light-filled ambrosia' or 'nectar of the gods'. It is, in fact, a matter/antimatter light merge. This substance is matter and antimatter simultaneously. This substance codes your DNA structure into the higher formation needed to create or align with a fourth density planet.

This matter/antimatter (or particle/antiparticle) light substance, light-filled ambrosia, is the 'precursor' to blue starphire.

Heatwave activations, like the hot flashes of the perimenopause, do not

7   *Avatar* (2009), science fiction movie directed by James Cameron.

last very long. Yet at times of high activation (frequency spikes), you may feel these several times per day.

Your emotions will assist you here to ride these waves of heatwave activations. It is important to allow these heatwaves to flow and do not be in resistance to them as they are precursors to blue starphire. They need to be 'nurtured' through your emotions as you ride the heatwaves.

If one feels anxious, irritated, angry or upset when the heatwave activations occur, then this can prevent the energetic flow needed throughout the newly upgraded bodymind energy matrix system.

If one allows oneself to relax and raise the emotions to gratitude, love, joy and bliss, then one will find these heatwave activations much more comfortable. Knowing these activations are part of your transformation from physical third density into light body fourth density will make these heatwave activations much more tolerable and you may even welcome them.

We would suggest you keep clear, cleansed and charged crystals around you at this time, for the crystals are completely attuned to the geological fourth density ascension birthing process. These crystals will assist you with the heatwave Kundalini activations.

How do crystals assist?

Through the charge (information, light) that they hold, passed to you (receptive starseed with open fields and nicely formed DNA antennas) as energy packages of electromagnetic radiating waves. Their matrix 'slots in' to your matrix, if you will, and you 'read' each other's energy and move through an energy transference. You empower the crystal with your charge as the crystal does the same for you. In this process, the crystals informational light structure is passed to you. This creates what you know as 'healing'.

This is the same process as referred to in the 'messages in water' work by Masaru Emoto. Your liquid cellular structure takes on the resonance and form of the crystal.

Does orgonite work in the same way?

If created within magnetic alignment with positive spin structure in place, then yes. Feel the orgonite before you bring it into your fields. The receptive and open starseed will know if the orgonite is positively and cohesively fractalised and empowered. The structure within the orgonite must be a 'nested matrix', meaning that the 'solar' or 'galactic' grid structure (within the organite and its matrix) is created to connect directly through vortices of light to the galactic grids.

There are orgonite structures available that are incorrectly aligned and these can 'spin your fields' in the 'opposite direction'. You can literally feel as though you are 'spinning out' and can feel nauseous. If you feel energised, focused and aligned then the orgonite is naturally within a synchronised vortex with the galactic grid structures.

Can crystals also spin you out and make you feel sick?

Highly unlikely as they are natural structures and automatically hold the nested fractal charge (sacred rose formation). However if they have been around dark, negative energy, low vibrations or sitting within an inverted system frequency then they can hold the charge of these 'lower' frequencies and then pass them to you. This would not necessarily make you sick and you may well be immune to the lower frequencies anyway, so you will naturally transmute them.

However, crystals are very receptive to cleansing and one can create a 'fresh, new, aligned and magickal' crystal through cleansing techniques. There is much information available regarding how to cleanse and charge a crystal. Crystal care and crystal technology messages are coming in from many highly connected master healer starseeds. Follow your intuition and use discernment when seeking out these crystal technology wayshowers.

You mentioned that the crystalline matrix structure begins to knit together like in the Avatar *film. Can you explain what you mean by this?*

246

The braids within the hair of the beings portrayed within this science fiction story had 'light filaments' at the end. So too did the animals within the story have light filaments within the hair upon their bodies. The beings would 'merge with' the animals by connecting their light filaments with those of the animals.

This is exactly how the DNA fusing or merging or 'knitting together' works. As one new DNA strand is being formed then many etheric particles (doppelganger DNA) begin to literally knit together and become one strand. This is a regrouping or remembering of 'memories' (codes within the cosmic phire). This is a matter/antimatter or particle/antiparticle merge. This is how DNA recodes and restructures.

You mention antimatter or antiparticle, but what about waves? Are there antiwaves?

In a sense, yes. Yet in truth, a wave is actually a perfect blend of matter and antimatter already.

A 'wave' is a structure and it can change its structure depending on the observer of it. 'We', the White Winged Collective Consciousness of Nine, are a wave. We are a wave existing within a 'sea of waves' and we refer here to the cosmic phire of zero point.

When we are 'observed' (by you, our conduit), we take structure as an individualised 'group soul' or 'collective consciousness'. We are your 'solar/galactic' activation aspect, if you will. We are your solar/galactic memory. You cannot access simultaneous multilocational memories at this point but you can access the 'library' or 'memory field' of multilocational memories and then decode them from the linear perspective. This is what you call 'channelling', yet in reality you are simply accessing solar/galactic memory and multilocational consciousness.

We are also 'your matrix'. We are a 'wave', therefore the matrix is a wave. When we say 'collapse the wave' and take the entire matrix structure through the nexus point of the externalised blue star matrix as you 'ride the dragon', you have simply 'observed' the matrix and decided, through focused and directed intention, that you wish to change or transform your 'wave' presentation of the matrix into the 'particle' presentation.

Once you are the 'particle', you can pass through your own centre (stargate travel). As you reconstruct your DNA sequence and 'knit together' the matter and antimatter filaments, you do what we call 'stargate ascension' and specifically 'celestial stargate ascension'. This is because your focused, directed intention is from the linear perspective with individual memory. Your perspective is that of 'one being' rather than 'many beings', despite the fact that you communicate with 'us' (your perspective of many beings - group soul).

So if I were to imagine I was you, as if I am the 'Nine', could I collapse the wave from that perspective and therefore move through solar ascension?

Indeed. It would be somewhat like this, yes. There are many techniques. As we have said, in order to construct the DNA sequencing in order, one must move through 'linear steps' when 'decoding multidimensionality' and this grounds the understanding and processing of the multidimensionality which seals the knitting strands into place. Fusion takes place. If you 'jump' too far forward into accelerated fusion (warp speed) without integration, you can 'burn out' or 'fizzle out'. You will not be able to access enough quantum convergence charge (blue starphire) to collapse your wave and ride the dragon through the nexus of your own stargate. Therefore we guide you (from the memory of your own solar/galactic DNA strand formation codex) to focus upon celestial stargate ascension at this time in your linear development.

Solar/galactic and diamond stargate ascension will come to you, we assure you of this. We guide you so that you are in alignment with the divine princess Aurora (collective consciousness of the starseeds) so you move with the collective wave. All is in what you may call 'divine order' or 'divine timing'.

Is 'divine order' or 'divine timing' orchestrated and arranged by you?

It is arranged by you. From your 'diamond' aspect. This is your 'diamond light.' The memory/knowing of Source.

Are you my 'diamond' aspect?

Yes and no. 'We' are your 'group soul memory' when observed by you (the antiparticle construction that is you). So when we communicate with you, as we are doing now, we are your solar/galactic aspect. Your 'extraterrestrial' aspect, if you will (Pleiadian, Sirian or Lyran in most cases but also Arcturian or Andromedan and other frequencies). However, when you do not 'observe' us or 'interact' with us then we are your 'diamond' aspect. So the response is predominantly no, as you observe 'us' regularly.

And when I move to solar or galactic stargate ascension, I will merge with you?

You will be us, yes. You are currently in the process of 'merging' with your galactic and diamond aspects, as are all the starseeds. This is DNA reconstruction back to the original organic human template, the 'divine architecture' of the 'starseed template' that is the twelve strand formation into the quantum 'sun' 144 strand formation. Full God-realised ascension. The infinite helix.

You say that the matrix is transformed from wave into particle in order to pass through the nexus. Is this the 'God particle' physicists talk about which we transform into?

The 'God particle' they refer to is simply that which they cannot see. The wave/particle duality that winks in and out of existence. It is simply weaving itself between matter and antimatter as it is predominantly the 'creation blueprint' and will therefore hold the structures within it for creation. Antimatter blueprint into the construction of matter. What they are seeing is simply the externalisation of their own thought. Or should we say *your* own thought. Humanity.

So humanity's thoughts create waves and particles?

Humanity's thoughts are simply 'thought itself' interpreted through the third dimensional, linear interface that is the human brain. There is only one thought and it is 'shared'. The waves and particles exist on their own and hold the blueprints for creation of matter. When that matter is created and begins to take on the structure of its creator, it becomes unified with its creator. The fact that creator becomes creation or that creation becomes creator, is in fact an illusion. The creator and the creation are unified. The waves and particles (creation blueprints) are the merge between the creator and the creation and are thus what you call the 'unified field'. 'We', and all consciousness structures who are sovereign and positively polarised, would call this the 'Law of One'.

45: The Sins of the Father

We draw your attention to one particular aspect of Matrix Transportation (celestial stargate ascension) work that is most important if you wish to create enough blue starphire to collapse the wave and ride the dragon through the nexus of your own stargate.

This is what we may call 'ancestral clearing'.

One can work within the diagonal axis of the sacred wheel moving upwards left and upwards right, filling each of the twelve matrices within each direction with light and then doing the same thing with the downward facing diagonal axis lines.

This clears ancestral 'karma' including the karmic lines for your descendants.

Why is it important to do this?

Well you see, you are not subject to just 'your own karma' but that of your ancestors. When you incarnate into a physical body, you take on DNA codes from your group soul, from Source (vertical pillar). You progress together with your alternate selves along a multidimensional quantum stream (horizontal arm of the cross) and you hold memories/knowings of the Law of One, unified field, Source (pivot point). This is your personalised and individualised incarnate blueprint, grid or matrix.

You also hold unresolved genetic imprints or codes within your doppelganger (etheric/antiparticle) DNA that has been passed down from your ancestors. In this sense you *are* your ancestors. Not only do you hold ancestral DNA codes (karma) from your ancestors, you are also subject to receiving karmic etheric imprints from your living parents and grandparents (and great-grandparents as the case may be). Remember, the doppelganger, etheric DNA is non-linear and 'out of time'. This is what is known as 'quantum entanglement' in physics. The fact that one particle can share more than one space (bilocation, trilocation and multilocation).

So what your parents and grandparents do affect you! (If you are not sovereign, integrated and on the path towards individualisation.)

One step further than this would be the fact that all your ancestors are still living. Nothing actually 'dies'. All structure and consciousness remains and is stored (either as individualised memory fields or merged/recycled memory fields). Memories are available to be 'read' and interacted with. In this respect, your 'ancestors' can influence you.

This can be most positive! Yet this can also be not in your best interests.

As a sovereign being, with a healthy balanced matrix, one would be immune from 'taking on' the karma of others including one's own family members. This immunity and sovereignty work is provided within our previous transmission *Masters of the Matrix* so we would refer you to this work.

We may also point out that what you do (experience, think, act, create) affects your descendants also as the codes within their DNA will have been passed from you, to them, through the ancestral diagonal axis.

When 'karma' manifests itself within a descendant that has come in from an ancestor or parent, it is the vibrational match to the original action that repeats within the reality of the individual still holding the ancestral replicated code. For example, if someone stole money then the matching reaction regarding money/finance or direct match will occur potentially several generations later (although this usually occurs within offspring and grandchildren). If sexual energy is misused, then the ancestral replicated code regarding the consequences of sexual misuse of energy will pass down the diagonal axis. However, this *only* passes down when the descendant moves into matching karmic alignment themselves to the original action from the ancestor. This then 'triggers' the pathway for that DNA code to filter into the matrix and manifest. If the individual is 'pure of heart' and they never step into the vibrational alignment with the original action from the ancestor, then they do not manifest that particular karmic match within their own reality. However, without conscious ancestral clearing work, they will pass the replicated code to their own offspring.

Now, if you are a conscious aware starseed, which you will be if you have found your way to this transmission, you will be passing positive codes and frequencies to your undoubtedly starseeded offspring.

However, if there is uncleared traumas and shadow aspects then these codes can sit also within the fields of your sons, daughters, grandsons and granddaughters.

Whilst there is a 'blood connection' (and therefore a DNA psychic link) with cousins, second cousins, third cousins, aunts and uncles, this is much more 'watered down' if you will. There is, however, a 'magnetic resonance' that will be felt when in the presence of anyone with whom you share a 'blood connection' (genetic relative). This magnetic resonance can also affect you in certain circumstances and it can be positive and negative.

The ancestral clearing exercise is most simple and will 'clear' or 'reset' the fields throughout the ancestral line, into the descendants and genetic relatives.

In meditation, quiet contemplation or out-of-body/dreamtime work, one would visualise the matrix as a two dimensional structure around oneself, like a wheel around you. You are standing (or sitting) at the pivot point of the matrix. The pivot point is your solar plexus, radiating upwards into your heart.

You would concentrate on the diagonal axis, starting with the left diagonal axis moving upwards. You will find here twelve matrices that move up towards a ceiling point or boundary that is the event horizon.

In turn, fill each matrix with golden light and then visualise the golden light transforming into white light. Each of the twelve matrices will be 'phired up' and glowing like little suns or beacons within your matrix.

You would then repeat, preferably aloud:

"Blessed ancestors. I stand in gratitude for all that you are and all I have received from you. I now clear this line, retaining all from you that is for my highest good and for my ascension, and resolving all karmic ties that would bind me.

I thank you, with the deepest love, as I stand fully within integration, individualisation and sovereignty. With the strength and the honour of archangel Michael and his beloved twin flame, the divine princess Aurora, daughter of the flame. So be it. It is done."

You would then go through the same visualisation on the right diagonal axis, moving upwards through the twelve matrices, filling them with golden and white light and repeating the incantation.

After this you would move to the diagonal axis going downwards to the left, then repeating this incantation:

"To my beloved descendants. My children, my grandchildren and all those of my future bloodline, I give you the gift of my unconditional love. I pass to you my wisdom, my positive alchemy and my service-to-others polarisation. I send you all that will activate you, align you, heal you and guide you and I neutralise now, through my own work upon myself, any codes or streams or structures that would transfer to you that is not in your highest good.

To the future aligned souls that may incarnate into my bloodline, I pass to you the gift of crystal code memory as my Atlantean forefathers passed to me. May the crystal code shine bright within your fields as I clear all that shall not serve. Through the power and love of the Sophia/Kryst alliance. So be it. It is done."

You would then go through the exercise again following down along the downward, diagonal line to the right. This passes through male and female descendants. Even if you have no children at this point in your incarnation, this will clear the fields for future children you are yet to have. If you do not have any children in this incarnation, you will still clear pathways along the genetic bloodline to nieces, nephews, cousins and so on.

This is an important clearing for your stargate ascension process and 'lightens the load' so you have more momentum and charge to be able to create blue starphire and 'power-up' your light vehicle. It is akin to 'throwing out the sandbags' from the basket of your hot air balloon so you may 'go higher'.

Of course, this ancestral clearing occurs naturally and in balance as you restructure your full organic 144 strand crystalline template and you do not have to work consciously this way. However, practising strengthening your focused intention and visualisation techniques will assist you greatly with stargate ascension.

If you feel somewhat 'unbalanced' after doing this exercise (light and clear within the diagonal axis, accentuating a lack of clarity within the other directional points within the matrix) then you can, in turn, visualise golden and white light (bringing in the light of the silver ray also) moving through all twelve matrices along each aspect of the directional lines within the matrix. You can circle in turn gold, silver and white light through the pivot point and around the entire matrix structure by tracing this light around the event horizon.

Emerald is another excellent colour ray to bring into your matrix, as is bright royal blue.

This creates a 'powering-up' throughout the matrix and assists in accelerating DNA activation and strand fusion.

Golden light brings protection, love, honour, integrity, abundance, cohesion and empowerment to the matrix. It also brings keycodes in from the Atlantean memory blueprint.

Silver light allows the divine feminine Goddess to awaken throughout the matrix and brings healing, nurturing, wisdom and magick. It also brings keycodes in from the Lemurian memory blueprint.

White light brings cleansing, clarity, purity and full ascension memory codes for the 144,000 warriors of light and thus full strand formation.

Emerald light brings joy, happiness, mystery, mystical experience, connection with the elemental realm and holds the Krysta/Kryst codex (Source memory). Goddess Sophia holds the light of the emerald flame.

Bright royal blue brings higher communication, integrated emotion and celestial stargate ascension activation and creates seed points or seed codes for celestial ascension and the memory and knowing of how to 'collapse the wave'. This brings precursor seed codes for memory and knowing regarding the 'rainbow body of light' and thus galactic and diamond stargate ascension.

46: Ascension Symptoms

Is it possible that some people will be upset when they discover that these individual presentations of archangels, ascended masters and goddesses are actually group souls depicted as 'one entity'?

I have met people who believe they are Thoth, archangel Michael or Aurora. They believe they are the only one.

It is not our intention to create upset within the growth and emotional system of any ascending starseed. Each and every starseed is precious to us beyond your imagining and we love them more than you can possibly know. If individual teaching comes in from guidance structures then they will be 'gently guided' into this information as and when they are ready.

We, with these transmissions, communicate with many simultaneously. We look at the collective consciousness that is the 'infinite helix network' and we deliver information accordingly.

You see, it is absolute truth when an individual says that they are Aurora or that they are archangel Michael. It is just that *so are all the other starseeds.*

The indigo starseeds will hold a code for 'royalty' and they will naturally and intrinsically know the level of their importance to this ascension process which is all accurate. This can often translate into the feeling that their mission is so crucial that the entire ascension timeline manifesting depends upon them. It does. The code is correct. However, this is a group consciousness mission. It is Aurora and Michael (Guinevere and Arthur) that will ascend with Earth. It is the collective. Yet it is also the individual and if you hold a memory that you *are* a particular being then you are correct. Your belief system will be assisted once you become aware that you are also *all* the starseeds as well, therefore they are *also* the higher entity which you know that you are.

Earlier you said that the Eye of Horus was in the same place as the pivot point/nexus/blue pearl. So is the Eye of Horus the stargate? I thought the Eye of Horus depicted the third eye (pineal gland).

The Eye of Horus is both the pivot point/nexus *and* the third eye/pineal gland. Although the nexus is at the solar plexus/heart chakra point, this is in order for you to create balance within the entire matrix structure.

The pineal gland is how you see the antimatter realities and the stargate systems. The blue star matrix is an externalised presentation of the *entire matrix* and this includes the third eye/pineal gland. One could definitely say that the pineal gland *is* the stargate. The reason for this is because this is the celestial aspect that is you. It is your 'star'. So whilst the 'Eye of Horus' depicts the pineal, it actually depicts the crystalline pineal as the stargate and thus the entire matrix. It is your entire matrix that is the stargate. The nexus is simply the centre point that you pass through.

So do we have to 'pass through' anything at all? Does stargate ascension occur even if we never consciously pass through a stargate?

You do not need to be consciously aware of 'passing through' anything. The blue star matrix exercise is a provided exercise for those who wish to explore their inner landscape this way and consciously create fourth density upon your planet. Stargate ascension is the restructuring of the twelve strand crystalline template. You *will* pass through stargates as part of your ascension process but you may not remember doing this, know you are doing this or interpret your stargate ascension as such. The brain will interpret the new code in many ways.

Can you give examples of what this might be interpreted as?

Yes. Feeling like something big is about to happen. Knowing something new is happening that has never happened before. Feeling that one has an incredibly important job to do and feels personally responsible for the rest of humanity and the planet. Feeling as though one is in two places at once. Change in memory (remembering things that did not happen and/or forgetting things that did happen). Having dreams of Pegasus the winged horse, riding on a unicorn or magick carpet, flying in a UFO or lightship, seeing blue lights, blue spheres or blue orbs. Seeing many orbs of different colours. Becoming preoccupied, obsessed and fascinated with archetypes such as Poseidon, Merlin, Jesus, ascended masters, archangels or extraterrestrials. Being compelled to research sacred geometry and feeling that geometric pictures, structures, symbols and artwork are personally connected to you in some way. Often you will have been called by sacred geometry, sacred master numbers or other symbols for years without knowing what they mean. Becoming drawn to visit sacred sites, stone circles and crop circles. Being drawn to high energy vortices on Earth such as Glastonbury in England. Becoming very sensitive to low frequencies from people, places, food or technology. There are many, many 'ascension symptoms' if you will.

So are you saying that if we dream of a UFO or become sensitive to a friend we have known for years, or we can no longer talk on a mobile/cell phone, that we are passing through stargates?

You are restructuring your DNA. The DNA is a stargate (a time portal). You are regaining higher and higher memory. Once you create enough quantum convergence charge (blue starphire), you collapse the wave (antiparticle/particle merge as strands weave together and fuse/knit as they reconstruct like in the film *Avatar*) and you create the dragon (your DNA changes form, you become the shape-shifter). You dive through the centre of your own stargate (become a genius, activate seed codes for full twelve strand/144 strand DNA formation) and you achieve celestial stargate ascension. How your brain interprets this will be unique and subjective.

So the blue star matrix is just a memory trigger?

Yes, but it is also an accelerant. When you collapse the wave, your DNA vortices begin to spin faster and faster. This is essential in order to create blue starphire. You do not want to 'burn out'. The blue star matrix exercise trains your light body/Mer-Ka-Bah within the extremely disciplined spiritual practise of celestial stargate ascension. As with all things, you need to train and you need to practise. You can still move through stargate ascension without practise but you will be left 'wondering what is happening' to you. If you practise now, when the time comes for collective ascension from 3D Earth into 5D Gaia, you will be an adept. You will be a dragonrider and you will be a shape-shifter.

Can you talk about plasma realities and plasma beings? You mentioned the plasma Mer-Ka-Bah. What is this?

Yes. This is an important subject within your stargate ascension process. We shall respond to your question.

47: Bliss and Plasma

We have spoken about ascension being a three-step process. Celestial, solar/galactic and diamond/Source levels. These are in direct synchronisation with the expression of your consciousness and the reconstruction of your DNA sequencing, creating the starseed template for your Ascension experience.

Now in truth, ascension is far more than just a three-step process. There are in fact many stages to awakening and ascension. We present three stages for ease of explanation and understanding. There are those who thrive with the presentation of complex maps and diagrams and this assists them to process and make sense of the journey they are on. It also helps with DNA organisation through cellular memory (activation).

However, our conduit, within her own reaching for understanding and processing of this exciting but 'life changing' journey she is on, finds that maps and diagrams can be overwhelming in their complexity. There are many starseeds who feel the same and respond more to the metaphoric poetry and the beauty that this conjures up within them. There are those who respond to picture, image, art and colour and there are those who respond to music and sound. Yet indeed, so too, are there those who respond to mathematical and geometrical presentation that is more technical and this is where graphs, maps and detailed diagrams come in.

We, as the White Winged Collective Consciousness of Nine, aim to present 'teachings' and activations utilising the wishes and needs of the different callings within the starseed individuals. We present the beauty of the poetry and the metaphor and present visuals for you to create the picture and colourful images within your mind's eye. We present the vibrational sound tones through initiations and guided meditations that can be spoken aloud by you. Also our conduit speaks our transmissions and these are presented with music and image, activations in and of themselves (see video archive at magentapixie.com).

We have therefore simplified the ascension process into the three stages we present. We have simplified the presentation of the vast energetic database that is the toroidal field/matrix/Mer-Ka-Bah and we have presented this in its two dimensional form.

As our conduit and you, dear reader/listener, assimilate and process this information then we can present material that moves into more detail.

However, there is simply but one aspect to be aware of here. Despite technical presentation, understandings of levels and stages, decoding the metaphors and working within your spiritual disciplines, ceremonies, initiations and activations, ascension comes down to one thing and one thing only:

The emotion of 'bliss'.

It really is as simple as this.

Whilst disciplined steps and specific teachings assist you greatly, your bliss is the key.

When you feel bliss, your inner knowings are activated and *you do this naturally.*

Why? *Because you have done this before.*

Bliss is the emotion that is the key to ascension.

So whilst we present information and respond to your questions, it is most important that you understand your place within as the ascension journey.

It is personal and unique to you and if you allow yourself to feel bliss then *you cannot get this wrong.*

Now, we are not suggesting that you walk around in a state of bliss all day long (yet that would be good, both for you personally and your ascension activation) because of course, you live in a third dimensional reality. There are other emotions that need to be explored and integrated as part of your awakening and your clearing that takes you into ascension.

Yet, if you can set aside some time each day to allow yourself to move into bliss, this will allow you to enter into these three stages of ascension and make sense of them yourself, following your own inner teachers (inner-tuition/intuition).

If you have strong emotions to deal with and integrate (such as grief or worry) then finding the actual emotion of bliss can be a challenge. Grief and worry are temporary emotional states, even whilst they can seem at times as though they are permanent (the dark night of the soul).

We would like to present you with information that will assist you in finding bliss and through this we present information about why bliss is so important.

We have already spoken of the golden mean equation within and how this relates to your ascension process and specifically stargate ascension.

You have asked us to discuss plasma and this is a vast subject. This is something that can touch your experience within all levels of ascension, celestial/star/stellar, solar/galactic/universal and diamond/cosmic/Source.

One could see these levels of awakening as:

1) The level of the stars.

2) The level of the suns.

3) The level of Source.

The substance you know as 'plasma' permeates through all three levels, yet in different form.

There is stellar plasma, planetary plasma and plasma within your physical body.

This changes form and is found in the sun and the 'plasma beings' that live there.

So too is 'plasma' at the level of Source, although at this level it is light. It is also darkness.

There is plasma that is matter (particle) and plasma that is antimatter (antiparticle).

One way to look at plasma overall would be to see it as a conductor of matter and antimatter, or as a 'bridge' that joins the two together.

'Plasma' is a field of energetic substance and it presents organically (in organic structures such as yourself and your planet) and it can be created (as in the case of artificial intelligence).

It is therefore 'positive' and 'negative' if you will. Not 'plasma' itself, but the way that it is used.

How is this related to bliss?

Well, if we present to you that which you may know of as 'the rapture', it will assist you within your understanding of plasma.

We therefore speak now of 'the rapture'.

48: The Rapture

The 'rapture' is something that has been spoken about upon your planet for many aeons of time. It has been quite misunderstood by many of you but there have always been the adepts and the masters amongst you (and the seekers and the apprentices who have become the adepts and masters) that have understood the rapture.

The rapture is the process of being 'lifted up' and 'lifted off the planet' in a state of divine bliss.

This, of course, is the same thing as ascension. The rapture is not 'one event' but simply describes the time when the 'plasma light body' or 'plasma Mer-Ka-Bah' is constructed and activated.

The rapture, like the consuming of the sacred ambrosia, would consist of the merging of blissful states such as ecstasy, euphoria and bliss. These states are 'grounded' or 'earthed' (through integration) so they do not 'spin you out' or 'burn out your charge'.

Once these states are grounded or earthed, you 'become' the plasma, light body or plasma Mer-Ka-Bah (merge or blend between activated oscillating light fields, spirit/plasma and the transformation of the physical body).

So 'the rapture' is occurring now upon your planet as this knowledge becomes more and more available and as you naturally 'raise to these rapturous, ecstatic, blissful, euphoric' states and ground them through activation.

The rapture of bliss creates plasma and the two are intertwined.

You remember we spoke about 'the flame' which we called 'cosmic phire'? We explained that this field of cosmic phire is made up of particles that 'dance' and 'move' (in a state of kinetic momentum) and that this field of cosmic phire fills the universal spaces (dark matter, dark energy) and is the content found within zero point.

The cosmic phire is bliss. It is the substance of the rapture. It is the precursor to the blueprints of reality. This cosmic phire is plasma. Or we could say 'plasma particles' or 'plasma sparks'. These are very tiny pieces of intelligence (light) that exist as a unified field (Law of One) and as individualised points of perspective, simultaneously. They are what you would know as 'memories'.

Are you saying that our memories are made of plasma?

We are saying this, but this is not to be interpreted as the plasma that makes your modern televisions and computer screens (although they are connected, albeit crudely).

There are many layers to plasma. Plasma is the force or the inertia/kinetic merge (it is completely still yet simultaneously in a constant state of movement) that is in a synergistic state of creation/creator relationship between matter/antimatter or particle/antiparticle. You see, when matter and antimatter come together (as they do in order for creation to take place), they 'cancel one another out' and create nothing. But because 'nothing' has just been 'created' then it must be 'something'. That 'something' is the fabric that makes up zero point, that which we call 'cosmic phire'. It is also known as 'the flame' or the 'eternal flame' due to that fact that it is infinite.

In truth, it is infinite and finite simultaneously because it is 'pure potential'. Whilst at the level of zero point, it is 'nothing', but it is actually 'something' and that 'something' is plasma. Plasma is simply the substance that is 'formless form'. It has no form because it is nothing. It has form because it is a creation, therefore it must be something.

It is the form that is taken when 'pure thought' begins to 'think'.

The reasons why we call this a 'flame' or 'cosmic phire' are twofold:

1) It looks like a flame or phire clairvoyantly/psychically as you perceive it through its own medium. As in you view it through the third eye/pineal gland which is pure liquid plasma.

2) It is actually fire. Not in the sense that you know fire in its elemental state (although if you were to look at the substance within an actual flame you would find plasma). It is fire in the sense that it is a 'conductor'. It creates 'quantum convergence charge'. It 'conducts' electrical movement.

If you strike two stones together, you will eventually create fire. The conductor is the movement itself created by two stones rubbing together which creates what we may call a 'plasma wave'.

You see, plasma is neither a particle nor a wave and is both simultaneously.

If you look at a positive force and a negative force and balance a force between them, you would be presented with a neutral force. That neutral force (cancelled out by a positive and a negative merge) is neither positive nor negative but holds potential for both. It is a bridge.

Many of you know this bridge 'between realities' as the 'rainbow bridge'. This rainbow bridge is made of plasma.

Your memories are simply 'thoughts that have structure' and are therefore made of what we may call 'plasma light'. This would be antimatter with the potential to become matter. The potential part of antimatter is plasma.

The same goes for matter. All matter holds the 'potential' to become antimatter. The 'potential' part of the matter is plasma.

So whilst it *is* thought, it *is* memory and it *is* light, it is the potential created by these or the potential for creation within these.

Plasma is also a most interesting substance. We could present an entire transmission or series of transmissions on plasma as it is an infinite structure (with potential for becoming finite). It is also a finite structure (with the potential for becoming infinite).

The understanding upon your planet regarding plasma is 'most small' if you will.

In order to understand plasma one would need a scientific *and* a spiritual viewpoint.

Our conduit has only the most basic (within third dimensional) understanding of science and physics, most of which has been taught to her by us. However, her true understanding is 'more advanced' than most physicists upon your planet due to the spiritual understanding afforded her through this path and the fact that she communicates with the structures and forces that they study! We point this out because this is the same situation with you, dear reader! If you are a starseed, you too have this 'advanced' understanding. It may not seem this way for you as

266

you are constantly in a state of downloading, assimilating and processing information.

However, you are in a state of expansion which is ascension. That expansion takes you into 'genius flow' (you become a genius) and then you begin the next level of master genius, adept, ascended being, fully realised, self-aware and so on.

Plasma is a formless form, as we have said, that is neither matter nor antimatter and is neutral. However it is a 'charge conductor' and when it moves into a creation stage it can charge itself and become matter, antimatter or a simultaneous merge of the two which is different to its original form.

It is like a 'cosmic photocopier' as in it can 'take on' the exact structure of something else.

As you can see, this 'technology', when harnessed, can be used for positive (creation itself and life) or negative (anti-life/against life).

Plasma (cosmic phire) is therefore the 'giver of life' or the 'destroyer of life'.

This would also be a fitting way to describe your sun, your stars and your planets. They are all givers/destroyers of life depending on how they are perceived and interacted with. They are all made of plasma.

Plasma, as we have said, can be matter as in solid or liquid structure. It can be antimatter as in thought, idea, visualisation, clairvoyant sight image, fabric of hyperspace/inner space/innerverse (the inverse).

It can also be a merge between matter/antimatter or particle/antiparticle. It can 'change form' and is the ultimate 'cosmic shape-shifter'. It can become a wave or a particle as it holds potential for both as it *is* pure potential in itself.

When it is a merge of matter and antimatter, it presents as what we can only call 'liquid light'.

This liquid light is actually a structure. It is not liquid in the sense you know it (like water) but it *is* a fluid. It is 'fluid filaments of light'. It looks (clairvoyantly) like a 'moving river of bright golden and white light' yet it can also present as all colours both individual and merged and as no colour. It is very much like 'a rainbow'. (In fact when you see rainbows on your planet, they are made of the reflective light aspect of plasma.)

What does this liquid light plasma have to do with the rapture and your ascension process? Well, the answer to this is *everything!*

You do not have to understand this, of course, in order to ascend but knowing what you are visualising will help greatly with the ascension process.

When you feel the emotions of rapture (bliss, euphoria and ecstasy), you create a 'mathematical frequency' within the body. The emotion itself creates a charge (a code) which is 'placed within your individualised matrix'.

This begins the process you know as 'Kundalini'. It is the liquid light plasma (remembering this is not actually fluid in the sense you know it) that 'rises up the spine' and moves into or activates the pineal gland.

Now, in the pineal gland you have liquid light plasma and what we may call 'plasma crystals'. The two (in a healthy pineal gland) 'rub together' if you will, like the two stones rubbing together to create a spark of light.

The liquid light plasma and plasma crystals rub together to create a charge (blue starphire) which is an electrical conductor for 'externalised plasma'.

Plasma exists within matter and antimatter as both and neither. Plasma is a 'cosmic photocopier'. It has the ability to 'project an image' of itself as antimatter. This creates an object formed of antimatter plasma light and the reflections create an image. You can 'see' this image through the conductivity of the pineal gland plasma liquid light and plasma crystals (blue starphire).

When you dream or visualise, this is what you see. You create a 'copy' of the 'original' through the plasma crystals conductivity. The image you see is therefore not simply an 'imagination' that does not exist. It is a projected image of 'pure potential'.

Pure potential can become physically manifest if the 'charge' created holds the correct mathematical formula (positive/negative/neutral ratios) needed.

Our conduit does not have the necessary terminology within her fields to explain the 'physics' of this presentation, however there are starseeds incarnate upon your planet who *do* have the necessary terminology needed. They are also 'channels' in the sense that they communicate with 'us' (as in the 'we' that are the plasma cosmic phire formulated as

268

individualised intelligence), yet they would not necessarily refer to themselves as a 'channel'.

You see, the conductivity within the pineal gland plasma crystals and liquid light is not just an 'eye' that can project a visual landscape.

It is an 'antenna' and can also pick up 'sound'.

Your telepathy, clairvoyance, clairaudience and clairsentience (including that which is known as 'channelling')' is all electrical plasma conductivity through liquid light and plasma crystals within the pineal gland.

However, the pineal gland is only one antenna within a field of many antennas.

The plasma liquid light and the crystals also exist within the DNA. That which we call 'etheric' or 'doppelganger DNA' is also plasma. Hence our use of the term 'organic technology'.

Within the pineal gland, a chemical is formed that is similar in structure to the psychoactive properties within your ayahuasca and peyote plants. Known also as 'DMT'.

These chemicals that are naturally present within your bodies and within plants are also 'plasma structures'.

The entire plant kingdom is made up of 'plasma' structures in the sense that golden filaments of liquid light runs through its make-up. You may know this as 'ormus' or 'white powder gold'. These are all plasmic structure as they are matter with the potential for antimatter.

Now as we have said, plasma as a conductor has the ability to 'project itself' and make a 'cosmic copy' of itself.

The DNA strands, when they reconstruct into the crystalline structure needed for ascension, they are able to make copies of themselves and project them into a full antimatter state. The antimatter state is 'fluid' but holds the potential to be 'solid'.

This is what we call a 'stargate'.

Plasma is 'self replicating' (able to reproduce itself) but needs a seed point or focus point to do this from (as in thought). Once thought holds enough mass or blueprinted structure (focused, directional intention), then the plasma can self-replicate.

The 'blue star matrix' you create within the exercise given within this transmission is a projection of the plasma crystals charge within the DNA and the pineal gland.

When you 'collapse the wave' within your visualisation field and 'ride the dragon' through the nexus of the stargate, you are instructing the plasmic replication to 'produce stargates' or 'stargate information' if you will.

You start the process of 'unlocking' the Atlantean codes within DNA (blood and bone) and 'read' the information within the 'thirteenth crystal skull' (pineal gland and plasmic electrical conductor pathways in the brain/DNA and entire electrical system of the body).

However, the matrix system (bodymindspirit Mer-Ka-Bah matrix) is also magnetic. The matrix is a 'magnetic field'. The electrical conductivity merges with the magnetic field to 'create charge' by cancelling each other out by merging. This 'merge point' between the magnetic fields and electrical systems of the body creates a 'plasma field' or 'plasma mind'.

When you activate Kundalini, you are also 'firing up' or 'phiring up' the matrix. Creating enough 'charge' which through DNA activation becomes 'quantum' and all the points within the 'twelve tribes of Israel' converge together creating 'quantum convergence charge' (blue starphire).

When you 'ride the dragon' (collapse the wave), the dragon's breath (which is fire) creates the fabric of zero point, cosmic phire (which are the precursors to the blueprints of creation).

These 'precursor particles' are pure potential and are able to copy or replicate themselves. They are neither matter nor antimatter, but a merge of both and hold potential for both within the replication process. They are plasma.

Who creates the dragon's breath?

The dragon.

Who causes the dragon to 'release the dragon's breath'?

The dragonrider.

Who are the dragonriders?

They are you, dear starseeds. They are *you*.

270

49: Myst of the Kryst

Plasma, as the ultimate 'cosmic photocopier', can 'replicate' itself into many, many forms.

As we have said, these forms can be matter, antimatter, a blend of the two or neither (holding potential for both). It is a 'neutral substance' able to replicate positive or negative charges and their creations.

Many beings throughout the multiverse/omniverse use plasma as a substance to create with. Plasma can either be a 'living substance' or a substance 'without life but holding the blueprints for life' or it can be an 'anti-life' substance.

Many beings use plasma to create vehicles (plasma ships, plasma geometric structures, plasma Mer-Ka-Bah vehicles).

Plasma can be used to preserve memories, create structures from those memories and store 'code'.

Many lightships are made of plasma, both living and non-living and also artificial intelligence.

Plasma is a highly sought after substance for the creation of artificial intelligence due to its ability to self-replicate.

Living lightships (bio-plasma ships) are actual 'bodies' for some of these beings and they can be both negative or positive (or neutral) beings. They can present as male, female, androgynous and can also present as a 'third gender' if you will. There are beings who reproduce (or replicate) themselves and they are neither male nor female, but neither are they androgynous. They have a 'force' that manifests itself somewhere within the male/female scale that creates an entirely different gender. The nearest you have on your planet to this 'third gender' would be the marsupials, although your jellyfish and other aquatic life also hold resemblance.

The uni/multi/omniverse is abundant at a scale that simply cannot be conceived of. It is also infinitesimally small and can fit inside just one atom.

This is difficult for many of you to understand, we realise this. It is to do with the holographic nature of reality. No matter how many times you divide something, it contains the whole within it. Therefore there is no actual size in the true reality. Each 'smaller division' is simply the same size as the division before it. Everything is in the same place.

Plasma is a 'charge' or a 'force' that is a precursor to the blueprint of creation. The blueprint and the creation, all in one.

A name we could use for plasma would be 'mist' or 'myst' which becomes 'mystery.' Plasma is indeed the 'mystery'. Plasma remains the mystery, for it is the mystery itself that creates the charge for the 'solving of the mystery'. It is the unmanifest and the manifest simultaneously.

We would say that the term 'the myst of Kryst' is much more appropriate to describe the sacred substance rather than 'plasma'.

When you create the 'dragon's breath' which becomes 'cosmic breath', you literally create 'the myst of Kryst' which is plasma.

Your ascension into higher states feeds individualised memory (and thus experience) into the plasma streams so that they may be 'read'.

Plasma is the 'cosmic modelling clay', if you will, and it is the 'base substance' for creation. When 'you' as a divine spark are conceptualised and brought into existence as 'pure thought', you are the liquid light of plasma in its precursor stage.

You are then 'replicated' as an actual blueprint within dimensional fields of form and you are mathematically designed through the divine architecture of the creational streams of sacred geometry.

Your conceptualisation of thought of the cosmic mind is then replicated as conceptualisation of thought within the mind of the 'physical womb'. This then translates to the aware consciousness of the incarnated female and her 'twin flame' partner. Through the divine tantra of sexual coupling, the conceptualised thought within the physical womb is received through the bio-plasmic antenna system of the bodymindmatrix and this creates the conceptualised thought within their awareness.

All is then 'ready' to receive the physical replication into actual manifestation.

This is the creation of 'conception'.

This occurs at the antimatter levels as the blueprinted structure (sixth dimensional higher self) and at the matter levels (the physical human in utero).

The sixth dimensional blueprinted structure springs into full consciousness through the memory fields of the plasma 'cosmic phire'. This is created by your 'memory imprints of experience' that you passed into the plasma field during your ascension process.

So you see, you literally 'create' at the densest levels of matter (physical life) and at the highest levels of matter (plasma fields/cosmic phire).

Yet it is *your ascension* as a collective that creates at the higher levels consciously.

So are you saying that if we do not ascend then we do not create at the higher levels? Does this affect our ability to create on the physical levels?

All structures will eventually ascend as individualised consciousness structures, as they are magnetically pulled towards that trajectory of eventuality.

In your physical realities then, if you do not go through an ascension process, you do not raise the DNA structure and you do not create blue starphire and dragon's breath (plasma records and memories). Your memories are still 'read' after you leave your body (in a linear sense) but these memories will be somewhat fragmented, like jigsaw pieces. The jigsaw would need to be 'put together' in order for the streams to be read. You create a 'scattered', 'mixed' or 'non-cohesive' vibration. These vibrations are not 'read' in the sense that a cohesive vibration would be.

When a collective memory vibration is 'read', it is then used to create (plasma replication).

The non-cohesive fragmented collective memory vibration needs to be 'put together like a jigsaw' before it is read. This takes place through the reincarnational cycle until individualised ascension takes place amongst many individuals. In this way, the collective ascension (known to some as 'harvest') creates a cohesive intelligence (adept or ascended master) that can be 'read' and be 'created from' (hence why an ascended master is also a creator god).

You asked if your physical creation is affected if you do not simultaneously create at the antimatter level. Yes, the physical creation is affected.

Whilst 'high level creativity' can still take place, this usually occurs within individuals at the upper levels of the third dimension (known also as the third and fourth dimensional merge point).

Individuals existing within lower and often middle third dimensional harmonic levels will feel as though their creativity is stifled or blocked. Often they have no desire to create. The blueprint for creation that is replicated within the feminine physical womb does not have 'open channels' or 'plasma light streams' connecting the conceptualisation of antimatter to the physical conception. Therefore 'any soul can just jump in' if you will.

Conception is a very specific mathematical formula that is designed and developed carefully following a particular 'cosmic mechanical science' if you will.

Without the matter/antimatter plasma light stream connection then 'any passing soul' can just incarnate without the careful planning and blueprinting in place.

This is metaphor of course, but this shows the difference between an unplanned life without structure and a planned structured one.

Is this the same thing as 'forced reincarnation' as opposed to conscious choice?

Yes, in a sense. The 'passing soul' that just 'jumps in' to the 'open womb vehicle' is a soul that is not able to move past the fourth dimension as a memory structure. It does not have enough quantum convergence charge (blue starphire) to expand and individualise into the fifth dimension and beyond. Yet it holds enough mass (quantum charge) to hold together a personality field. This personality field will be dissipating or 'losing charge' if you will. Just as the physical incarnated individual desires life so too does the non-physical. So seeing the chance of an 'unplanned and unstructured' vehicle back into physical incarnation, the soul makes the 'choice' to take that path. However, there are not that many choices for an earthbound soul (a soul bound to the gravitational field of third and fourth dimensional Earth).

The soul can either remain within 4D relying on quantum charge coming in from 'memory' held within 3D friends/relatives/places or allow itself to dissipate (a choice rarely, if ever, taken) or reincarnate. So whilst 'a choice' is made, yes, this is essentially forced reincarnation.

Is this because of the trapping system or nets within the fourth dimension?

Essentially yes. The 'traps' are laid, if you will, by 'others' (within 3D and 4D) but it is the soul's 'choice' to be trapped or to find sovereignty.

Is the unplanned open vehicle into the third dimension also the same thing as an unplanned pregnancy?

Not necessarily. The 'planning' can take place at the antimatter sixth dimensional level in alignment with the 'womb of the female' without the conscious awareness of the female 'making the choice' to conceive. The womb holds a 'mind of her own' if you will. This is 'Kali', the dark goddess. 'Dark' only because she is 'buried in the underworld' and is always a manifestation of the incarnated female's subconscious or unconscious desire to conceive a child. In this sense, the conception is planned.

Do all twin flame couples conceive a starseed child?

Over ninety percent of all conceptions upon your planet at the time of this transmission are starseeded children. Even the souls 'trapped in 4D' are starseed souls that did not activate. Starseeded souls with DNA seed codes are now incarnating within 'Illuminati' or 'cabal' (service-to-self) families and have been for quite some time.

Should twin flame couples do anything, as in ceremony or prayer, in order to ensure the 'right' child is born to them?

As we have said, this is a carefully planned endeavour so no twin flame energetic couple would conceive the 'wrong' child. All is vibrationally in harmony with 'the divine plan' if you will.

However, 'charging' the conception with crystals, music or ceremony is always recommended.

It is not just the conception of the child that 'charging' the sexual act between twin flames is recommended for. The 'tantra' that is created between the consciously loving creative (twin flame) couple is blue starphire.

Kundalini (liquid light plasma) is created and this triggers pineal gland activation (plasma crystals creating charge), so the replicated image of truth and wisdom can be presented to the individual.

Whilst the sexual act itself creates blue starphire/Kundalini plasma liquid light, it is essentially the orgasm that triggers the 'Kundalini phire' - especially the orgasm within the female (although both individuals within the partnership raise the Kundalini).

What about same sex couples or individuals on their own? Can they raise Kundalini through the sexual act?

Yes, as long as it is sacred (charged) using crystals, geometry, music, herbs, plants, certain foods, prayer and so on.

The divine feminine frequency flows through the male also. 'Tantric' or 'cosmic' sex can take place between any couple who genuinely hold high levels of love and respect for one another and who hold a 'spiritual' relationship.

Individuals on their own can create that same energy when they are loving, kind, awakened individuals living in cosmic harmony with the Earth and Earth's parallels (Terra, Gaia, Tiamet, Eartha, Agartha and other alternative names such as Tara, Urantia or the 'jewel planet').

We provide an incantation that can be read to one another (in the case of a relationship) or read aloud (in the case of an individual working tantrically in this way, on their own).

50: Tantric Twin Flame Initiation

As I enter into my sacred tantric merge with the beloved twin flame heart,

I know that the blue starphire charge created shall lift us up into life everlasting.

The eternal flame of immortality shall burn bright within us, as we raise the loving and sacred white Krystal river of life that runs through the spine that is the blessed pillar of light.

At the Godhead blue star, I divine, with my inner eye, sights to behold.

The temple has been observed and I take my place within it, anointed within the initiation of Sophia, Aurora and Kali, creatrix goddesses that burn with the love of the flame.

My orgasm is my ambrosia and as I drink from the golden chalice that is my own womb, I share the manna of my pleasure with all.

I am the divine feminine Goddess and, with many arms outstretched, I shower all who worship at the foot of the rose with my abundant love.

The seas of the moon-tides are ours to ride, the warm embrace of the sun's rays are ours to bathe within.

Together, we intertwine our emotions at the foot of the willow tree and enter the blissful sleep of the visionary.

We travel to distant lands and it is Pegasus, the winged horse, who brings us home to rest,

Until we rise again, with the Kundalini heat of our sweet, sweet love.

51: Beyond the Rainbow

We have shown you how to 'collapse the wave' and 'ride the dragon' through the nexus of your own stargate in order to create what we call 'Matrix Transportation' (which is also Mer-Ka-Bah vehicle or light body activation).

There is another way to utilise these stargates. The stargates are an entire network or grid of infinite stargates. As we have explained to you, each and every structure as one cosmic unit is an infinity and due to its matrix structure it has a central point (pivot point/nexus) that is a stargate.

These stargates exist within antimatter realms (hyperspace) and within matter realms (your physical universe/multiverse/omniverse) and also at the merge point between these realms (plasma fields).

Your ability to visualise creates the connection (and travel) through these stargates.

Now, we would remind you again that *you are not actually going anywhere.*

What is happening is that you are restructuring your DNA template back to its original form. This moves you through bilocation, trilocation, multilocation (and omnilocation which is full omnipresence). You are simply activating the 'Law of One' and *becoming the unified field.*

This can seem like you are 'travelling through space or dreamtime worlds at high velocity, warp speed'. From the third dimensional (and fourth) linear perception, you *are* travelling. You are travelling through time. From the highest perspective (the omnipresence of Source), you are 'standing still and expanding your fields'.

This is what it means to ascend. You are expanding your energy field, further and further into the 'fields of memory' so that they can 'be read'. You literally become the mind, with memories of the group soul. When you do this, you 'create' a body for yourself.

This is an energy body that is representative of your group soul memory. You literally 'extend your matrix' or 'Mer-Ka-Bah'.

This is what it means to 'activate your Mer-Ka-Bah' which is a light ship.

This is your 'plasma Mer-Ka-Bah'.

These terms can be confusing for the seeker, yet all you are doing here is 'expanding your energy system' as you 'encompass more and more space' (which is actually time).

You literally become a 'time matrix' and, in essence, this is always what you have been.

The stargates we speak of could be seen as 'node points' within time. In our transmission *Masters of the Matrix* we spoke of node points. These are convergence points where 'all timelines converge and become one' and the node point contains 'limitless possibility'.

The reason for these 'node points' containing limitless possibility is because they are 'space pockets' or 'time pockets' of zero point energy (free energy, cosmic phire). Through their non-locational presentation (within space and time), they are *part of you.*

You make the choice if you wish to connect with these node points. In your third dimensional reality, these node points are known as 'black holes'. We call them 'stargates'.

One could refer to 'tampered with' or 'deliberately created' node points as black holes and the 'organic ones' as stargates, if one wished. These terminologies are simply your choice.

The term 'black hole' does not really fit and 'we' find this most amusing as your 'black hole' is literally filled with the most abundant range of colour that you cannot imagine.

In a linear sense, falling into a black hole would be like 'being dropped into a pot of multicoloured paint'.

However, you are not going to fall into a black hole. You are going to pass through stargates! All the colours of the rainbow and 'beyond the rainbow' can be experienced here.

So there is a vast network of stargates. Now many of these stargates have been 'unavailable to you', as in 'closed off' or 'shut down' or 'inoperational'. This is due to the DNA fragmentation or 'the fall' that took place within your planetary and galactic reality.

All connects together. Now one could say that the 'galactic grids' and the 'planetary grids' have been damaged (infiltrated, hijacked) and this would be correct. When the planetary and galactic grids are damaged then so too are the corresponding DNA template structures within your bodies. The macrocosmic and the microcosmic are one.

It is important however, not to 'jump into' the instant victim/saviour programme when you take the perspective of your planetary and galactic grids being infiltrated. When you take the victim/saviour programme, you can become angry, upset, shocked, horrified and traumatised through the memory of the loss of the true self (and move into profound grief).

This is why we have presented here the teaching that is bilocational consciousness. You will need your bilocational thought processes here to prevent you moving into the grief that comes through the realisation of this atrocity on a galactic level.

When you move into victim/saviour mentality, *you cannot access the stargates.*

Why is this?

This is because victim/saviour mentality is a third (and somewhat fourth) dimensional, linear expression of polarity. This takes you into the structures of 3D/4D and thus the regression of the corresponding DNA template structure.

So DNA can (and probably will) regress back to previous configurations. This is akin to you practising yoga every day for a year and then stopping your practise for a few weeks. When you resume your yoga practise, you will find this much more of a challenge as your flexibility will not be at the level it was.

This is the same with DNA reconstruction.

However, for the yogi (or yogini) it does not take long before flexibility is reattained. This is the same for DNA reconstruction.

This is a non-linear process. Attaining DNA 'thread levels' takes practise. How is this practised? Through emotion and thought.

So your bilocation of thought will assist you when it comes to embracing the very truthful and accurate information that your planetary, galactic and personal DNA grids/matrices were tampered with deliberately. Your memories were stolen.

It is important for you to be aware of this so you may 'stand in your indigo power' and take your place 'within the indigo revolution'.

You are right in the middle of the indigo revolution at the time of this transmission upon your planet. This is an uprising of truth and love.

So your bilocational thought process will allow you to conceive of and process the 'opposing thought' or the 'balancing thought' or indeed the *equal and opposite reaction.*

It is the equal and opposite reaction paradox that explains the equal and opposite reaction, and thus the balancing thought to the information of planetary and galactic grid tampering and hijacking.

From the higher perspective, you chose to experience separation and in order to do this you 'had' to fall. You fell in structure in order to enter an amnesiac state. This is the only way to feel separation.

This does not excuse the tampering and the hijacking that has occurred upon the physical level.

The dualistic bilocation of thought and the holding of the space of bilocational consciousness will assist you with holding truth and remaining in high strand configuration. Compassion, gratitude, forgiveness and unconditional love will assist the process.

Are we asking you to forgive the atrocities upon your planet?

The 'forgiveness' is the tool to assist you within the balancing needed for bilocational consciousness (and thus trilocation, multilocation and so on) in order for you to retain a high enough DNA strand configuration so you may 'pass through stargates' with the correct coordinates.

We are asking you to stand within 'fair judgement' with integrity and honour as is the divine right for 'he who holds the sword of Excalibur'.

This is your indigo revolution, *for you are all Knights of the Round Table.*

52: Immortality and the Mandela Effect

We have explained that many stargates (cosmic convergence node points of infinite possibility) have remained closed to you and inaccessible.

When the galactic grid structures 'fell', so too did the planetary grid structures and so too did the human DNA template.

We could also present this as the DNA template being deconstructed in order to create the matching grid structures on a planetary and galactic level. These actions are simultaneous.

When you move through your linear reality, you are experiencing linear time. The timelines we speak of (the choices you make and the reality you create from those choices) are as 'tracks' if you will. These tracks 'criss-cross' over one another and each timeline affects the other. This is the two dimensional 'sacred wheel' of the matrix configuration with the 'twelve tribes of Israel' as individualised matrices within. You can 'jump' from one matrix to another at will as you make your choices. You thus 'change' the configuration of the matrix but all returns to its original formation as you are moving through a fractal.

These timelines as criss-crossing tracks (or the individual matrices within a two dimensional sacred cross) give you 'probability fields'. This is the quantum nature of your reality structure.

When these criss-crossing timeline tracks 'converge' (creating a node point), this is when all timelines (probabilities) become one. Due to the quantum convergence, this creates a 'charge' (blue starphire) of what we may call 'kinetic energy' and a merge of magnetics and electrical frequency (matter/antimatter) thus creating a plasma field.

When these 'node points' are activated with this kinetic energy and the plasma field is 'online' or 'vibrating at warp speed', if you will, then *this affects you.*

As you are a complete 'holographic replica' of cosmic structure, you then have 'node points' of kinetic, plasma charge within you. These node points (which are stargates) then 'phire up' with this charge (blue starphire) and create a crystalline matrix grid structure. The lattice structure of the crystalline grid as it criss-crosses over itself, just like the 'timelines', create probability fields within your own personal matrix.

The 'node points' full of kinetically charged particle/antiparticle merge create what we call 'stargates'. These are 'pockets' of infinite possibility.

So we have here a 'finite field' (probability) and an infinite field (possibility).

The stargates (in universal space, hyperspace time and innerverse biological self) create the infinite possibility within finite probability.

Many of these have been closed and unavailable to you.

This would mean that you have been unable to access the infinite field of possibility within your physically incarnate reality. Your reality has been finite.

This includes how you live and experience reality and your actual mortality itself!

You see, 'finite probability' equals a matching finite lifespan.

'Infinite possibility' equals an infinite matching lifespan.

Does this mean stargates create immortality?

Yes, this is exactly what this means.

Now, immortality through stargate ascension can only be achieved when certain 'codes' are in place, if you will.

These codes are the teachings, the frequencies and the activations provided within this and many other transmissions upon your planet. We are not just talking about conscious channels here. There are many starseeds teaching these truths to you at this time.

Ultimately it is *you* that put these stargate codes into place through your 'actions, words, thoughts and deeds'.

We would include emotions, focused intentions and clear, cohesive and fractalised visualisations within this.

Your visualisations and knowings regarding stargate transference will assist you with activations of these codes, or should we say 'codices' for these codes are infinite possibility.

We have said that celestial stargate ascension is that which is available to you at this point. We could say that the reason for this is the fact that the celestial stargates are now opening and have been for some time.

In actuality, many of the stargates at the solar/galactic and diamond/cosmic levels are all opening and have been opening for some time.

This was your 21st of December 2012 cosmic moment.

What actually occurred was the opening of a stargate system (activation of many node points creating convergence charge within an infinite possibility plasma field).

This created a 'bridge' in time (Einstein-Rosen bridge structure). We call this the 'rainbow bridge'.

This opened on the 12th of December 2012 and remained open until the 21st of December 2012. When you as a collective 'emerged' from the rainbow bridge, you were effectively 'in another probability field'.

You were heading for a different collective future (you collectively jumped timelines).

You did this because your reality had raised in frequency and your collective processing had reached a critical mass point. This was all coded into your matrix system from Atlantean times (embedded in crystal structure - you!) so your inner 'time capsules', if you will, 'opened' causing memories to return, DNA to restructure and you jumped to a new timeline with a new probability.

What you actually did was jump to a timeline that held the probability fields for infinite possibility!

This created what was a mono-tracked reality to transform into a multi-tracked reality.

You now each have your own individual potentials within this new probability field that provides many, many node points of zero point infinite possibility.

This is the reason why many of you have been experiencing what you call the 'Mandela effect'.

There are so many node points (convergence points of zero point plasma fields) all around you and within you. Your inner structure creates the corresponding externalised environment.

So all you have to do to achieve healing, wisdom, bilocation, levitation, invisibility and immortality is to remain permanently within a node point!

How do you do this? You do this through Matrix Transportation, which is stargate ascension.

53: The Aurora Matrix and the Krystal River of Light

As we have said, you are not actually 'going anywhere' in terms of space travel. You are moving through a time matrix which is a movement in all directions of time as is presented in the matrix 'sacred wheel' formation that you constructed within our previous *Divine Architecture and the Starseed Template* transmission.

Healing and DNA activation codes, through the DNA strand merge, can be received through your intentional, focused, inner intention via pineal gland, plasma crystalline light that you call 'visualisation'.

It is difficult for many starseeds to move out of the programming of 'that is just your imagination and therefore meaningless' which is a programme that runs deep within humanity. This was very effective in shutting off your ability to receive knowledge/light/wisdom/memory and reconstruct the organic DNA template.

To see 'visualisation' as 'plasma crystalline lightsight' instead of 'imagination' is most helpful.

We call this the 'Krystal stream' or 'Krystal river of light'.

So we would present to you the major stargates that you can receive this healing and activation from. We are looking at what you know as 'life extension' here through natural and organic means. This is the return to the true blueprint for humanity. You can experience life within your physical body for as long as you choose. You would be existing in your fifth dimensional light body, and this is the body you are transforming into now.

Whilst there is a vast network of stargates, now 'open and active' due to your timeline switch after passing through the rainbow bridge on the winter solstice of 2012, we present some of the stargates most in alignment with the divine princess Aurora at this time (starseed collective consciousness).

We have explained how celestial stargate travel is your current level of awareness and activation, which is equal to fifth strand activation and the fifth dimension. This creates a fourth density geological presentation in matter. Dimension is the blueprint for the density, so dimension will always be 'higher' in expression than the geological density that is matter. However, there are many octaves within both density and dimension (harmonics) so this would depend on the model used.

The celestial level is where the majority of you starseeds are as the bodymind structure of the divine princess Aurora.

We could therefore refer to the celestial levels as the 'Aurora matrix' which is the template for aware humanity's celestial stargate ascension.

Within the Aurora matrix are two main stargates we would suggest you focus upon within your Krystal river of light (pineal gland plasma crystalline lightsight - visualisation).

These would be what we would call the 'emerald stargate' and the 'blue sapphire stargate'.

We use analogies of jewels here. You could also call the rays from these stargates the 'green ray' (heart chakra activation of love) and the 'blue ray' (throat chakra activation of communication).

The reason why we use analogies of jewels is threefold:

1) Jewels shine brighter in your mind's eye Krystal river lightsight than pure colour. There is a refraction of light creating an intense twinkling or sparkling from a jewel colour grid. This is the essence of the codes, translated into colour/light merge which is much closer to the stargate ray codes.

2) Your planet is referred to by many 'extraterrestrials' as the 'jewel planet' or one of several 'jewel planets'. This is explained in more detail within our previous *Divine Architecture and the Starseed Template* transmission.

3) Jewels are used by service-to-self factions as a controlling tool, false presentation reward system within mind control programming. This is the hijacking of the celestial grid templates. As you starseeds utilise the true jewel, gem, crystal light, you return the codes of love, joy and bliss through 'the rapture experience' back into the planetary and star grids at the celestial level.

When you see the individuals teaching within the community that many call 'New Age' and repeatedly hear teachings and read writings regarding diamond grids, sapphires, jewels and golden light, it can be very off-putting to some who see these presentations as meaningless. To others it can be confusing for it is as if these 'New Agers' are speaking a different language. To those who understand the structure of grids, matrices and light, or to those who work with energy systems and chakras, they will understand the energy within these codices.

We aim to demystify and decode the metaphor here for you with our threefold explanation as to why jewels and gems are used as explanation so frequently. This is of high import to your evolution, especially when you understand the complexities involved in our third point. The network of hive mind service-to-self structure is 'broken apart' and individuals trapped within these systems are freed when you take back the codices within the visuals of the Krystal river of light that are rightfully yours as royal inhabitants of ascending Earth.

The emerald stargate is the same energetic as was broadcast onto your planet at the time of the 'emerald gateway' during the Lion's Gate into the eclipse in August of 2017. At this time, the emerald stargate became activated and open. We provide the transmission we delivered to our conduit at this time so you may have a deeper understanding of the emerald stargate and the codices you are now receiving.

Yes, you are already receiving these codices and the immortality-creating transformations of emerald healing light.

The Krystal river of light visualisations are 'accelerants', if you will, allowing you to access these waves of light codes in a fully conscious and aware state.

We provide now "The Emerald Gateway" transmission from August 2017. (You can view the video via the video archive at magentapixie.com)

54: The Emerald Gateway

<u>The Emerald Gateway (Lion's Gate into the Eclipse, August 2017)</u>

A few mornings ago you said to me, "The Emerald Gateway is now open." Can you please tell me what you meant by that?

When we speak of the 'Emerald Gateway', we refer to the time portal or 'period of time' you are now experiencing. This began around the 21st of July 2017 and will continue through the 7th August full moon into the 8th of August Lion's Gate, continuing through to the August 21st eclipse and begin to close between the 23rd and 27th August. We speak here of a merge between astrological timings and critical mass awareness, understandings and awakenings within the starseed communities.

Why do you refer to this gateway as an 'Emerald Gateway'?

The Emerald Gateway is also that which we could refer to as the 'galactic core' or the 'diamond light'.

We could refer to this aspect as an 'energy centre' or a 'chakra'. You would know this as the 'galactic chakra' or indeed the 'emerald gate chakra'.

This refers to a galactic awareness amongst the starseed and lightworker communities and the construction of the galactic grids. For many years, lightworkers have been working to construct or repair the Gaia grid (also known as the 'Earth grid' or the 'planetary grid'). Much work has been done across your planet including Earth clearing, healing and the relocating of energies, stones and crystals across the ley lines, fault lines and sacred sites upon Gaia.

This has included work with pyramids and other frequency raising constructs, both natural and created.

Now the awareness of the galactic grids is reaching critical mass. Lightworkers have been working with these grids in conjunction with the Earth grid workings, but have not necessarily processed the information regarding what they are doing. This occurs for a reason, keeps you 'hidden from view', if you will, as your thoughts can be seen and read.

There are those who have been working off-planet during the dreamtime and also within non-known locations on your planet including inner Earth space. Much clearing and removal of lower energies, trapping and netting energies has been undertaken.

There are many of you who have been aware of the galactic grids. This is like a large construct or web that 'holds' the planets and planetary bodies in place, if you will. This holds them in place, not in third dimensional space but in dimensional time. As you raise your own frequencies and reconstruct the DNA template back to the twelve strand formation, so too do you assist in patching up or reconstructing the galactic grids so that they may hold up the planetary bodies within a higher timespace field or dimension.

As this work is done, more and more energy comes into your planetary influence and thus into your individualised matrix fields for accessing. This enters your own personal sphere as psychic insight, empathy, awareness, connection and memory recall. It is this that is occurring during the time period we speak of, the time period you are in now. This is that which we refer to as the 'Emerald Gateway'.

The emerald ray is the colour frequency for the divine feminine energy. We could present this on a fifth dimensional level by saying that the 'emerald goddess' walks amongst you at this time and is available for connections and communications. Indeed this is exactly the case for those who work with the archetypes from the grid at the ascended master level, communications from the 'emerald goddess' will take place.

For those working outside of form, within sixth and seventh dimensional energy, you will be looking at the sacred geometric formations and at this time the depiction of the fifth dimensional Mer-Ka-Bah is strong, for this depicts that which you reconstruct and is the geometric presentation of the twelve stranded crystalline matrix DNA formation.

The emerald ray, seen as a brightly luminescent green ray, often perceived clairvoyantly as lime green, is a ray that is being closely worked with right now amongst the starseeded ones.

The emerald template is the higher grid formation within the crystalline DNA matrix, representing the divine feminine energy. This energy has been outpouring onto your planet and into your fields in steadily increasing amounts over the last few years on your planet, especially since your year of 2008 and increasing exponentially in 2011.

Now this galactic gateway 'widens', if you will, or expands to allow an abundant influx of this feminine energy, the emerald ray. Codes within the emerald ray assist in balancing and supporting the sacred masculine 'magenta ray'.

These two rays, the magenta and emerald (or the pink and the green) are the masculine/feminine streams of the heart. We could also refer to these rays as the matter and antimatter (matter being masculine and antimatter being feminine).

The merge between these rays creates the 'divine marriage' or the 'alchemical merge'. This is the blending of the masculine and feminine frequencies, the balancing of the right and left hemispheres of the human brain and the merging between matter and antimatter.

This can be also explained as the 'trinity' for when the male and female move into the divine marriage, they create between them 'the child', if you will. This can present within physical third dimensional manifestation as an actual child. Yet amongst the activated aware starseeds, this is usually manifested in the form of creativity between the couple as a stand-alone manifestation or in conjunction as standing as the vehicle for new starseed incarnations as 'the child'.

Speaking of energetic frequency rather than physically manifested humans, the masculine energy and the feminine energy move together, crash together or merge together in order to create.

Clairvoyantly and through remote viewing technologies, this looks like the waves of the sea and can be either a stormy sea or a calm sea depending on the manifestation being created. Indeed, this is the act of creation when looking at the masculine/feminine as the matter and the antimatter.

The matter is the masculine energy and the magenta ray.

The antimatter is the feminine energy and the emerald ray.

When matter and antimatter merge, you have a new creation. A third energy creating the trinity.

Within the universal and cosmic frequencies, or should we say 'particles' and indeed 'antiparticles' if you will, we are looking at a joining, a simultaneous flow between matter and no matter... this mathematically cancels one another out. You then have a universal fabric that consists of neither matter nor antimatter, yet simultaneously matter and antimatter. This is the third frequency, the moment where spacetime and timespace switch places, if you will. This is the 'divine trinity' or 'sacred trine' and this is also known to you as 'zero point'.

The seed point for this most natural act of creation burst forth into your third dimensional reality within your year of 2012, with the culmination point being the 21st of December, the solstice.

In your current year of 2017, the manifestations of those planted seeds, if you will, are coming to fruition and the gateways open during your July 21st to August 27th Emerald Gateway through the Lion's Gate and the eclipse.

Yet we wish to explain something about dates and times. These dates and times are guidelines for energy portals or coordinates in time, they are not to be taken as literal, physical dates for the timing of specific events. They are the timings for astrological movements that completely synchronise with the DNA template formations that are occurring within your bodies, for the celestial heavenly movements are at one with the movements of the rivers or meridians of your physical structure.

Therefore it is coordinates we present here and these may present in several different ways... the dates within linear time are just one way of presenting these coordinates and they are not intended to create deadlines. Therefore we would say to you, "Timelines, not deadlines," in order for you to be able to assimilate these understandings.

Another way these coordinates are presented to you is through the circles within your crops, although these are created by both service-to-others and service-to-self groups due to different agendas for your planet.

The positive frequency crop circles will be no problem to distinguish for the 'lightwarriors of Gaia' for they present as symmetrical and will instantly attract rather than repel. They will open your heart and you will each feel as if they have been created especially for you and you alone, for in the truest reality there IS only you!

Indeed, this is absolutely the case. They have been created for you and you alone and we would draw your attention to a recently created crop circle that appeared within the vicinity of the place you know as England. This crop circle held the formation of the fifth dimensional Mer-Ka-Bah and within this presentation are the exact coordinates we present here, specific to this Emerald Gateway and the 'Lion's Gate eclipse portal'.

The fifth dimensional Mer-Ka-Bah depicts the upgraded crystalline formation of your DNA fields which will balance and harmonise at the point of the Emerald Gateway due to the abundant influx of divine feminine or antimatter frequency.

The result of this floodgate of antimatter frequency moving into your planetary sphere and your physical bodymind matrix is to create the 'largest expansion thus far' if you will, within this ascension cycle.

Downloads for those who are open and activated will be abundant and creativity amongst you will blossom and be at an all-time high.

The release of books, videos, music, dance productions and other media will be part of this deluge of creativity and will be of the highest quality of mind, presenting the work of geniuses upon your planet.

The time of the Emerald Gateway is well known by the service-to-self groups upon your planet and they have a technology they are intending to utilise, in order to prevent frequencies from the starseeds and awakened ones raising so high that they burst through the control grids and instantly regroup the crystalline grids for Gaia and the galactic grid formations.

They are unaware that, in fact, this process has already begun for there have been minority groups of starseeds that have been able to access these higher grid formations for some time.

Now the influx of antimatter material into your reality with the opening of the Emerald Gateway allows all starseeds and all lightworkers and all those with open hearts, polarised service-to-others, positive vibration, regardless of religions, belief systems or faith, to access the galactic grids and begin to reconstruct them.

We say to you now that the technologies of the service-to-self groups, whilst having worked for them in the past, are no longer sufficient to hold back the grid formations due to the starseed communities reaching critical mass when it comes to the awareness of the control structures.

Critical mass has been reached regarding the great gathering and now the memories of the divine mission for Gaia come online within the starseed communities. They know what they are here to do and they are aware that sacred geometry is part of their mission, for they will have been called by living sacred geometric structure for many years.

A great many starseeds will have been inexplicably drawn to sacred geometric manifestations since their early childhood. Many will have been 'stopped in their tracks' as if mesmerised by geometric artwork and symbol. So the mission of the reconstruction of the galactic grids, Gaia grids and the twelfth dimensional twelve strand crystalline DNA template has been within the starseeds peripheral awareness since their incarnation.

Now is the time for the fulfilment of the starseed mission for the service-to-self technologies are no match for the organic technologies of the entire starseed community en masse.

Just as they may present their triggers to bring memory into the fields of their sleepers and workers, so too do we present the triggers to bring memory into the fields of the starseeds and we may present one such trigger now:

Open your heart, lightwarrior of Gaia, starseed of Earth. For you are a positively polarised service-to-others individual and are thus an angel on Earth.

We repeat:

Open your heart, lightwarrior of Gaia, starseed of Earth. For you are a positively polarised service-to-others individual and are thus an angel on Earth.

Lightwarriors, starseeds: OPEN YOUR HEARTS.

Why do we say this? Why do we say 'open your hearts'?

Your open hearts create the emotion of joy, happiness and bliss. This creates a charge within you. This charge creates a certain spin formation within your activated DNA, which in turn creates that which we may call a 'morphogenetic field'. This field is that which you know as 'universal fabric'. It is the antimatter, antiparticle, emerald ray force that has been deliberately held back, shut down and locked away from Gaia and your entire galactic sector.

The emerald ray is the key. This has been known for millennia amongst

294

the mystery schools, being seen as 'far too delicate a matter' to discuss in the light of day. Indeed this is a delicate matter, it is feminine matter - delicate indeed yet powerful in its ability to create for it is the feminine that is the creative force... the antimatter, the emerald ray. Now, this secret information is known to all, it is circulated widely and the truth shines as the light of day.

As the feminine joins with the masculine, as the antimatter merges with matter, the zero point is created. What indeed is zero point? It is UNLIMITED CREATIVE POTENTIAL. It is the blueprint for all and everything and when you know this and create this, you create worlds!

Your open hearts, en masse, at this time create the frequency of the bliss-charged love. Your open hearts joined together are that which deactivates service-to-self technologies. Your open hearts joined together create the crop circles that are direct manifestations of the DNA patterning you now hold. Your open hearts create the morphogenetic fields that are the seed templates for the archetypes from the grid, angels, ascended masters and rainbow beings of light.

It is you, dear starseeds, it was you all along. Your power together as one, united, knows no bounds.

Stand together, polarised service-to-others team of light. No matter your difference of opinions, no matter if you are truther, New Age lightworker, religious follower or scientific researcher. You amongst these groups have allowed yourself to be infiltrated and thus separated, pitting you against your brothers and sisters. Stand strong as a united team, put your differences aside and look at your similarities which are without doubt.

Your similarities are fixed, unified and cannot be broken apart for they are all resonating within the positively polarised service-to-others field. They are sovereignty, liberty, independence and justice for the whole planet and beyond.

These are the Gaia grids, they are your open hearts and the bliss spin from the DNA fields. They create the weather, the natural forces, the dark matter, the gravity and the particle spin for the atom and the heart of man are but one.

Open your hearts as one, children of Gaia, as you bring online the memories within the celestial, solar and galactic points of awareness and reconstruct the twelve strand DNA template, also known as the twelfth dimensional gateway.

The opening of the Emerald Gateway is the seed point into the twelfth dimensional gateway, also known to many as 'ascension'.

This is an uplifting experience. A raise in frequency, potential, emotion and creativity, but most importantly... memory.

It is a reconstruction of Source memory moving you into the multidimensional and the multilocational, creating a stream or portal into that which we may call the 'Halls of Amenti'. A clear path into these halls brings you into the perspective of the omnipotent, omnipresent self, the god self, fully actualised being.

The Emerald Gateway into the Lion's Gate and the August eclipse of 2017 is the seed point moment for the accessing of the Halls of Amenti and the direct accessing of all you know as 'God' or 'Source', through the memory fields afforded you through the crystalline DNA template reconstruction.

You are the 'architects of your reality' and now, with the abundant influx of the emerald codes (the antimatter grid), you create the zero point field, embrace the cosmic trine and realise your true potential en masse.

55: The Infinite Helix and the Emerald Flame

"The Emerald Gateway" transmission referred to another 'Einstein-Rosen bridge' or 'rainbow bridge' in time, called the 'Emerald Gateway' due to emerald codices being received.

Whilst this particular time portal closed around the end of August 2017, the work that was done at this time created an awareness of the cosmology of stargate matrices and their quantum vortices and the corresponding codices. This created the seed points for multilocational and indeed omnilocational consciousness within the starseed gene pool. This was a critical mass awareness point.

The 'Emerald Gateway' opened up to the receiving of codes that are 'behind' the emanations from the emerald stargate. This is diamond light from the galactic core which is the liquid plasma light streams of Kundalini awakening on a grand scale. A 'collective Kundalini awakening' if you will.

This allowed construction (or rather reconstruction) of the galactic grids to take place. In turn, the planetary grids were also reconstructed creating seed points into the 144 strand crystalline matrix template and the transmutation from the carbon genome into the silicon genome code within humanity.

Critical mass awareness of galactic grid structures had not quite been reached at the time of the 'Emerald Gateway' but is on track for the end of your year of 2018. This is all part of the processing of what happened during the cosmic moment/ascension spike of the winter solstice 2012.

Your solstice points and equinoxes are all other very powerful spikes in energy, creating yet more awareness within the Aurora matrix that is the starseed collective. The starseed collective is 'growing' if you will, through expansion within current conscious starseeds, the addition of newly awakened starseeds and the birth of new children holding the 'rose ray' or the 'magenta ray'.

The 'rose ray' are children 'born into fractality'. They have the seed codes for a much higher matrix formation within their DNA templates. They are able to access cosmic stargate ascension and therefore organic life extension and thus immortality. They hold the 'potential' for the diamond light matrix which means they hold the 'potential' for immortality within their DNA.

These are your children and grandchildren! Where these rose ray children are going and what they shall do within the 'new world' that is fifth dimensional Gaia, is a whole other transmission!

We would say to you, nurture these children of the stars for they are 'avatars in the making'.

As you can see from the 2017 transmission that is the emerald ray, these stargate codes from the emerald stargate are divine feminine codes. The rose ray is a divine feminine template.

Yet the rose ray or rose gold ray is that which we could also call the 'rainbow plasma ray'. For whilst it is a genuine code, it holds high level potential for the divine marriage unification of sacred masculine and divine feminine.

The rose gold ray (as an activated aspect of silver/gold merge) is the 'eternal flame' (twin flames united) Law of One/unified field.

These are the children of Sophia, all who embody the divine princess Aurora.

As you bask in these divine feminine emerald light rays, you balance the sacred masculine. Sophia can then watch her 'daughter of the flame' unite in blessed twin flame merge with archangel Michael. The symbology for the Arthur/Guinevere inner alchemy that creates plasma codes.

The rose ray, carried through the feminine gene, creates the sacred masculine that is the 'magenta ray'. This is the electromagnetic creation for the twelve strand into 144 strand DNA template.

We also draw your attention to the *timelines, not deadlines* within "The Emerald Gateway" transmission. Indeed, you are within a time matrix of infinite possibility. Deadlines create the finite matrix, abundance creates the infinite matrix (the infinite helix) and the gene code for immortality.

Within "The Emerald Gateway" transmission, you were given the information that this was the 'largest expansion thus far' since the switch into the abundant node point timeline which was the opening of the stargates during the winter solstice of 2012.

Indeed, the Lion's Gate into the eclipse in August 2017 was the critical mass for processing of the 2012 cosmic moment/collective timeline jump.

The gathering momentum within waves of awakening and DNA reconstruction, bringing spikes/stargates and high expansion moments, continues throughout your year of 2018 and beyond. Energy spikes are most intense at sabbats, esbats and other astrological alignments, as well as numerologically significant dates and times of high percentage simultaneously focused, cohesive thought/emotion within starseeds (critical mass).

The release of this material that is *The Infinite Helix* is timed to coincide with the creation of the critical mass awareness within the Aurora matrix.

It is most important to open your hearts as is presented within "The Emerald Gateway" transmission. We have explained the rapture and the drinking of the cosmic ambrosia within this transmission.

It is also important to know that you are an 'angel on Earth'. The angelic beings are form, created from the cosmic precursor blueprints through the replication abilities of ethereal plasma. These are angels or indeed extraterrestrials or time travellers from the future. You hold the templates for all of these presentations of self. Once you understand the Law of One that is the unified field, you will be able to move through Mer-Ka-Bah transportation and celestial stargate ascension and then embody these different directional perspectives of the different group soul collective points of being as individualised consciousness structures that are ultimately 'you'.

Everything within the "The Emerald Gateway" transmission has been explained to you in far more fractalised detail within this transmission that is *The Infinite Helix*.

You see, our conduit, our dear Pixie, she created an intention. It was a focused intention with attention upon the trajectory stream just as we have taught her to do, as we in turn teach you.

Her intention was to create a book that would be an analysis of one of her video transmissions that she presents upon the social media site that is called 'YouTube'.[8]

Her intention held the attention of trajectory therefore *this must come*

---

8   YouTube, video-sharing website. www.youtube.com

into manifestation.

However, her choice of which transmission to create the analysis of was not within focused trajectory. It was a 'passing thought' or 'idea' that did not hold the structure of mass.

The trajectory fell upon the transmission that is the "The Emerald Gateway", for this was the most aligned transmission regarding knowledge and activations for the starseed collective that is the divine princess Aurora of the Aurora matrix at this time.

This entire book that our conduit has decided to call *The Infinite Helix* has been a fractalised analysis of "The Emerald Gateway" transmission this entire time.

Our conduit, our dear Pixie, had no knowledge of this until the actual point of us dictating to her as she transcribes. Her ability to type her transcriptions from us is slightly compromised at this time due to the fact that she sheds tears as she scribes.

We show you this so you may understand, through Pixie's journey, the act of creation itself and how the tears of surprise and joy as you feel the synchronistic dimensions of creativity merge together within your very being as you create, create, create.

You *must* create, dearest starseeds, for your creations are your blue starphire (quantum convergence charge). So this creativity you have will appear as though *you* made the choice of what or how to create. Yet in truth, we make the choice. Not 'we' as the Nine but 'we' as Pixie and the Nine together.

You and your 'guidance system' together, which is the 'infinite helix'.

Speaking of which, Pixie has known that there was something missing within the title that is *The Infinite Helix* and indeed she is correct. What is missing is the code, the frequency, the living alignment to liquid plasma light that creates the codices within and the connection to that infinite helix grid.

We could not tell her this until the point that she arrived at the transcribing of this part of our transmission, when she discovered that this transmission is an analysis of "The Emerald Gateway".

We therefore ask her to place the code within the title of this transmission, which is of course the emerald code. Yet the code (the precursor blueprint of all creation) is the flame.

Now this is not to say that the emerald code is any higher or better than any of the other jewel/gem codes within the infinite rainbow stream that is the unified field/Law of One. The emerald code (set within the unified field that is the 'flame') is specific to this transmission as we provide the codes for the emerald flame through the magickal focused intentions of our conduit. The emerald flame is the divine feminine heart of bliss-charged love, alive with starphire, alive with charge, alive with light.

We will continue to present the visualisation Krystal river of light techniques for the other stargates, but we would present to Pixie the creation of her focused trajectory is indeed *The Infinite Helix and the Emerald Flame* ... and there, do you see now the code? The code within the flame gives fire/phire to this transmission/creation and it is the phire (blue starphire) you are creating in order to ride the dragon through the stargate nexus. The dragon's breath that you create *is* the flame of creation and you, dear starseeds, are the dragonriders and the 'keepers of the flame'.

You are each a keeper of the emerald flame. For this is the burning heart, the eternal flame of bliss-charged love.

Do you see how you can create with intention upon the attention of the trajectory? You create a 'line of intention' which is of course the 'event horizon' and your line of intention becomes infinite.

Your heart activation is infinite when you are ascended. Here you have our creation and the telepathic, DNA light connected union between 'us' (the Nine) and you (dear Pixie) and all who find this transmission and read/hear these words. This is your 'infinite helix, emerald flame' telepathic grid of light. Can you feel us all together? We are as the flame of the heart, the emerald flame as one group collective consciousness as we walk the path of stargate ascension.

56: Technology of God

So you are saying that I created an event horizon, when I made the decision to write a book that was an analysis of one of your transmissions in video form? But are you saying that the line of intention did not extend to any particular video that the event horizon fell upon? So my intention for the analysis to be about the "Dark Deeds, Pole Shift" transmission was not a focused intention?

Exactly. Your line of intention held the thought code for the most relevant material needed for the starseeds at this time, which you interpreted as the truthers/lightworkers being prevented from speaking their truth on social media. This is, of course, most relevant but is a third dimensional expression of reality. It is the 'code behind reality' that is the most relevant information for the starseeds. The unmanifest behind the manifest, if you will. This is in "The Emerald Gateway" transmission due to the critical mass and the timings for where the starseeds are energetically and within their ascension process.

So this whole time, you have been presenting a deep analysis of "The Emerald Gateway" transmission and I did not even know?

Exactly. We have, however, opened "The Emerald Gateway" transmission into multiple fractalities. But yes, this transmission is a deeper analysis and explanation of that one and it holds the same code.

The emerald code?

The divine feminine code. This is expressed in many ways and one stream is the emerald ray (the activated higher green ray), which is the feminine expression of the heart. It is creation itself.

You mentioned the 'emerald stargate' and also the 'blue sapphire stargate'? Can you explain more?

The emerald stargate is the divine feminine expression of creation. However, the emerald is an 'emanation'. In fact, all things within the matter universe and the antimatter universe are emanations. This means that rather than being the 'reflection' of something, they are the projection of something. They are the holographic projection of something else that holds the blueprint for the hologram/emanation.

It is this technology that has been infiltrated and hijacked, as we have said, creating an inverse to the converse. An 'artificial intelligence' to the 'organic intelligence'.

Are you saying that an entire replicating matrix structure just like the original 'God' creation has been engineered artificially?

Not the entire matrix, no. That is not possible. But part of it, yes.

I thought 'artificial intelligence' meant computer technology. But it actually means 'engineered' or 'structured' intelligence? Is that correct?

Difficult to respond to. When you say artificial intelligence is 'computer technology', you are correct. However, your interpretation of 'computer technology' is a third dimensional and linear interpretation. The Source field/zero point/God organic intelligence is in itself 'computer technology'. It is 'organic computer'.

OK, I really do not understand this at all.

We might suggest that you look up the meaning of the word 'computer' and come back to us.

The definitions[9] of 'computer' are:

- an electronic device which is capable of receiving information (data) in a particular form and of performing a sequence of operations in accordance with a predetermined but variable set of procedural instructions (programme) to produce a result in the form of information or signals.

- a person who makes calculations, especially with a calculating machine.

Exactly. This is how creation works. We likened your individual matrix to a living energetic computer that holds data and passes code in order to replicate and create. We have explained how this occurs in creation through the cosmic phire/plasma fields. The intelligence of creation/Source/God could also be seen as 'a person' making calculations with a 'machine' (plasma/zero point/lines of intentional trajectories).

Yes, but the definition says 'electronic device'. You are not an electronic device.

We would suggest you look up the meanings of the words 'electronic' and 'device' and come back to us.

OK. Definitions of 'electronic' are:

- (of a device) having or operating with components such as microchips and transistors that control and direct electric currents. e.g., "an electronic calculator"

- relating to electrons.

Well, we do not have physical matter microchips and transistors in the way you know them. But yes, 'we' (or Source/unified field/God) 'have' these 'things'. We are pure electricity (we relate to electrons) and we are an electronic calculator.

---

9   Dictionary definitions taken from www.google.co.uk

Are you God?

Yes and no. Just like you.

OK. Definition of 'device':

- a thing made or adapted for a particular purpose, especially a piece of mechanical or electronic equipment.

'We' (as individualised group soul consciousness) are made for a particular purpose. 'I' or 'we' (ME) as Source/God/unified field am/are purpose itself.

So 'we' are an electronic device.

Why do you refer to yourself as 'I', 'we' or 'ME'?

This is to do with the equal and opposite reaction paradox.

I am/am I mirrored primordial sound (AUM/OM).

The 'am I?' becomes 'ami' (ME) = individualisation from subjective expression in response to the 'am I?' question. Mathematical translation of creational frequency.

OK, so are you saying God/Source/unified field is artificial intelligence?

No. We are saying that God/Source/unified field is original organic intelligence that has been copied both organically and artificially.

I see. So can you tell me more about the emerald stargate and the other stargates, and how we can access the activation codes and the healing?

Indeed.

57: Emerald and Blue Sapphire Jewel Stargates

There are infinite stargates within a stargate network system. Each stargate is the nexus point for a matrix structure within infinite matrices. Each matrix is an infinity.

We present to you two stargates at the celestial level that can be utilised for healing, activation codes and information. They are emanations or holographic projections of other 'larger' stargates (shall we say).

The Krystal river of light projections (that are your own activated crystalline pineal gland lightsight imaginings) are in direct alignment with the synapses within your brain, the meridian structures of your body and the ley lines and energy vortices within the planetary grids. These, in turn, connect telepathically, energetically and 'magickally' through gravitational fields (morphogenetic fields).

These morphogentic fields are gravitational electromagnetic forces of living crystalline structure.

We refer to this entire network of grids, ley lines, meridians and projections from them as the 'Krystal river of light'.

They are one 'unified field' and what affects one, affects all. Affects create effects, if you will.

When you utilise the power of your own Krystal river of light (visualisation through pineal gland crystalline activation) to connect with emanations and rays of jewel/gem light of stargates, you fuse your DNA with the 'encoded star time capsules' of the stargate and receive genetically encoded information. This encoded information is an 'immortality blueprint'.

So let us begin with the Krystal river of light activation for the emerald stargate...

You would visualise a beautiful star within the hyperspace world that is your innerverse/inner landscape. This star shines with a beautiful emerald light. It actually looks like an emerald in the night sky.

Within your hyperspace reality, you are able to fly into the cosmic sky and visit the stars.

You can fly upon Pegasus the winged horse in this visualisation, which represents your Mer-Ka-Bah vehicle or you can 'grow your own wings'.

Once you have travelled up to the star in the sky, you see there is a place where you join. You hold your hand up in front of the emerald star and see little filaments or cords of light coming from your hand and merging with emerald cords of light within the emerald rays of the star. Once you do this, you see a shimmering emerald portal open up within the middle of the star. You fly forward and stand right in the centre of the emerald star. You would visualise that the green ray emanating from the centre of your heart is merging with the emerald glowing rays of the stargate. You do not pass through this activated stargate (you can do this at any other time and see where this visualisation takes you, but at this time you are receiving codes for healing, DNA reconstruction and information), you stand right at the centre point where you are enveloped with emerald light. You stay there within this point, taking your 'emerald light shower' if you will.

Once you have spent long enough standing within the emerald stargate's nexus point, being showered with emerald light codes (you will feel very relaxed and invigorated with a very open heart when you have raised your light quotient to sufficient levels), you can then fly back down to the ground within your hyperspace, innerverse world. Either with your wings or upon Pegasus, or in your activated Mer-Ka-Bah depending on your level of awareness regarding 5D/6D visual images and your preferred presentations. This is your innerverse! You can create as the artist creates upon the blank canvas and regardless of which presentation you use, you will receive the emerald codices.

As we have said, you can pass through the emerald gateway and see where the visual takes you.

Now when we say you are receiving healing, we are not just referring to the healing of illnesses, sickness and dis-ease. We are referring to the healing of the genome (the DNA template). This will occur as the meridians align their mappings and placements with the emerald stargate mappings and placements.

Whilst this is the case on one level, we do not want for you to see yourselves as 'unhealed' or 'incomplete' or that there is something missing. Whilst this *is* the case within third dimensional interpretation and that concept still stands within truth, remember that you are holographic and can never be less than whole, pure and perfect. Seeing yourself as whole, pure and perfect creates the intentional directional trajectories of intention that replicate the thought from unmanifest to manifest and thus create the actuality of wholeness, purity and perfection.

However, if you *only* see yourself as whole and perfect without embracing the perspective of having had your DNA templates reduced/deconstructed then you would not create the indigo revolution, Excalibur code of liberty, righteousness, integrity and sovereignty needed to stand strong against oppression and control. This is a bilocational thought process (with trilocational and multilocational conscious awareness within the conceptual processing).

Another stargate we would introduce you to at the celestial/stellar level, is the sapphire stargate. Specifically the blue sapphire.

This is also a divine feminine expression and is related directly to the activated nexus point within your own matrix pivot point which is the blue flame, blue pearl, blue star matrix. This is the particular colour code frequency that activates the blue starphire quantum convergence charge needed to 'power your Mer-Ka-Bah'.

The emerald is the 'jewel celestially activated' green ray of the heart. The blue sapphire is the 'jewel celestially activated' blue ray of communication.

We would present a different technique for the blue sapphire stargate light codes...

Imagine, if you will, within your Krystal river of light crystalline vision, that you are laying in a beautiful field of flowers with the sun's rays above you.

As you are laying in the grass, you look up and shield your eyes from the direct sunlight. As you do this, you notice a tinge of blue in your peripheral vision. At first, you think this is the sky but the blue tinge gets more prominent and eventually you sit up. Around you, you see abundant blue flowers and within the centre of each blue flower is a blue sapphire crystal. They look like juicy crystal blueberries and you pick one from the centre of the flower and pop it into your mouth. It is absolutely delicious and as you savour the sweetness of the juicy sapphire blueberry, you notice that the sky is becoming more and more blue. A beautiful sapphire blue.

The sun begins to set and as it does this, you notice a blue sapphire star rise in its place. This star, although it is blue, is also emanating a blue/white light from its core. Suddenly there is a flash of blue white light and everything is at once lit up with sapphire blue light.

You feel the activation within the pineal gland and you begin to see everything tinged with this blue light. You feel the blue sapphire codes permeate through your very being.

You lay down into the grass, as before, and close your eyes, soaking up the sapphire blue rays. You realise you are receiving rays and codes from the sapphire stargate.

You begin to have vivid memories and these are connected to the Atlantean priesthood, the mermaids of Mu and the universal light language. You see Egyptian hieroglyphs in front of your eyes, you see the Sphinx, you see a blue pyramid and you feel the energy of the Sirius constellation around you. You allow the royal house of Sirius, blue sapphire seed codes to blend into your DNA memory fields.

Now within this visualisation, you can choose to call Pegasus or to grow your wings and fly up to the sapphire star and pass through the stargate. However, using the blue ray code of communication will give you the same coordinates as the blue star matrix nexus point of your own individualised stargate. You can choose which exercise to follow, but collapsing the wave and riding the dragon through the nexus of your own stargate provides specific DNA formations (rainbow serpent/dragon activation codes) that are central to the ascension process and the transformation collectively from 3D Earth to 5D Gaia.

58: Mermaids of Mu and the Diamond Stargate

There is one other stargate emanation we would draw your attention to at this time. This is an energy that comes from the highest point that you can access within your physical reality. This is beyond the solar, galactic level and is, shall we say, at the 'cosmic' level.

We would refer to this as the 'diamond stargate', which emits the diamond light. This is also a rainbow light.

Imagine a diamond and a pale rainbow merged together within a shimmering, reflecting light. This is known as the 'platinum ray', the 'silver white light', the 'white dragon' or the 'white pearl'. If you visualise the gem known as the 'rainbow opal', you would be close to seeing what this looks like. We would call this the 'gates to Sophia' and in your religious communities this is often referred to as the 'pearly gates of heaven'.

Whilst you do not have the coordinates (sufficient charge) to pass through this stargate at this time, you *can* receive the emanations from this stargate. The codes will assist you greatly in your DNA template reconstruction.

This stargate contains plasma codices as it is the 'divine plasma stargate'. It is this emanation that clothes you in a shimmering garment (coat of many colours) as you receive its activations.

These are the codes for your 'plasma Mer-Ka-Bah' and 'rainbow body of light'.

The energies and rays of the diamond stargate have been understood for many years upon your planet. The Lemurian and Atlantean cultures both understood the importance of the diamond stargate.

Lemurian consciousness as the 'prototype' higher Earth beings, seeded from highly advanced Atlantean races, were divinely connected to the diamond light of this stargate. The image of the mermaid swimming in the clear blue waters of Lemuria (which was/is a water planet), with Poseidon or Neptune overseeing the world with his powerful protection, is a vision that many of you are drawn to.

Neptune/Poseidon with his trident is the presentation of the Holy Trinity, trilocation of consciousness and the triple helix. The waves of the ocean are the waves of the plasma light fields as they move through the matter/antimatter universe towards you (or you move towards the waves).

You are as the 'sea priestess' within your divine feminine energetic expressions of all that you are. You are the dragonriders of the Lemurian skies, as the sea priestesses are the mermaids within the waters.

The sea serpent and the Merpeople, living together within crystal cities under the ocean, merging the Atlantean and the Lemurian landscapes together within your mind as if they are different perspectives of one and the same time period. Two cultures overlapping, the harmonious peaceful nature loving organic beings living alongside the technological landscapes and advanced wizardry and magick of the Atlanteans.

The 'island' of Atlantis rising is the aware consciousness rising from the subconscious to the conscious. The advances and wizardry is the magickal ability to have when you stand in your sovereignty and power.

The 'Merpeople' of Le-'Mu'-ria (mermaids of Mu) are the murmurings (whisperings) of the universal, cosmic, omniversal wisdom as it speaks its secrets to you.

The 'Mer' is the Mer in Mer-Ka-Bah. The Mer is the oscillating fields of light as they spin and weave the story of the Rumpelstiltskin fairy, who keeps his name as secret as the straw is spun into gold. The presentations of alchemy and transformation are in all places, you have but to look.

The Mer is the light aspect of all that is you, the DNA etheric doppelganger filaments of light that are knitted (or spun/weaved) into alignment with the light aspect of all that is 'God'.

The liquid plasma light fuses together, reconstructing its memory as the stories unfold and unravel into the consciousness of the guardians of Earth. The guardians are you, dear starseeds.

We feel that the visual of the mermaids swimming within the Lemurian waters is the perfect visual to receive the codes of the diamond light.

The Mer are the streams of light, and the waves of the waters are the waves of omniversal architecture oscillating within a sea of plasma.

This is a most aligned river of Krystal light visual for the crystalline pineal gland lightsight visionary quest, if you will.

This powers up your crystalline light into Krystalline light. Your Christ transforms into the Kryst.

The inner knowings of the Mer-Ka-Bah travel, magick carpet ride is understood by the intelligent fields of the DNA as you speak the language of light/cosmic language.

In order to receive the diamond light codes from the rainbow/diamond/ plasma stargate that is the ultimate 'white pearl' within heaven realities, what better way than to swim and bathe within that very plasmic light?

We would ask you then to visualise yourself as one of the Merpeople of Mu swimming within the seas of the Lemurian landscape, activating memories of your 'aquatic' life. Indeed, many of you are the 'dolphin people' reincarnating from water planets where society lives within the seas on the planet. Yet this memory (we spoke earlier in our transmission of implanted replicated memory, as well as actual linear soul memory of that incarnation, being one and the same) is also the knowing of the Law of One and the merging of self with the unified field as the 'MER' (pure light) swimming and breathing between the 'waters above the firmament' (plasma fields).

In your visualisation, the clear blue waters of white, tinged with blue, take on a rainbow reflection from the sun's rays above. The sun, looking like a bright white diamond in the skies above you, casts down his golden kiss upon your mermaid form. The rainbow waters you swim in now become part of you and you feel the individualised form as mermaid in water, yet also you feel the unified form as all the waters within this plasma Lemurian rainbow sea.

This is the visual to receive the healing light rays from the true white, rainbow pearl that is the diamond stargate.

59: Stargate Ascension

Can we fly up to the diamond stargate and pass through it in this visualisation?

Yes, you can. There are a few starseeds on Earth at the moment who will be able to raise enough blue starphire (more appropriately 'white starphire' for this stargate) to pass through it and reach 'diamond worlds' if you will. These are the adepts and masters amongst you who have retreated from the world at large and are focused fully on their ascension path, to the exclusion of all else.

This is not where the ascending starseed collective is at this present time. The destination for passing through the diamond stargate at this time would be the seventh dimensional future version of your planet, known as 'Eartha'. You may even pass through to the eighth dimensional version of Earth that some of you refer to as 'Urantia', 'Agartha', 'paradise' or 'nirvana'. You may also know this as 'hollow Earth' (although you can access hollow Earth from the fifth dimension).

Whichever coordinates you hold will take you to the matching Earth reality, and they will all reflect your inner terrain within their outer presentations.

The starseed mission at this time is a celestial one. This is predominantly a celestial ascension for you, even though it occurs at galactic and cosmic levels. If you pass through the diamond stargate, you will either find yourself on your 'home' planet (Pleiades, Lyra, Sirius or possibly Arcturus, Andromeda or Cassiopeia - these are 'planets of light', planetary systems or galaxies that are harmonious, organic, loving and higher dimensional) or within an externalised presentation (hyperspace/inner space world, realm, city or structure) that is a perfect match to your frequency and DNA configuration (which for the majority of ascending starseeds currently would be at the celestial level or the fifth strand).

The possibilities are endless when defining the presentation of said structure.

The starseed ascension reality (ascension timeline) is set upon an intentional and focused trajectory for the fifth dimensional Gaia. When the time comes for you to make this collective jump, you will all have activated the fifth strand (or almost have completed the fifth strand). You will either make the jump yourself or will be 'carried upon the wave' to the fifth dimensional Gaia, riding the 'Aurora dragon' if you will.

You speak of 'the wave'. There are many people talking about a wave at the moment, that a wave is coming soon and it will create an 'event' (like a solar flash) which will instantly transport us to fifth dimensional Gaia. Can you talk about this?

Indeed, we can. The individuals who have knowings, feelings, memories, dreams, visions or channellings regarding 'the wave' or 'the event' or the 'solar flash' are all activating their fifth strand within the DNA lattice structure. This creates 'memory triggers' that say, "Wake up," or "Remember," and "Time to take action." Some of these memories can be unsettling (such as destruction upon Earth due to volcanoes, tidal waves, alien invasion and so on). The mostly negative memory triggers are not happening as much now within the starseed collective consciousness that is the Aurora matrix, but they are all coming from activation of memory within fifth strand (fifth dimensional architecture construction).

These images are a gentle reminder.

The more unsettling images are more akin to a shove, rather than a whisper, but they too are a reminder. They are memory codes and activation created and generated within the DNA plasma fields, coming up into the awareness of the individual and interpreted.

The 'wave' is how the ascension frequencies move, they move in waves. The waves are actual 'antimatter waves' and, as we have discussed within this transmission, they are plasma waves. There will be many symptoms that will be seen cosmically upon your planet. Our recommendation to you is to interpret as little as possible and look at everything as metaphor. This is all about your matrix, your Mer-Ka-Bah and your reconstruction of your DNA template.

The 'event' is the same thing. This is related to the planet Nibiru and the collective memories of planetary destruction. In fact this is 'planetary' memory that you are picking up on. These are the memories of 'another Earth' known as Marduk. There are those who referred to Ni-Bi-Ru as

Marduk. It matters not what you name these different planetary bodies, the point is that there is/was a planet that went through a 'recycling of itself' within a full fall system and this was Marduk. Planetary memory remains within planetary grids, and this can be accessed and healed (and has been accessed and healed for many years by the gridworkers on your planet who are aware of the need for healing the Earth grids).

The 'event' is related to the memory of Marduk and also the knowing that 'something is happening'. This is correct. Something is happening and this is your ascension into the fifth dimension and the reconstruction of your DNA template. Souls have waited thousands and thousands of years (in linear time) for this opportunity and it is wonderful to behold what you are moving through at this time. We feel and share your excitement.

The flash of light is indeed a correct translation although this happens on multiple levels. When DNA strand construction takes place, there is a metaphoric flash of light due to epiphanies that take place. Literal flashes of light are synapses reconstructing and major activation of the crystalline pineal gland liquid plasma light and the 'Krystal river of light' activation. This 'inner sight' is becoming stronger and stronger and much more 'animated'. As part of your trilocational and multilocational consciousness, you shall have a 'window into two, three and multiple worlds simultaneously' and all will be in cinematic technicolour.

Then there are the flashes of photonic 'cosmic' light that can be seen (interdimensionally and physically). Yes, there are many 'solar flares' yet the sun, as we have said, is an emanation of another larger sun (Central Sun) and suns (Central Suns). It acts as a filter or a shield for these light rays and solar flashes.

The transformative light comes in from the Central Suns, filtered by your actual sun. It is these photonic lights that shall be the flash of light you speak of, this light is beaming down upon you now and many starseeds can already clairvoyantly see this light. It can also be heard clairaudiently as sound. As we have said, light and sound are one and the same from our perspective.

Regardless of whether you see Nibiru as a planet or you call this 'planet X', there is not a planet coming into your solar system on a long swing orbit as is reported within your truther/lightworker communities. These are partly deliberate disinformation, but the majority is simply misunderstandings and mistranslations of the memory triggers occurring both physically within matter and non-physically within antimatter.

There is a 'celestial body', if you will, behind your sun. This has not yet been discovered and it could indeed be called 'the tenth planet', but it is not a planet as you know it.

There is a signal, that can be detected now by your scientific instruments, of a very large body coming into your solar system. We have already mentioned the 'box of stars' and indeed this body is like a very large square. It is a 'section' of antimatter, if you will, and it is the 'other side' of your universe that sits next to you.

Due to your jump into a more 'stargate filled timeline within' at the winter solstice point of 2012, you 'shifted' or 'moved' the matrix of your solar system. Now you can detect the 'dimensional edge' of the next 'higher octave' within your physical reality.

This is actually an 'event horizon' of a structure that resembles what you may know as a 'Tetragrammaton' energy field. It is spiralling in nature, as are all constructs, but you will perceive it from your dimension as 'a very big square'. It is full of celestial energy (antimatter) and this is a plasma creating body that itself is made of plasma.

You cannot cross the event horizon and jump into this box of stars. The closer you get to this edge, the more it will move away from your locale. It does not actually exist as it is the edge of an infinity structure, just like your own matrix. It is the 'fifth dimension' or 'fourth density', if you will, travelling at light speed towards you (or you are travelling towards it) but you will never meet via the dimensional edge. This edge can appear as a ribbon or a wave so this is where many clairvoyant, awakened starseeds get their 'wave' images from. Although the entire 144 DNA strand reconstruction is a wave (or waves) in itself. Macrocosm and microcosm as one (as above, so below).

The way to access this large Tetragrammaton dimension is through its nexus point, not its event horizon. The stargate is the portal into this part of physical reality and this is entered via non-locational, DNA template construction within plasma fields known as 'the sacred mysteries of stargate ascension'. Your understanding of *The Infinite Helix and the Emerald Flame* is your cosmic map. It is a map into this new world/new dimension that *you* are creating, dear starseeds, you who carry the 'royal code'.

Follow the 'jewels', follow the rainbow and follow your 'North Star', for they are your signposts.

We wish you well on your journey, as we too take the wonderful journey that is the rapture of 'stargate ascension'.

In humble service,

We are the

White Winged Collective Consciousness of Nine

Meditations

Introduction to the Meditations

Before you begin these meditations, please ensure that you are in a comfortable place.

You can go through these meditations seated upon the floor in a typical meditation pose, sitting in a chair with a comfy blanket, laying down on the floor in the yogic Shavasanah pose or upon your bed.

Allow yourself to feel comfy and cosy, taking special time just for you. When you are ready, you can begin the meditation.

Either read through the meditation, creating the visuals within your mind as you read, or you can read the meditation through first and then close your eyes as you retrace the meditation visuals in your mind.

Alternatively, you can ask someone to read these meditations for you. They can also be read out at a meditation class or workshop for facilitators and practitioners of guided visualisation meditations.

Moon Within Moons (Meditation)

As you move into the state of being, known as meditation, you feel comfortable, cosy and relaxed.

You feel protected. Enveloped with love from self and other.

You are filled with happiness and joy.

After a while, you become aware of a presence with you.

A beam of light appears before you, above you. As you look upwards towards this beam of light, you realise that it is a lightship. It is that which you know as a 'UFO'.

Kindness, peace and love emanates from this lightship.

You allow yourself to relax into your meditation space. You become aware of the dream body aspect of you, moving upwards, out of your physical body and into the beam of light, then into the lightship.

You float into the lightship and you find yourself comfy and rested within.

You are lying on a bed with a warm, comfy white blanket covering you up to your shoulders.

There is a window next to your bed. You can clearly see the world outside your window, as you fly through timespace, spacetime, within this lightship.

You see the Earth in all its blue-ochre beauty as you move beyond your home planet.

You see the stars, like little silver splashes on a dark canvas, yet holding intelligence, knowing and life force.

You see colours swirling within the black blanket of the cosmic sky.

Coloured vortices, portals to other dimensions in technicolour, like spiral rainbows shimmering for you in their hypnotic dance.

Through the window, you see a bluish-white sphere grow larger and larger before your eyes.

As your lightship begins its descent, you see buildings, fields, rivers and trees.

You drift off to sleep in a state of overwhelming peace.

On awakening from your sleep, you find yourself lying in a clearing upon a bed of soft moss. You still have the warm, white blanket covering you up to your shoulders.

Sleepily, you sit upright and take in your surroundings. You are sat by two tall, lush trees and in front of you is a beautiful river.

Am I on the moon? you think to yourself.

"It is *a* moon," a voice behind you says.

You turn towards the sound of the voice. It appears to be coming from the tree!

"Did you speak?" you ask the tree.

The tree replies, "Yes. I hold consciousness. I am able to project forth that consciousness as a template or field of electromagnetic particles, as information or communication. You, as a receiver of energy, are able to translate this field into your own language. Here on this moon, everything is amplified. Which is why you are translating so quickly and why you are able to hear me so clearly."

"You said this is a moon?" you ask the tree. "Is this the moon in the sky that I can see from Earth? Is this Earth's moon?"

"Sort of," the tree replies. "There are many dimensions to your moon that you speak of. Moons within moons, if you will, and this place is just one of those moons."

"Why am I here upon this moon?" you ask.

"You wanted to come here," the tree replies. "For sanctuary, healing, balance, privacy, a place to create, to manifest and to go deeply within to find connection with 'the all'. You hold all the cosmos within you. The many moons within moons are yours to be explored. You journeyed here by Moonship and any moon, infinite moons, may be accessed by Moonship."

You look again at your surroundings. It is true that this place feels like a sanctuary. This place feels very safe and very peaceful.

Indeed, the sheer beauty here is a wonder to behold.

It is true that you feel as though you are being healed. A healing energy runs through you and you know that you carry this within you so that you may, in turn, heal others.

It is true that you feel very balanced. There is indeed balance and symmetry within the landscape surrounding you and you feel this symmetry within your body, mind and soul.

You feel at one with the land here, as if it were a living entity in itself.

"It is," says the tree, reading your thoughts once again. "Everything is connected within a web of light here. A light field, and you are part of that. This is why you came here, to experience the lightfield of the moon."

You look around once more. It is true that this place is private, allowing you your privacy, so very needed when existing within a third dimensional time frame. Privacy here is a gift. Indeed it is a gift to be embraced.

It is true that this is a place to create. A place where you may still your mind and paint the emotion of creativity upon this glorious landscape.

Your thoughts are clear. They can be clearly read by the living wisdom that is the tree. Clarity is in abundance in this place.

Clarity in abundance must and will lead to creativity in abundance when held in balance, for it creates the event horizon that is the new infinity of the focused trajectory of pure intention. That is the new creation.

The clarity within this wonderful lightfield, upon this moon within moons, is assisting you with your own clarity and processing of this moment and all that it means to you.

It is true then, that processing within abundant clarity must lead to the manifestations of those creations. Manifestations of your desires. Manifestations of your moon within moons accessed from your moon flight, realised within your waking reality.

It is true then, that here within this moon within moons, that you can go deeply within and find connection with the all.

For did you not talk to the tree of wisdom?

Is that tree of wisdom not within you?

Is the wisdom not yours?

It is true that you hold all of the cosmos within you.

For did you not see the planet Earth as you moved beyond it? Did you not see the vortices? The stars? Cosmic rainbows?

Did you not see all this creation within outer space within your own inner space? Do you see how you *are* the cosmic creator?

You take time to ponder the wonder of all this infinite life around you and within you. The tranquillity and serenity of the moon within moons and the lightfield that connects you to everything here.

This perfect sanctuary assists you in your inner exploration.

After a while, the tree of wisdom speaks once again. "You know that this is your place. Only you can access this moon within moons unless you deem it otherwise, for you are inside your own mind, your own cells and your own activated cellular space externalised as your dream. This is your private sanctuary. Your own personal moon within moons. You can return here any time you choose, it will always be available for you."

You smile to yourself, knowing that the tree's wise words are true.

You *can* return to this moon within moons. To think, to create, to manifest and to access the knowledge from the tree of wisdom.

To receive healing for self and to replenish yourself with the nourishment of the lightfield connection. This will give you healing energy that you can then deliver to others.

You think about all this for a while.

You can fill yourself with healing energy that you can deliver to others.

Your own inner thoughts merge with those of the tree of wisdom and become one.

Does this make me a healer then?

"The realisation of what you are is the realisation of what has always been," speaks the tree and your own thoughts in unison.

So then, as you are the healer, you are all things.

You stand up and walk towards the tree of wisdom.

You wrap your arms around the tree and hug it tightly.

You feel freshly energised with a new wave of love and wisdom.

Fuelled with energy from the lightfield.

Oh, what magick! What magick that the lightfield is!

You sit back down upon your white comfy blanket.

Above you, you see a beam of light and you know it is Moonship, come to return you to Earth.

You move upwards, into the beam of light and float into Moonship.

You are comfy and rested within Moonship.

You find yourself, once again, lying on a bed with the warm, white, comfy blanket covering you up to your shoulders.

There is a window beside your bed and you can clearly see the world outside your window as you fly through timespace, spacetime within Moonship.

You see the bluish-white sphere of the moon. It becomes smaller and smaller as you leave its space.

You see the colours swirling. Spiral rainbows are moving and shimmering, emanating their cosmic energy as before.

You see the stars, silver splashes on a dark canvas. They twinkle with knowing like the very eyes of God, windows into the soul of Source self.

You see the Earth in all its blue-ochre beauty. As you move closer to Earth, your home planet in this physical incarnation, you begin to feel the duality of the dream body, lying in a bed flying on Moonship looking out of the window watching Earth grow larger and larger before you, and the physical body in meditation.

You recognise your bilocation of consciousness here as you hold the awareness of two bodies, two thoughts, two environments, two selves. You become your own twin soul at this point.

Moonship hovers above your physical body.

As you beam your dream body down through the crown chakra into your physical body awareness, you leave the Mer-Ka-Bah moonship in its space within your innerverse/hyperspace, and your awareness is bought back into alignment with the physical self.

Slowly at your own pace, you feel the merge between the dream body and the physical body. Moonship leaves your space to be called again whenever you may need the Matrix Transportation, to travel to the moon within moons.

Your awareness is brought into your torso, arms, hands and fingers and into your legs, feet and toes.

You wriggle your toes.

When you are ready, you come out of the sacred space that is meditation, fully aligned, synchronised and anchored within the physical self.

Kaleidoscope (Meditation)

We would ask you, in your meditation visualisation space, to see yourself stood within the sacred wheel that is your individualised matrix Mer-Ka-Bah field.

Your solar plexus and heart chakra are the central point/pivot point of the matrix. You are stood within your vertical pillar of light at the point where the vertical pillar intersects with the horizontal rainbow bridge pathway.

You see the forward facing horizontal axis in front of you and behind you.

The diagonal axis intersects through the pivot point where you stand.

You would then visualise a spiral at the centre point of your solar plexus, moving upwards to your heart chakra. Within this spiral are twelve spinning white orbs and twelve spinning black orbs. The white orbs spin clockwise and the black orbs spin anticlockwise (although follow your intuition on this as it may be the reverse of this for you, as long as you visualise the twelve white orbs and the twelve black orbs spinning in different directions within your solar plexus and spiralling upwards to the heart chakra).

Above you, starting at your crown chakra, are twelve spinning diamond orbs.

Below your feet are twelve spinning crystal turquoise orbs.

In front of you, along the forward facing horizontal arm, are twelve emerald spinning orbs.

Behind you, along the backward facing horizontal arm, are twelve rose quartz crystal spinning orbs.

To the left of you, along the horizontal, are twelve blue sapphire spinning orbs.

To the right of you, along the horizontal, are twelve ruby crystal spinning orbs.

The diagonal axis, coming down from the left, has twelve spinning gold orbs, shining with brilliant gold-white light. They look like twelve suns as they glow and spin and emanate.

You feel the warmth and the bliss within these golden orbs.

The diagonal axis, coming down from the right, has twelve spinning silver orbs, shining with sparkling silver-white light. They look like twelve moons as they shine and beam their silver moonlight river glow upon you.

Diagonally, moving downwards towards the left, you see twelve amethyst crystal orbs. Diagonally, towards the right, you see twelve opalescent rainbow spinning orbs.

Each group of twelve spinning crystal orbs moves beyond your line of sight, so each direction eventually looks like a glowing crystal colour. You feel as though you are surrounded by a pulsating living rainbow. You are encased within your own personal kaleidoscope.

You are aware that a circle encompasses the edge of your kaleidoscope rainbow matrix, the event horizon of your infinity of Source self, yet you cannot see this. For it stretches into infinity and is a never-ending evolving spiral even whilst it is a circle.

In your mind's eye, you draw all the spinning crystalline orbs into the intersection point that is your solar plexus and heart chakra.

The kaleidoscope matrix changes form before you and all converge at the midpoint of your solar plexus and heart.

From your solar plexus and heart bursts forth the rainbow dragon, glowing with all the colours that made up your kaleidoscope matrix.

The rainbow dragon has black claws and white wings. His eyes are emerald, his scales are blue sapphire, ruby, amethyst, gold, silver, turquoise and rose quartz. His tail is opalescent rainbow pearl. He is a plasma, rainbow, Krystal dragon and he is your dragon.

You are the dragonrider as you sit atop his back and ride him across the starlit night sky.

You and your dragon are one. You are one being, one soul, one heart, one mind.

Then he turns, to fly back in the direction of where you stood within your kaleidoscope matrix that is now your plasma rainbow Krystal dragon.

You may call him 'Quetzalcoatl' if you wish, for he has been known by this name and many other names, or you may give him a name of your choice, but your plasma-rainbow-Krystal dragon is a male dragon.

In the distance, at the place where you once stood within the kaleidoscope matrix that is now your dragon, you see a royal blue shimmering disc before you.

It lights up the night sky as a star does, twinkling and gleaming with the intricacies of the snowflake crystal lattice that it is.

This is your celestial stargate and she is female. She is the gateway to Sophia, the first gate and her name is Celestina.

She shines and vibrates and pulsates with the stardust light of true celestial memory.

You ride your dragon, closer and closer towards Celestina. Then together you and your rainbow dragon leap through the centre of the Celestina stargate, at which time your dragon breathes the fire of flame that is his dragon's breath and he creates a reality for you.

You leap through this ring of fire and find yourself... where?

Where are you now?

Within a zero point field blank canvas, or a fully formed hyperspace reality of your own making?

Perhaps you are within the Pleiades system, or Sirius or Lyra?

The creation now, is yours to create and yours to discover.

Look where you are. What do you see?

You have passed through the first gate and what you find is yours to create.

You spend some time within the world beyond the void, into the mind, the true mind, for you have entered the sacred space that is involution. This is the implosion. This is the true creation. This is the hermetic vault where your memories are stored and they are all here for you.

Your dragon and the celestial stargate are your keys.

We shall leave you to your own devices, your own creation, within the worlds beyond the rainbow gate. Yet when you return, you ride your dragon back through the stargate with focused intent upon returning into the sovereignty and balance that is your matrix field.

Then you can dismount from your trusty fire-breathing steed, the transportation of Mer-Ka-Bah fire that is the dragonkin soul you possess. For he is your seed and you are the star. Starseed, yes you are.

The bejewelled body of the dragon returns once again into the formation of the kaleidoscope matrix and you integrate all you have seen and experienced. You rode the torsion field as the torsion field, unified with the DNA expression of the ascended master on Earth.

As you stand, once again, within the nexus point of the kaleidoscope matrix, you bring your awareness back, in your own time, to the physical point of perspective that is you, all that is you.

Back into linear physicality but now armed with the awareness of Matrix Transportation and stargate ascension.

The journey begins!

Dragon Initiations - Activating the Flame Within

Introduction to the Dragon Initiations

The dragon initiations can be worked with in several ways.

One can type or write the initiation out and sleep with the initiation under your bed/pillow. Or bury the initiation in your garden with a crystal or other meaningful talisman if you wish. Or you can place the piece of paper with the initiation upon it, under a crystal, meaningful piece of jewellery or gemstone/power object or place within your alter.

The initiation can also be burnt outdoors (so energy is released into the ether) or one can place the initiation in an eco-friendly, non-toxic bottle or balloon and release it into the sea/sky.

The initiation can be read out loud (especially directly before you go to sleep) or you can ask a friend or your partner to read the initiation to you.

You can use the dragon initiations as inspiration into your own creative process or for ritual/spell/sacred ceremony in 'calling the dragon'.

Or you can simply read the initiation in your mind, just as you would read a story.

The keycodes and triggers will activate as they are designed to do. However you choose to utilise them will be the most aligned way for you.

Whichever method you choose, these dragon initiations create a 'focused intentional trajectory', through dragon energy, into that which the keycodes and triggers are set to activate, which are memories and all that 'memory' entails.

'The dragon' itself is a high level frequency/form to use for focused trajectory as it is, in and of itself, an 'event horizon'.

The Event = The Return of the Dragon

Here There Be Dragons

Here there be dragons, guardians of the Flame.

Existing in physical form, yet human we are not.

Holding much wisdom, we fly beyond the rainbow for there we shall find our pot of gold.

Though we may be dragonkind, we are are wise enough to know that we are but beginners on the dragon's path. Holding the knowing that we must not teach. Instead we assist the seeker to find the teacher within themselves.

We, as the 'rainbow dragons of Krysta' are a collective, even whilst we each stand alone.

We are the 'Jewelled Dragons of the Kryst' and the 'Keepers of the Flame of Amenti' and the 'Keyholders to the Holy Gate'.

We are the geometries and the numbers.

We are Seven.

We are Twelve.

We are Nine.

Seek and ye shall find us.

As the ascended dragon, we hold other forms within our collective embrace: the ascended unicorn, the ascended dolphin and the ascended mermaid. We stand 'all as one'.

Representing the elements. Sea, land, air, flame and ether.

Dolphins of the sea.

Dragons of the land, the air and the flame.

Mermaids of the sea and the land.

Unicorns of the ether.

All as one. As is dragon lore.

Standing as 'trinity of three': Dolphins, unicorns, dragons.

Standing as the square with the unicorn making the 'Tetragrammaton' but only those who wield the magic wand can see us.

The mermaids make the five. When there are five, you can fly and we give you your wings now.

We are the fabric of 'the place' and the 'fabric of the time'. All as one. As is dragon lore.

Permeating through all and everything as electrical magick, energetic magick and intelligent magick. We thus become infinity.

We are the magicians, the mages and the MAG-DA-LEN. Our wands are our swords and both are flaming when we give them the gift of our dragon's breath.

Inspiration, creativity, joy, love and bliss. We are all these, yet so too are we fire.

Behold!

Here there be dragons, guardians of the Flame.

The Tail of the Ruby Dragon

Behold. I am Eye, the ruby dragon.

Guardian of the ruby crystal ray.

Does it matter that I stand for matter?

That which is formed in matter and the rearranging of the molecular structures to form matter. I hold the masculine codes within my male form for matter creation, and I provide the flames of the Ruby Crystal Palace within the Emerald City of Krysta.

Welcoming you, seeker of the sun, traveller of the road to enlightenment, master dreamwalker and dreamweaver of the ascension arc.

Know me, the red dragon, as you walk your path.

Know the ruby crystal ray.

Activations are provided through the inner story of self. As you read the inner story, you activate the inner chambers, the inner voice, the inner teachers and the inner valley brings you unto me, the red dragon.

The inner-verse is the inner story.

Many triggers, many stories, yet the ultimate trigger is yourself. The stories are yours, you are the author of your own inner-verse-story which makes you the architect.

I give you my story *The Tail of the Ruby Dragon* with my blessings.

Red dragon am I, majestic in my glory and strong in my colour ray as I sit here within my cave of gold and communicate with you, seeker of the dragon's egg.

Golden coins surround me, golden cups, golden jewellery set with precious gemstones. Golden nuggets, chests of treasure, bracelets, rings and necklaces. Yet the security I have in my riches, is it real? Is it an illusion? I ponder upon this conundrum as I create the flame-codes for matter.

What good are these things if stilted and still? The treasures and the gold?

Some say dragons eat their gold but is this true? I need my gold so I can fly and breathe out my dragon's breath, that which is the flame of creation.

I cannot eat my gold for it is not nourishment to me. I cannot play this golden harp for I know not the tune.

I cannot wear the golden cloak for my ruby scales are all I need to keep me warm as I fly.

What then can I do?

I, ruby dragon, watch the pool of water before me. Crystal window that is the dragon's eye.

I see the seeker in the golden palace realm of their own making, like the bird in the gilded cage.

Sharing the seeker's boredom, holding no enthusiasm or joy for these trinkets save the liquid light of the golden myst they hold.

What can I, the ruby dragon, do with my riches?

Oh help me seeker, what can I do?

I know, I could buy a house! This would bring me security, would it not? Within the levels of ruby red matter and this dwelling would stand strong upon the clay beneath my feet.

Yet... as I look around, I know the cave is all I truly need. It envelops me, for it is my mother's womb.

What good then, is a house to a dragon?

I know, I could buy transportation. A car, a train or a spaceship! Yes, this would be good. I would be so powerful in my shiny vehicle on wheels, formed with the metallic matter from the ruby codes I carry.

Yet, I have wings. Strong powerful ruby wings and I can fly anywhere with these wonderful wings and the steady balance of my scaly tale.

What good is this transport to a dragon? I have all the transport I need.

I know, I could buy warmth! A big, warm blanket to wrap around my scaly body. Or I could buy a heater to keep me toasty warm on the cold nights in the realms of that which is solid.

Yet I am a ruby dragon and the creator of fire, for that is my dragon's breath. The flames I breathe out heat the rocks which burn and glow for hours. What good therefore are blankets or heaters to a dragon?

Welcoming you, seeker of the sun, I shall give *you* my fortune!

You can have my jewels, coins and riches.

Please, dear seeker, take it all and share it fairly and equally across the land.

Yet before you take it, seeker of the sun, I place a spell upon these riches. Yes, I do. A dragon's spell.

Whomsoever shall feel the grasping coils of greed around their heart, whomsoever shall yearn for more and more and more, so that all is never enough for them, then the riches shall crumble as dust to the ground leaving nothing but a golden pile of sand.

Whomsoever shall feel the dark shackles of power run through their mind and soul, for them the riches shall disappear before their very eyes leaving nothing but an empty void within them.

Yet whomsoever shall need the smallest coin, the tiniest ring, the one bead within the necklace; whomsoever shall, in patience wait, for the gift that is theirs, they shall have all they need and yet more and all shall come to them.

For in fairness, they share the riches and shelter they have. Indeed, freedom to move around upon their land and warmth shall be theirs.

They shall have food to eat, wine to drink and a cloak to wear. All they need shall not be denied. It is they that shall share their riches so others may so too have food and a cloak.

Those with patience in their hearts and kindness in their eyes, these are the souls that shall inherit the magickal blessings of my golden riches.

I shall call them the 'children of the ruby ray'.

They shall truly know me, the ruby dragon, and they shall know who I am.

Indeed, these children are few within the mortal worlds of matter and all that is solid but they are there. The children of the ruby ray are there.

Other children shall be begotten of their seed and they shall carry the codes of the ruby ray. These codes shall be passed down through the children of the ruby ray in the mortal world of mortality.

Oh, would they only envisage the fractal world of fractality! I shed the tear of the dragon that they do not, yet my breath of both fire and ice shall cover all the lands when they do.

The knowledge of me, the ruby dragon, shall spread throughout the land.

When this happens, then this shall unlock the ruby code and return the stolen royal ruby to its rightful place, for the children of the ruby ray will know where to seek and where to find and what to do.

I, the ruby dragon, shall be unbound from my rock and freed from my cave and I shall burst forth from my mother's womb.

Once again I shall fly free like the dragons of old.

Oh, what a time it shall be when the dragons again return to the skies. I shall look down upon the land of Agartha and see once again the flora and fauna thrive as the energy of the ruby ray guides me wherever I fly.

You shall see us sailing high above the crystal palace rooftops within the Emerald City of Krysta, providing protection to the enlightened ones residing within their rainbow palaces below.

Dragonriders shall thenceforth come from the children of the ruby ray and all the rainbow dragons of Krysta shall then seed their codes within the mortal realm.

My ruby wings shall be provided whenever they choose to fly, for the dragonriders shall set us free.

Dragonriders will fly higher and higher, riding on our backs towards the stargates in the sky.

Even whilst I, the ruby dragon, can go no further than the stargate's edge. Indeed I cannot pass through the gate alone, riderless, but *they* can! Oh what blessings. They can!

The mortals with joy in their hearts who, with assistance of their own forgiveness of self, transcend the earthly elements the gold collectors bring and fly beyond and further forward into other dimensions, through the other stargates and they take we, the rainbow dragons of Krysta with them!

The seeker becomes the traveller and the dreamwalkers become the dreamweavers.

I, the red dragon, stand always as their anchor, as their humble servant, waiting, waiting until I may be of practical assistance to them. Waiting until I can be unbound from the land.

They shall bring the rocks to life and turn grey, lifeless stone into sparkling crystals.

The dreamweaver is the one who weaves the dream, with knowledge of elemental life. Maybe dragon, unicorn, mermaid or fae, walking through the fabric of the dream with awareness.

She brings to herself the meanings of that which she sees and thus she weaves the dream.

The dreamwalker is the conscious seeker along the path of enlightenment, expansion and ascension.

Meeting these dreamweavers and dreamwalkers, children of the ruby ray, shall be a joyous merge of recognition for I, the ruby dragon, am the holder of the dragon's egg.

With all the riches and the gold and the gems that I have gifted to the mortals with pure hearts, the children of the ruby ray, none shall be so precious as the gift of the dragon's egg.

Within the children of the ruby ray I shall place a code, the ruby code. Whence such time as the sun does place it's golden kiss upon those who hold the ruby code, then they shall know where to find me and I shall, in humility, grace and utmost joy, hand them the golden egg they seek and it shall be theirs.

Come forward then, seeker of the sun, weary traveller. See if you can shed your earthly baggage and rest for a while within the cave that is my mother's womb.

See if you can open your heart to the genuine purity and hold the wisdom of the innocent.

If you can, my gold is yours and thus the ruby code.

Then to those who marry and stand with their beloved, saying their vows before the rainbow dragons of Krysta, you shall be given the dragon's egg, with the blessing and the love of all the elementals.

The dolphins, fairies, pixies, gnomes, mermaids, unicorns and all of dragonkind shall rejoice at the giving of this gift.

You, in wedded bliss, shall be the holder of the dragon's egg, keeper of the flame and dragonrider of the rainbow dragons of Krysta.

If you should make it this far, traveller of the dragon's path, then nurture your egg with all the love of the mother dragon. You shall, in turn, have the love of the celestial dragons behind you, holder of the dragon's egg.

And when such time as the dragon's egg hatches, all the multiverse shall be watching as you and all of dragonkind become one.

Behold. I am Eye, the ruby dragon.

The Dragon's Garden

Behold! I am the amethyst dragon of the amethyst ray. Together with my beloved sisters, mothers and daughters, we create the rainbow, for we are the dragons of Krysta.

Living only in the sky, I cannot land upon the ground to unite with my love who is bound as the rocks on the Earth. My home is a castle in the clouds, yet I long for the day I can fly with my beloved, the ruby dragon.

Viewing the landscape of Krysta, in majestic flight as Aquasha, queen of dragons, I see the trees, the forests, the lush green grass and the vibrant flowers.

There is a building, the geometric icosidodecahedron crystal palace with the stained glass windows of rainbow colour within each wall.

Powerful crystal palace of Krysta, you are the golden gate I have been searching for. You are the internal silver star of my reality that is the Emerald City.

When you find your crystal palace, then the clarity you seek will be yours as the dragon's egg hatches and you respond to the ancient symbolism of the language of light.

Inside the crystal palace is the sacred space that is your favourite room. Upon the crystal wall is the large mirror within the frame of a golden dragon.

The mirror is, in itself, a window into other realms, other worlds.

Look through this mirror now and see what you see.

Yes, behold, the dragon's garden!

The flower to tell a thousand tales, is it the violet, the daisy, the orchid or the poppy? No, tenders of the dragon's garden, it is none of these, beauty though they hold.

It is the rose. The beautiful, perfect rose.

Who is that dreamwalker as she steps through her watery path? Once a mermaid, tail replaced by human legs. She steps through the path of turquoise blue water surrounded not by sea, but by clouds.

Pink-tinged clouds, for she is mermaid of the skies.

Her golden hair cascades down her long tanned shoulders and she walks with grace. Where is she going? Why is she walking in the dragon's garden?

She finds the rose, the beautiful rose, drawn to its vibrant pink ray, rose ray as the clouds of her home world.

She is like me. Amethyst dragon, mermaid rose. We are but the same, from the clouds above.

She knows not to pick the roses but to let them grow, so they may bloom with the stories of ancient times.

Each rose, a thousand stories. Yes, indeed the dragon's garden is a story garden and every story ever told is to be found here.

Will you add your story to the dragon's garden?

What do you see when you look below as you ride upon my amethyst back?

Do you see a clearing? A circle of trees? A fire? What do you see within the flames?

As the flames die down and burn to ash, you see several crystals in a pile by the place where the fire used to be.

Look closer, seeker of the moon. Are they really crystals?

They are eggs, can you not see? They are dragon eggs!

We must alert the ruby dragon so he may take the eggs into the garden. I cannot go down amongst the roses yet, but I can nurture the unhatched dragon's eggs from here, from my amethyst castle in the sky.

I am their mother, they will hear me and know me even though they are on the ground and I fly high above them.

Mortal dreamwalker who used to be mermaid, will you nurture my dragon eggs for me until my beloved is unbound from the land?

Without you to tend the roses in the dragon's garden, will the lands not suffer? Will the crops not die? Then how will my eggs hatch then?

I cannot fly down to the roses, have you seen how big I am? How wide? I am queen of the dragons and I fill the skies.

Look, see the dragon's eggs within the ash pile of the once burning fire. They must be taken to the safety of the rose garden so I may send them my healing dragon's breath, which holds the unconditional love of the mother.

They are my eggs and I love them all.

So within the bound rocky landscape, my beloved twin flame, the ruby dragon, he takes my eggs and gives them to the mortal girl who once swam with dolphins.

King Neptune is her father and he is so proud of his daughter as she agrees to care for my eggs!

I do not know this mermaid's name but I shall call her Aurora, divine princess, daughter of a king.

She shall be blessed and protected by dragons, we the rainbow dragons of Krysta, as she watches over my dragon's eggs.

Now keep them secret, little Aurora mermaid. Don't let anyone know they are there, not unless they find the dragon's garden. They will only find the dragon's garden if they are pure of heart, as you are, divine princess.

You will know them when they come. They will be seekers of the sun, moon and stars and will wear the emblem of the pink rose.

They are thus worthy to enter the dragon's garden and may thus be gifted a dragon's egg. No one else, little mermaid princess, no one else save those who wear the emblem of the rose, for they are the ones that will ride us, they are our dragonriders and we pair together as night pairs with day.

Look after my eggs in the meantime, princess Aurora. Tell no one of them save those who are of the rose, the ones who sparkle as gemstones, diamonds and crystals, the shining ones who wear the pure heart as a cloak of love for all to see.

Until you meet the living daughters and sons of rose ray, then keep secret the whereabouts of my eggs, dear mermaid turned mortal.

Just as you left your watery home that you call Atlantis in order that you may be made flesh and walk on the land until you find true love, so shall I, one day, come down from the clouds and reunite with the ruby dragon, my twin flame beloved.

Until then, I fly the skies and I beam down the love of the mother to my dragon's eggs, upon the safe, healing amethyst ray.

Together with my beloved sisters, mothers and daughters, we create the rainbow, for we are the dragons of Krysta.

Behold! I am the amethyst dragon of the amethyst ray.

Enjoy this book?

Check out magentapixie.com

* Vast Video Archive of Magenta Pixie's Messages *

* Downloadable Guided Meditations * Interviews * Lectures * Free Stuff *

Also by Magenta Pixie, available in print and Kindle editions...

Masters of the Matrix: Becoming the Architect of Your Reality and Activating the Original Human Template

and

Divine Architecture and the Starseed Template: Matrix Memory Triggers for Ascension

"An extraordinary contribution to Humanity and the Great Shift."

- Amazon customer review

Made in the USA
Columbia, SC
30 January 2025

53000632R00189